GENTLEMAN SPYMASTER

How Lt. Col. Tommy 'Tar' Robertson
Double-crossed the Nazis.

Also by Geoffrey Elliott

I Spy

From Siberia With Love

The Mystery of Overend & Gurney

The Shooting Star

Secret Classrooms: An Untold Story of the Cold War
(With Harold Shukman)

Kitty Harris – The Spy With 17 Names
(With Igor Damaskin)

GENTLEMAN SPYMASTER

How Lt. Col. Tommy 'Tar' Robertson
Double-crossed the Nazis

Geoffrey Elliott

Methuen

First published in Great Britain 2011 by
Methuen
8 Artillery Row
London
SW1P 1 RZ

www.methuen.co.uk

1 3 5 7 9 10 8 6 4 2

ISBN 978 0 413 77706 5

A CIP catalogue record for this book is available from the British Library.

Typeset by SX Composing DTP, Rayleigh, Essex

Printed and bound by CPI Group (UK) Ltd, Croydon, CR0 4YY

For Fay
in celebration

Contents

Illustrations

'The British national character, as conceived by themselves, is honest, straightforward and even a little simple. It is all the more a source of pride that they have been the greatest deceivers in history.' Anonymous reviewer in *The Times Literary Supplement*, June, 1973.

'All warfare is based upon deception', Sun Tzu, 6/7th century BC Chinese general and strategic thinker, in *The Art of War*.

'The suicide bomber who killed seven CIA agents in Afghanistan was an Al Qaeda double agent . . .' BBC World Service News Report 5 January 2010.

1

Overture and Beginners

This is one man's story. It is also the story of the extraordinary contribution to victory in the Second World War that Tommy 'Tar' Robertson and his colleagues in British counter-intelligence made through the 'Double Cross' system. In the words of the authorised history of the British Security Service, MI5, of which it was a key component, 'No agency in British history, probably none in the history of intelligence, has ever devised such a wide range of ingenious deceptions with such a high success rate . . .'[1] To Hugh Trevor-Roper, the historian who became one of the secret world's stellar wartime academic recruits, Tar was 'its original architect . . . whose genius guided the whole machine throughout the war . . .[2]

From inauspicious beginnings – a purloined German wireless set operated from a cell in South London's Wandsworth Prison – Double Cross's intricate and elegantly executed mission was to turn the Nazi's espionage efforts in Britain inside out, to the point where, from their base in an anonymous office building close to London's St James's Park, a small team of professional counter-intelligence officers, backed by academics, lawyers, an art dealer and even a circus proprietor, recruited for wartime service on the rightly renowned British 'Old Boy Net', controlled every agent German intelligence believed they had in Britain. Through a collective concentration of cunning, imagination and intellectual firepower, and unparalleled coordination of the complex Whitehall machine – not least the code breakers at the Government Code and Cipher School ('GC&CS') and the Secret Intelligence Service ('SIS') – Double Cross evolved into a cornerstone of the massive deception plan known as 'FORTITUDE', which hoodwinked Hitler and his Generals about where the Allied forces would land on the beaches of France on D-Day in June, 1944. Londoners in particular should be grateful to Double Cross as the subterfuge by which a desperate Nazi régime was deluded into shifting the target points of the V1 and V2 rockets, Hitler's 'secret weapons', away from the heart of the city.

Most biographers set out on their lonely mission fretting that they might not find enough new material to bring their subject to life. They ferret for long hours in libraries and archives, rustling pages ever faster in the quest for insights undiscovered by others. Internet search engines hum as every conceivable combination of likely words is tried to see what new leads might be revealed, and friends and family are questioned for fleeting scraps of memory. For 'Tar' Robertson's wartime exploits, the problem is rather different. As John Bowen remarked in a review of a recent life of Charles Dickens[3] the problem for his many biographers is that 'Dickens got there first' by incorporating versions of many of the key episodes in his life in his own classic novels.

Tar Robertson wrote no novels. He left no memoir and only a handful of papers. But many other authors have 'got there first' with bits and pieces of his story. There are official and unofficial histories of MI5 and many accounts of the individual deception cases, their complex and delicately inter-linked scripts, the adventures and misadventures of the motley crew of agents, and the crowning achievement of the D-Day deception strategy. In the scholarly journals and at the symposia which rightly take the study of intelligence as a serious and fertile topic, academics have focused their professional laser beams on the place of deception and Double Cross in the history of espionage; it has even been the subject of a Ph.D thesis. Tar himself has an impressive tally of index entries in books ranging from Ben Macintyre's enthralling picture of the roguish Eddie Chapman, Double Cross Agent ZIGZAG, and the same author's insights into 'Operation MINCEMEAT', to Professor Christopher Andrew's authoritative history of MI5. Tar's name also appears frequently in the files of the wartime Special Operations Executive, created by Churchill to 'set Europe ablaze'. Thousands of pages of case files have been released to the National Archives at Kew albeit several tagged as 'Summaries' or 'Selected Papers', and all studded with coy, and with the passage of time, redundant redactions.

So those who want detail can find plenty in the Archives and library bookshelves, as the Bibliography demonstrates. And should they want more than the printed word, Operation MINCEMEAT and Eddie Chapman's rambunctious saga have been reinvented as films, the first as *The Man Who Never Was* and the second as *Triple Cross*. In the latter, Tar's rôle is played by Trevor Howard, sporting a moth-eaten ginger beard more appropriate to a Chekhov play, and wearing, even indoors, a Homburg hat of the kind much favoured by 1930's Tory politicians. Both features are singularly out of keeping with the man whose life and career we will follow. The BBC also told some of the Double Cross story in their *Timewatch* series, which in a technical sleight of hand that would have bemused the Second World War generation, is available on every computer screen in the world through the medium of 'YouTube'. It might also have bemused Robertson himself since he does not rate a mention.

The impression created by all this material and even the idiosyncratic films, is of Double Cross as an exquisitely orchestrated Beethoven-scale symphony, everything in perfect harmony, point and counter-point crafted to crest to a magnificent finale as the Allies thundered ashore on D-Day .

But in its early stages, it was much more a series of impromptu pieces, performed by a talented but largely amateur ensemble, improvising as they went along.

Despite all these one-off sightings, Tar's colourful personal story has not been told as one coherent narrative. Even the new and meticulously detailed History errs by some 20 years in the date of his death.[4] In narrating it, faced with all those twice and thrice told tales, we will take the approach advocated by Lytton Strachey when he tackled the lives of several already copiously documented figures of the Victorian age,[5] namely to 'row out over that great ocean of material, and lower down into it here and there, a little bucket which will bring back up to the light of day, some characteristic specimen from those far depths, to be examined with a careful curiosity.'

Our first 'specimen', though one on a coelacanth scale, is found in the archival cache of papers on the agent code-named SNOW. Though it and the related files are a daunting agglomeration of records, Tar is centre stage and many of the notes were dictated by him in a fluent, factual style which belies the pressure under which they must have been composed. As in the other more celebrated cases, he is directing a louche supporting cast – the sly and seedy SNOW himself, CELERY, a serial conman who earned Tar's trust, BISCUIT, SNOW JUNIOR, LILY, GW the polyglot policeman, and the nervous CHARLIE; the script includes cameo appearances by The Infrared Man, Obed From Aden and the sad Piccadilly restaurant manager William Rolph. Though its twists and turns are more convoluted than any fiction writer would dare to confect, SNOW's story, fascinating in itself, is even more important as the cornerstone, or in the donnish words of Tar's wartime colleague Sir John Masterman 'the fons et origo' ('source and origin') of the Double Cross conjurer's cabinet of magic and illusion.[6]

The second specimen, the case of the temperamental TREASURE, is in marked contrast; it ran much later in the War and played its part in FORTITUDE, the complex D-Day deception plan. Also unlike most of the Double Cross cases, its central character is a woman. TREASURE, the codename given to 'Lily' Sergueiew,[7] was an adventurous, impetuous French-educated Russian émigrée, who deceived the Germans into sending her to England as their agent, and then worked hard, putting herself at considerable risk, as a Double Cross agent, only to threaten to jeopardise the entire FORTITUDE plan because she convinced herself that Tar and his 'gang' had caused the death of her much-loved dog. She was one of the few people who did not like him. Whether or not she got the better of him in the end, is an open question. Whatever else she achieved, she was surely the only Double Cross agent to have interviewed Hermann Goering. Other already much publicised cases will be mentioned in less detail.

But at the price of some eye-rolling by those who have more interest in the personalities and the tales of derring-do, to put Tar's story into context we also have to digress to look at the Service he joined, how he came to join it, and its wrenching evolution into a powerful Second World War asset. We need also to explain the complex network of resources without which Double Cross could not have succeeded, notably the real-time insights provided by Britain's super secret ability to crack the supposedly unbreakable radio traffic of the German Intelligence Service, the Abwehr. Referred to in security shorthand as the 'Most Secret Sources', and much later known to a wider world as ULTRA, they put Tar and his colleagues at the centre of what one post war commentator saw as 'a virtually perfect intelligence system'.[8] To round out the story we shall also touch on the machine's sometimes awkward relationship with its counterpart in the British Secret Intelligence Service, or SIS. 'Sometimes' is an important qualification. SIS' rôle in talent-spotting potential Double Cross agents abroad, and even more in watching and 'babysitting' them when they went off to neutral capitals for risky encounters with their supposed German con-trollers, was an essential contribution to success.

We need also to understand the strengths and failings of the Abwehr itself and how, despite successes elsewhere, its officers allowed themselves to be so comprehensively outplayed by Tar and his team.

As a side issue, though an important one in terms of the attribution of credit where it is due, it may surprise those whose image of Anglo-French relations in the Second World War is of a running skirmish in a fog of mutual suspicion, the pioneers in running double agents against the Abwehr in the 1930s were the French counter-espionage service, which had a close relationship with SIS. One senior SIS officer told his French counterpart 'You are our teachers'.[9] But we will first take Lytton Strachey's advice literally, and head out to sea.

Notes

1. Andrew, *The Defence of the Realm*, p. 285
2. Trevor-Roper, Hugh Redwald, later Baron Dacre of Glanton, 1914–2003, like Tar a pupil at Charterhouse, Regius Professor of Modern History, Oxford, 1957–80, Master of Peterhouse College, Cambridge, 1980–87. See his Foreword to Montagu, *Beyond Top Secret U*. See also Sisman.
3. *The Times Literary Supplement*, October 2009
4. Andrew, *ibid* p. 318.
5. Lytton Strachey, Giles, 1880–1932, elegant historian, biographer and a

leading light of the Bloomsbury Group.
6. Masterman, Sir John Cecil, OBE, 1891–1977, sportsman, scholar, Whitehall 'mandarin', Provost of Worcester College, Oxford 1946–61. One of MI5's heavyweight wartime academic recruits and himself the talent-spotter for several other key players.
7. The Francophone spelling of her Russian family name which more usually would end in a 'v' or 'ff', 'Lily' was her preferred abbreviation of her first name Nataliya.
8. See Hindel et al.
9. Paillole, p. 126.

2

Two Men In a Boat

We start our voyage in Grimsby, on Britain's north east coast, one of the country's biggest fishing ports. It is 21 May 1940. Britain had been at war with Germany since the previous September. Just a few days earlier, on 10 May, the nerve-wracking lull the newspapers had christened the 'phony war' had come to a crashing end when the Wehrmacht unleashed its 'Blitzkrieg' against Belgium and Holland and Winston Churchill took over the leadership of his beleaguered country. A fighting nation needed to be fed, so the depleted fleet of weather-beaten trawlers (many had been commandeered by the Royal Navy as minesweepers) was encouraged to chug into the Humber Estuary from Grimsby's two 'fishing docks', and thread its way through the defensive minefields to the cod and herring rich grounds of the Dogger Bank, the vast sand shallows which begin some fifty miles off the coast and stretch half way across the North Sea. For the trawlermen the war was already far from 'phony'. British newspaper reports of those early months have frequent accounts of Grimsby trawlers coming under fierce machine gun or bomb attack by German aircraft, with the loss of many, often young, lives.

As seagulls keened and wheeled in the smudgy dawn light the 130 ton trawler *Barbados*, registered number GY 71, its black hull flecked with rust, a Union Jack painted on its funnel, and a Red Ensign fluttering at the stern, cast off from the North Wall and burbled its way out into the chilly sea past the 309 foot high Dock Tower, proud relic of the Victorian age, and alongside Spiller's Flour Mills, skirting merchant ships waiting to join the next convoy, tramp steamers bringing in Swedish wood pulp and pit props, colliers and iron ore carriers heavy in the water. On board were the captain, who knew what was going on, a brave crew of nine fishermen, some of them just boys, in oilskins and heavy sweaters, and down in the cabin, a fug of diesel fumes, cigarette smoke and the briny reek of fish, two edgy passengers. One was Arthur George Owens, known to Tar Robertson in London as his Double Cross agent SNOW and to the German officer in Hamburg who thought he controlled him, as JOHNNY, a diminutive, sharp-featured Welshman with false teeth and a false heart. His travelling companion was Sam McCarthy, a petty drug smuggler and confidence trickster, turned police informer and now code-named BISCUIT. The *Barbados'* bows smashed through the green rollers at about eight knots, the crew performing their professional ballet routine – getting the nets ready, checking the floats and the winches, stripping the tarpaulin off the First World War vintage Lewis machine gun and checking that the box of 47-round pan magazines of ammunition was not waterlogged. The gun was no more than a morale booster; against the 7.9mm machine guns and 3.0cm cannon of a Messerschmitt 109, it would have been as effective as a peashooter.

At a forward Luftwaffe base on the island of Sylt, on Germany's North Sea coast, a Swastika flag snapped in the wind above the sentry boxes which flanked the gate. A nervous Nazi intelligence officer checked and rechecked his maps and the weather forecast, made doubly sure that the German anti-aircraft and fighter defence systems knew all about his flight, and finally gave the 'thumbs up' signal to his pilot to gun the engines of the Dornier 18, the long-range coastal reconnaissance flying boat. The two 888 hp BMW 132 motors, mounted, oddly to modern eyes, back to back in a nacelle above the fuselage, one a 'pusher' the second a 'puller', roared into life and it lumbered into a clear sky. His objective, far-fetched and dangerous, was to rendezvous with the *Barbados*, land alongside it, pass over sabotage gear and collect one of the two passengers who would be taken to Germany for training as a spy. The German, a well-built man of forty or so with thinning hair, a man who would pass unnoticed in a crowd, had wrapped a heavy civilian overcoat over his Luftwaffe uniform. He knew the flight would be long and cold but he was also keenly aware that the Dornier might run into a British fighter patrol and be forced down. And though he trusted

JOHNNY, whom he believed had set the whole thing up, there was always a risk in these complex games that the operation had turned into a British trap; if he was captured he wanted to be treated as a uniformed POW, and not shot out of hand as a spy. He was taking a risk; he was not just an intelligence officer, a catch in himself if he fell into British hands, but knew more than was good for him about Hitler's plans to launch an invasion of Britain. The FBI too were keen to get their hands on him after his indictment as a co-conspirator in a much headlined US espionage case.

The Dornier zigzagged from one cloudbank to the next, to reduce the risk of being spotted. The German officer's version of the story is that when it reached the area marked in red on his chart there was no sign of the trawler. They circled and searched but failed to see any sign of it. Though a souped up version of the Dornier crammed with extra fuel tanks had set a record in the late 1930s with a non-stop 5,214 mile flight from Start Point in Devon to Brazil, this was wartime and the Germans could not risk running out of fuel so close to enemy airspace.

The *Barbados'* captain reported later that he had seen an aircraft circling, and dropping signal flares but he could not tell whether it had been British or German. It does not matter ; the sortie was abortive. The spymaster returned to Sylt, disappointed, chilled and half-deafened by the engine noise.

A few hours later a dispatch rider from the German Intelligence HQ in Hamburg brought him a radio message from JOHNNY, 'Had to go to ground. Captain under surveillance.'

The fascination in this strange episode is that both Tar and the German thought the little Welshman was *their* man, the potentially lethal ambiguity that is at the heart of all the Double Cross stories.

As the *Barbados* rocked and rolled back to Grimsby, Thomas Argyll Robertson was sitting nervously in an office building at 58 St. James's Street in the heart of London's 'clubland', its supposed anonymity contradicted by the armed sentries outside and the festoons of barbed wire around it. A few months short of his thity-first birthday, he was remembered by one of his wartime colleagues as 'immensely personable and monstrously good looking', attributes of which he had taken full advantage as a 'man about town' in his twenties, and by one of his agents as 'Hollywood's concept of a dashing military type'.[1] When the Robertson family looked back in later years they remembered the genial, joking sheep farmer, absorbed in stamp collecting, village cricket, golf, and his extended family, and like his father a deft wielder of the embroidery needle. His rôle in the Double Cross system tended to come out as anecdotes told to amuse rather than for history. Appearances can be as deceptive as Double Cross operations. Even those closest to him failed to appreciate his style – cunning, charming, imaginative, unruffled, a master of detail, a deft Whitehall operator and a shrewd discriminator between the good, the bad and the ugly with whom he had to deal, starting with the two men he had sent off on the trawler. Last but by no means least, ruthless when he needed to be.

To use Christian names in telling someone else's story is open to criticism that the author is being a touch presumptuous; after all, they say, 'you never met him'. But surnames can be even more off-putting in their formality, their echoes of a school register being called. He was 'Tommy' to his adoring family, 'Tom' to his early friends and, from his initials, 'Tar' to his admiring wartime colleagues.[2] We shall start with Tommy and switch to Tar once we follow him, like Orpheus, into the counter-espionage underworld.

He looked the epitome of what at one level he was, an officer from a crack Scottish regiment, his character forged by the chilly class-rooms and even chillier playing fields of an English public school, drilled and buffed into leadership material at the Royal Military Academy, Sandhurst. A man who had sown his wild oats in London night clubs arm in arm with his charismatic contemporary, the film star David Niven and who, as far as the world knew, had settled down to a hush-hush but humdrum staff job behind a desk in the War Office. A casual acquaintance might well assume that when better times came he would take over as Laird of a five-thousand acre family estate in the Highlands, salmon glinting in its clear streams, roe deer roaming the hillsides, birds of prey wheeling high above the heather.

Not so. Like so much else in this story. He had actually spent many more years in British counter-intelligence than he had in the Regular Army, and had been born half a world away from the Highlands under a sweltering sky in Medan, Sumatra, a bouillabaisse of races and cultures, where the Rivers Deli and Boboera merge in a muddy swirl. It was 27 October 1909, just a few days before the start of the monsoon season. To understand where Medan fits into the story we have to tug at one of the brightest strands in the tapestry of British colonial history, the extraordinary contribution the Scots made to building, running and defending London's Imperial dominions. In the mid nineteenth century the American mantra for those in search of their destiny was 'Go West, Young Man'. Over several earlier centuries, while many young British fortune seekers and adventurers had fought, scrabbled, and died for richer or for poorer in North America, Southern Africa, or Australia, many more had looked eastwards. The Scots were prominent amongst them, as teachers, doctors, plantation managers, Army officers and hardboiled rank and file soldiers, government officials, traders, bankers, lawyers, nannies and missionaries, and not infrequently, spies. Theirs was a formative presence over centuries, a human tide described by one historian[3] as a 'relentless penetration, which transformed centuries of English conquests around the world into the British Empire'. Generations of Robertsons were part of that canny, hard-working Diaspora, who turned their backs on family and friends, rain-slicked granite, grey skies, hellfire and damnation preachers and limited professional horizons to embrace the challenges and romantic uncertainties of the Far East, where in Rudyard Kipling's words, 'the sunshine and the palm trees and the tinkly temple bells . . .' and the comfortable trappings of Colonial expatriate society made an agreeable setting in which to advance in one's career. If fortune smiled and health held up, hard work would translate into capital to provide a good education and an inheritance for the family's sons, a decent dowry for the daughters and a comfortable retirement back home.

Tommy's grandfather John Hutchinson Robertson, born in Edinburgh on 21 May 1829 was certainly a hard worker and bright too. He was just 20[4] when he qualified at the city's Medical School, the first such Faculty in the English speaking world, though it was actually set up by doctors from Holland. From there he went north in 1850 as a House Surgeon to the small hospital at Elgin, named after the Dr Gray who funded its construction in 1807 with a grant of £20,000 – several millions today. Over the centuries it has evolved into a sizeable regional medical complex, though the original stone clock tower still stands. Via the 'A' roads and motorways which have sliced across the Highlands, the 173 mile journey can now be made by car in about four hours, roadworks and stops to take in the scenery permitting. But for the newly qualified young doctor, with his portmanteau of clothes and his Gladstone bag of ivory-handled knives, clamps and drills, the trip must have been more daunting than scenic. An 1840's railway map shows no rail lines north of Edinburgh. Though the English speculative mania for railways would soon spread north of the Border, the line to Elgin was not fully opened until March 1858 with the completion of the Findhorn Bridge. So John Hutchinson Robertson had two equally uncomfortable choices. On the one hand, the two to three day stagecoach jolt across the Highlands via Inverness, crammed inside with sweaty strangers, or for a lower fare, crouched chilled to the bone and wet, on a seat on the coach roof. On the other, he could take his chance on the unpredictable North Sea – shading by the minute from blustery to benign and back again – to sail up the coast on one of the 100 ton schooners which ran between Edinburgh and Garmouth, about 15 miles from Elgin. Today Garmouth is a charming cluster of weekenders' seaside cottages. Back then it was still the busy harbour and shipbuilding centre it had been since the 1500s. In the 1600s it had given a guarded welcome to the future King Charles II, when he came to Scotland to seek alliances in his father's civil war with Cromwell's New Model Army.[5]

Elgin itself had charm and a long history, a street plan unchanged from the Middle Ages, the brooding sandstone ruins of a 13th century cathedral, and fine old houses, in one of which, Bonny Prince Charlie, the 'Young Pretender' sheltered in April 1746 before riding off to his final defeat, and the collapse of the Jacobite cause, some 30 miles away at Culloden. It was home to a genteel society of lawyers, bankers, merchants and drapers, in which a newly arrived, handsome young doctor would have been a social 'catch' – much as in Mrs. Gaskell's 'Cranford'. But behind the fine old houses the poor lived in ragged squalor, without running water or drains; stinking gullies down the middle of the street served as sewers.

It is hard to imagine John Robertson's daily ward rounds in Victorian Elgin. Medicine and surgery were advancing, but chloroform had been introduced only three years earlier and it was not until Queen Victoria led the way with the birth of her eighth child in 1853 that it began to be used in obstetrics. The deadly rôle of dirt, germs and bacilli was not yet understood and it would be another twenty years before the principles of antiseptic surgery were widely accepted.

Opium, mercury, even strychnine, saltpeter and deadly nightshade were 'remedies' of choice, along with leeches and castor oil. When the remedies failed, and surgery was unavoidable, it was a terrifying ordeal. 'A patient preparing for an operation was like a condemned criminal preparing for execution.'[6] In Dr Gray's Hospital the operating theatre, as in other infirmaries of the era, was literally that. Galleries rising above the scrubbed wooden table set centre-stage, on which the patient was strapped, provided a ghoulish vantage point from which students and other doctors could watch, and hear, the knife, drill and saw at work, and blanch as the blood bubbled under the yellowish light of a gas-powered chandelier. John operated not in a sterile white gown, a face mask and rubber gloves but in a frock coat and blood-stained apron. He must often have been as frightened as his patients, let alone the spectators.

Two years of bone-sawing, screams, incurable diseases, women dead in childbirth, and the winter winds slicing off the Moray Firth were enough. Supported by a new wife, Mary Anne Murray, daughter of a prominent member of the Edinburgh intelligentsia, John set off for Singapore, a fast growing Imperial outpost whose strategic and commercial importance had been realised forty years or so earlier by Sir Stamford Raffles. Dr Gray, the Elgin hospital benefactor, had made his money in the lucrative (for its officials, not the natives they controlled) service of the East India Company in

Bengal[7] and John may well have picked up a sense of the opportunities and challenges that awaited the courageous on the other side of the world.

'Going to Singapore' nowadays means little more than the high anxiety, intrusive screening and misleadingly-styled 'Duty Free' shopping of an international airport, and long hours in the air. The Robertsons faced the perils of a long sea voyage. Though the giant tea clippers were still ploughing between India and London under billowing sails, grizzled military men and mottled planters, unmarried girls of good family in search of husbands, nervous governesses and hopeful young couples like the Robertsons could now travel eastward with Peninsular and Orient Lines, who for some years had been running their steam ships, powered by paddle wheels rather than propellers, from England through the Mediterranean to Alexandria. From there, with the Suez Canal still ten years in the future, as yet no more than the bold desert mirage of Ferdinand de Lesseps,[8] eastbound passengers clambered onto a rickety train for a furnace–hot ride across the sands to Suez, where they would board another boat to sail down the Red Sea and into the Indian Ocean. The whole adventure must have been a heady cocktail of excitement, fatigue, wonder, sea-sickness, and, these being British ships, socially stratified claustrophobia.

Singapore itself was not just half a world but more like a galaxy away from Elgin, a garrison and a busy trading port in whose dense jungle hinterland tigers still stalked and killed. While the red-coated soldiers drilled and bugled, Singapore bought and sold.

Iron, porcelain, medicines, sewing machines, cotton goods, gabardines and guns came in from Britain. China, what was then Siam, the Malay States, Vietnam and islands and peninsulas in between shipped in spices, silks, gold, tin, rattan, mother of pearl, camphor, silk, and opium, that powerful source of sweet dreams, sweeter wealth, diplomatic manoeuvring and, in 1839 and again in 1856, even minor wars. It was hardly surprising that piracy in the surrounding seas by well-armed fleets from the Philippines and Northern Borneo was a major enterprise in itself, and a serious threat.

In Commerce Square, European, Chinese, 'Jewish', Arab, Armenian and American trading firms each had their own warehouses, often with the owner and his family living upstairs, and their own wharf. The faces the excited young Robertsons saw in the crowded streets were predominantly Chinese. Most were immigrant coolies with their mutual support system of secret societies, though as business prospered, so did the community of increasingly wealthy Chinese entrepreneurs and middlemen. Disease lurked in the rusty hand-cranked water pumps, the drains and the middens. The Singapore military garrison had its own medical staff, but the many European mercantile families and their 'outriders' – the chandlers, bankers, auctioneers, shipping agents, lawyers, teachers, and clergy – had to look for help to private practitioners, the first of whom opened his surgery in 1826. At the bottom of the social scale, the ragged tide of sick seamen, mostly Chinese or Indians, often carriers of smallpox and cholera, and much afflicted by scurvy, eye infections, yaws, venereal disease and 'gun shot and spear wounds received from pirates', had to rely on the decrepit General Hospital or clinics run by Scottish and American missionaries.

By 1846 there were four private doctors. One, J. I. Woodford, clearly had a hard time making ends meet and took to advertising help for those who might, so to speak, have similar problems by way of a booklet on '*Sex Preservation – on the Secret Infirmities of Youth and Maturity with 40 Coloured Engravings*, sent in sealed envelopes. Personal Consultations by Post.' He later went bankrupt, after which, following his calling to its logical end, he became an undertaker.

A more successful practitioner was Robert Little, with whom John Robertson went into partnership, advertising their association in the *Singapore Free Press* in July 1858. The evocative history of Singapore medicine in that period by Y. K. Lee shows that like any closed and competitive 'shop', all the more one operating in a sweltering, gossipy, status-sensitive climate, the medical profession was rife with jealousy and backbiting. In 1860 and 1861 both partners found themselves with enough spare time to indulge in verbal fisticuffs with colleagues. After a ding-dong battle in the newspaper correspondence columns, Little had to eat humble pie for seeming to question the credentials of another doctor. For his part Robertson entered the lists with a passionate polemic against the 'defective' evidence given in a murder trial for the prosecution by a doctor whom he castigated as 'incompetent'. Had the evidence been accepted there would in his view have been a serious miscarriage of justice. He took his complaints to the press, including three Scottish papers, and to the Governor, but the fuss soon died away and the partners' public outbursts did not exclude them from invitations to Government House; both were guests at the Balls marking Queen Victoria's birthday in 1860 and 1861. Though they sold their Dispensary they continued to be available to patients 'from 10.00 a.m. to 4 p.m. daily, Sundays excepted and at other times at our private residences.'

The Robertsons had five sons, one of whom died in infancy, and three daughters. The sons had the Far East in their blood. Alan became a doctor, practising in what were then the Federal Malay States. Thomas Murray Robertson, also a doctor, became a Coroner in Singapore. The other two sons broke the medical mould, but stayed rooted resolutely East of Suez. Farleigh became a planter and the youngest son, John Argyll Robertson, Tommy's father, also born in Singapore in September 1871, emerged as a canny banker. But he too navigated by the same exotic if schizophrenia-inducing lodestone, his career a gazetteer of one teeming Asian city after another. But he never forgot his roots, his kilt or his bagpipes.

It is John Argyll Robertson, whose journey we follow next. But first we need to explain 'Argyll.' Medical literature connects 'Argyll Robertson' to an important eye problem, in its day most commonly associated with syphilis, but still part of the modern medical student's curriculum. It was the discovery of one the most distinguished ophthalmic surgeons of the Victorian era, the resoundingly named Douglas Moray Cooper Lamb Argyll Robertson, born in Edinburgh a few years after John Hutchinson Robertson.[9] Though they were apparently unrelated, they became friends, cementing their friendship with a pact reminiscent of a Victorian novel, that each would pass on one of the other's names to one of his children.

Douglas Robertson died childless, but John Hutchinson fulfilled his part of the compact and gave the 'Argyll' name to Tommy's father John, who in turn passed it to his children. That at least is the story as it has been handed down through generations. It leaves tantalisingly open the point that Douglas' father was also named John Argyll Robertson.[10]

Notes
1. Personal papers and Popov, D., p. 23.
2. One official letter amongst the thousands of papers in the National Archives is addressed to him as 'Robbie', though the writer does not seem to have been someone with whom he was in frequent contact.
3. See e.g. Devine, p. xxiii et seq.
4. Courtesy Edinburgh University Archives.
5. Courtesy National Archives of Scotland and Elgin Public Library.
6. Courtesy Old Operating Theatre and Herb Garret, London.
7. As the Elgin History puts it blandly 'Like others in the Company he was able to take advantage of local trading opportunities to amass a considerable personal fortune'. And as Devine cites, 'in North America and India they claimed not merely a reasonable but a quite indecent share of the spoils'.
8. Ferdinand, Vicomte de Lesseps 1805–84.
9. Robertson, Douglas M. C. L. 1837–1909. Oxford DNB, doi:10.1093/ref:odnb/35778.
10. Douglas Robertson himself was not immune to the lure of the East. In retirement he took into his care the eldest daughter of one of his former pupils, a high-caste Indian, made several visits to her father's home and died out there in 1909; his ward's father lit the funeral pyre on the banks of the Gondli River. See DNB ibid.

3

Drawn to the East

Nineteenth century medical wisdom decreed that because of the risk of disease and the rigours of the climate, children – Anglo-Saxon children, that is – should not be kept out in the Tropics beyond the age of eight. Often that meant prolonged separation, as it would years later in Tommy's case, but John Hutchinson Robertson's family seems to have come back together in the 1880s, to live in an imposing four storey granite-faced house at 15 Great King Street, in Edinburgh's prestigious New Town.

Tommy's father, John Argyll reminisced to his own children that family life in Great King Street had been 'kindly but strict . . .' His parents were addressed in high Victorian style as 'Mater' and 'Pater' though if they wanted to reprimand him for some minor transgression, he would be called 'Robertson'. They believed in 'the Presbyterian ethic of honesty, integrity, and hard work . . . no flamboyance and not huge fun. No whistling on Sundays and no noise, take your hands out of your pockets, butter or jam but not both together, and so on'.[1]

But there were good times too, like the Highland holidays, where John Argyll learned the subtleties of salmon fishing, how to read the river, to choose the right length of rod, the weight of his line, and decide which flies would work best. Should it be the traditional 'Meg in Her Braws' or 'Kinmont Willie', or perhaps the 'Silver Doctor' and the 'Blue Charm'? He also mastered the age old skill of 'guddling' or 'tickling' trout, a manoeuvre not without parallels with Tommy's own later career. The guddler has to wade nimbly into cold fast flowing water, balance on slippery boulders, and then wait, and wait. And wait. Finally as the speckled target slides slowly past his legs innocently foraging in the weeds, the guddler's hand slips below the surface inch by inch, closing in on the feasting fish with enormous patience and the lightest of touches. The infinitesimal tightening of the fingers, the climactic feather light tickling, all an intimate interplay between man and fish which can set up such a bond that the trout is often thrown back into the water rather than tossed into the creel to be taken home for gutting and grilling.[2]

John Argyll Robertson was enrolled at Edinburgh's George Watson's College, established in 1741 as a charity hospital and converted into a boys' school in 1870. Its initial roll was an impressive 1,000 pupils, a hard place for a boy to find his footing. As with Tommy later, success in sport, rather than schoolbooks, was the key, and John Argyll's height – he was well over six feet tall in adult life – and speed made him a powerful rugby wing three-quarter.

University seems not to have been an option, but when it came to a career, that fizzy *Irn Bru* of Scottish energy, interconnection and a touch of nepotism produced the entry ticket, one that would lead John Argyll back to 'faraway places with strange sounding names, far away over the sea . . .' He was to be trained as a banker, but a banker of a now-forgotten era, one who dealt with real money, real people and real business. He was to become a 'cadet', an entry level candidate for management, at the Chartered of Bank of India, Australia and China,[3] introduced there by his uncle William Dougal, manager of the Bank's branch in Singapore, no doubt at the gentle nudging of his wife, John Argyll's Aunt Maggie.

The Bank was the vision of James Wilson, Scottish entrepreneur, farsighted politician, public servant and founder of *The Economist*.[4] In October 1852 it raised a sizeable initial capital of £500,000 to take advantage of the growing flows of trade and finance between the old and new worlds. A shrewd Scottish voice can be heard in the commitment in the share prospectus that while the new Bank would undertake all forms of legitimate banking business, 'All other transactions will be strictly prohibited, and especially the making [of] advances on landed or other immovable securities or growing crops or acting in any other way in a mercantile capacity.' Many twenty-first century bank shareholders, not least those of other once proud pillars of Scottish finance, might wish that their management had been guided by similar principles. The Chartered Bank story is another reflection of how British 'Dominion over palm and pine' was reinforced. It opened its first branches in Bombay, Calcutta and Shanghai in 1858; Hong Kong and Singapore followed in 1859. The opening of the Suez Canal in 1869 and the extension of the telegraph line to China in 1871 gave further boost to what was already a thriving business, financing trade in cotton, indigo, rice, sugar, tobacco, hemp and silk. It also had high hopes of profiting from the flow of gold from the new discoveries in Australia.

The Bank's Archives show that John Argyll joined on 15 December 1890, when he was 19. He spent four years in London, learning how to write up ledgers in a neat, round hand, the principles of double entry book keeping, the rudiments of foreign exchange, and how, in the language to the times, 'to spot a wrong 'un' when assessing the character of a prospective borrower, hard enough to do in one's own territory and hugely more difficult when dealing in other lands and cultures. For relaxation he played rugby for London Scottish, the elite club formed in 1878 (it seems fitting that the inaugural meeting was held in MacKays Tavern in the City). He also played the pipes in the London Scottish Rifle Volunteers, a Territorial Army unit originally formed in 1793 as 'the Highland Armed Association of London', (a title which in Tommy's later career might have had him pricking up his ears), and reinvigorated in 1859 by the Highland Society of London and the Caledonian Society.

In July 1894 he was posted to Singapore and Bangkok as 'sub accountant' and in 1896 to Calcutta where again the 'daily round and common task' of banking was agreeably punctuated by sport – including athletics, an activity for which the climate was singularly unsuited. John Argyll paraded his piping prowess for Scottish high days and holidays, as well as rugby matches; rugby's Calcutta Cup is said to have been cast from the silver rupees held in a Chartered Bank vault by the 'Calcutta (Rugby) Football Club' when it was disbanded in the late 1870s. There were also less sporty evenings with a 'chota peg', Anglo-Indian slang for a whisky and soda, and billiards at one of Calcutta's opulent clubs. We do not know at this distance which of them as a junior bank employee in that stratified society he would have been invited or expected to join. There were several choices – the Calcutta Cricket and Football Club, said to be the oldest cricket club outside Great Britain, the Racket Club, set up by the East India Company in 1793 so that 'noble gentlemen could flex and exercise their muscles . . . and keep their sweaty portly bodies free of the dreaded vapours,' the Royal Calcutta Golf Club with its breeze-wafting punkahs swaying hypnotically from the ceiling, or the Turf Club. All sound convivially if restrictively colonial.[5]

A gap in the records prompts a 'fast-forward' to 1908, when John Argyll took advantage of a spell of home leave to get engaged, and in October, married, to Sarah Lilian Pitt Healing, then 30, one of eleven children of the owner of a substantial grain mill in Tewkesbury. The Healing daughters were sent to Cheltenham Ladies College, where Lilian, known to her extensive family as 'Mim', would have been a pupil towards the end of the 48 year reign of its driving force, Dorothea Beale. The sons went either to Cheltenham College or to Clifton College near Bristol, both outcrops of Britain's nineteenth century fervour for applying architectural exuberance to the creation of new temples of 'muscular Christianity'.

Their honeymoon, the last sight and scent of Scotland for perhaps many years, perhaps forever, was spent at the Fishers Hotel in Pitlochry, on the River Tummel, fringed by the Grampian Mountains. The railway had arrived in 1863, so they would have had an easier journey than John Hutchinson Robertson's expedition to Elgin. Their hotel, first built in 1830 in an eclectic mix of Scots baronial and French chateau styles, is still welcoming guests today. Though it now fronts a busy road, a Victorian era photograph shows it standing in rather splendid isolation. By December the newlyweds were on their way from Scotland to Sumatra. The Robertsons understood the demands of duty and the lure of the East. For the Healings, it may have been harder. A daughter was expected to get married, but even in those heady days when overseas territories were a prideful part of the fabric of British life, not yet 'the white man's burden', it must have plucked at the heartstrings to wave farewell to a young woman setting off with her new cabin trunks to the other side of the world, prey to fever, worry and loneliness, with 'Home leave' granted only every few years, and the only contact via sea mail, which at best took more than a month to arrive. Lilian would have been much missed. She sang prettily, played the violin, danced well, and could turn her hand to fancy embroidery as well as mundane domestic needlework. She played golf and tennis, and, a rarer trait, understood and enjoyed cricket. She would have been amused to see Tommy's wartime triumphs against the Germans described by an Anglophile American intelligence officer as 'the greatest Test Match of the century'.[6] It is nice to set against this image of all round delight that in the view of one of her children she was lucky to have lived her entire life supported by domestic staff as she 'couldn't even boil an egg!'.[7]

Now she was to be a colonial banker's wife, and Tommy's mother.

Sumatra, then part of the Dutch East Indian Empire, is today the largest in the giant sprawl of islands vast and small which make up modern Indonesia. Medan, pronounced 'Madan' was its fast growing commercial centre. Its original name was 'Medan Poteri,' which translates evocatively as 'The Princesses Field', commemorating the daughters of the local Sultans whose playground it was before Dutch tobacco planters and Chinese entrepreneurs seized on the agricultural potential of thousands of square miles of fertile soil, and the hot, humid climate. Tobacco was the region's main crop, but palm oil and rubber also poured their profits into Medan's coffers, including the vaults of the Chartered Bank, whose 'sub-agency' was now John Argyll's responsibility. His predecessor Mr. Campbell (no doubt a fellow Scot) had left at short notice, whether as a result of disease, drink or defalcation, the three demons of colonial banking, we do not know.

By the time Tommy was born in 1909, the 'playground', now linked by rail to the harbour at Belawan, forty miles away on the swampy coast of the Strait of Malacca, had become an elegantly laid out bustling township. Blank out their shady verandahs, and many of the larger houses could have been transplanted from a prosperous Dutch suburb, and the 'sanitary system' was claimed to be 'the equal of any English town.' Risks still lurked. Only a few years earlier a cholera epidemic had forced postponement of the planned opening of the Chartered Bank's sub-agency. There were two good hotels (to judge from a contemporary photograph the dining room at the De Boer would not have been out of place in Edwardian London's West End), a 'handsome' railway station, tennis courts and football pitches. The central square where the Sultan's daughters once danced, 'now has its beauties heightened', one writer observed, 'by the fashionable costumes of the ladies of Medan; in the morning equestrians and equestriennes trot or canter around it. At night a band plays cheerful music and all in all Medan is a very pleasant place, a joy forever.' Had Tommy been able to take them in, his infant images would have been of palm trees, the town's road roller hauled by a plodding long-tusked elephant, spruce Dutch Colonial policemen, buffalo tugging wooden ploughs through the paddy fields, Indian washermen sluicing laundry in the river, and the glittering magic of the chandeliers, ornamental mirrors and silverware on display in the *Warenhuis*, or General Store, which also offered its customers bespoke tailoring and dressmaking services. We can get a sense of the Chartered Bank sub-agency from a contemporary photograph of the headquarters of a Medan trading firm. It was an all-male affair – no coquettish secretaries or pert receptionists. The manager, at the rear of the open plan room, from where he can keep an eye on things, is in shirtsleeves, with a dark tie as a badge of rank. The male clerks, mostly Indian, are in high-collared crisp white linen suits. A pith helmet, that totemic combination of protection and privilege, sits on top of one of the cupboards. To the side squats a solid safe, and in the foreground a letter press. In the days before duplicating machines and Xeroxes, letters were copied by laying a moist sheet of tissue paper over the text and pressing the two pieces of paper in a heavy press which might have belonged to the tool kit of the Spanish Inquisition.

Life outside the office had its social compensations but running the sub-agency was not an easy job. Beyond the complexities and sensitivities of granting or refusing credit in a small community, the daily business had a special 'eastern' edge. Local transactions were settled in a mix of sterling Bills of Exchange (commercial IOU's with which Tommy would become familiar later in life), well-travelled and highly sought after gold Mexican dollars (in which the Chinese 'Coolies' cannily demanded to be paid), Spanish silver 'Carolus' coins and the sycee, a popular small ingot whose value was determined mainly by weight but also by the delicacy of the silversmith's engraving. Their relative prices fluctuated sharply with the ebb and flow of trade and the far-distant London markets, and the sharp minds of those Indian clerks and the clicking of the abacus were essential. The sub-agency stuck firmly to financing the trading needs of the tobacco and tin merchants. True to the founder's precepts, they avoided the loans against plantations and mines which brought competitors such as the Oriental and the Agra Banks to their knees.

The overall impression from that office image, like that of Medan itself, is one of orderly prosperity. Unlike the world outside. The town's hinterland was spectacular, a range of mountains, blue in the haze, capped by two volcanic cones, one of which, nicknamed 'Sulphur Mountain', blazed briefly and brightly yellow as it was lanced by the rays of the morning sun. But the country was also untamed; tribes still fought in the rainforests with bows and blowpipes, and had been known to lunch, Lecter-like on their enemies' livers, (one of the nearby conflicts, in Aceh, has persisted to the twenty-first century). Tigers, six or seven feet long, padded through the underbrush stalking wild boar, tapir and deer. Sumatra blood pythons, deadly kraits and heat-seeking pit vipers lay coiled in the lush leaves, and crocodiles rippled the dark waters of the local lakes and rivers; deaths in their snapping jaws were so common that the Medan newspaper only reported incidents if at least two unfortunate locals had been killed by the same beast. The town was growing fast. Between 1905 and 1913 its population doubled from some 13,000 to 27,000. The 1,400 Europeans, mainly Dutch, were in a minority. They held most of the economic reins but entrepreneurs in the far larger Chinese community were beginning to make their own powerful mark as planters, astute property developers, bankers and traders. Each ethnic group – as well as the Chinese, the official records listed 'natives', Arabs, Indians and 'foreign Orientals' – was housed in its separate segment of the town and lived its own life, many of the plantation and factory workers with hopes and dreams sustained by opium, still then a trade flourishing in the hands of local dealers. It was not until 1912 that the local Government, for whom it was a major source of tax revenue, took over the trade and began efforts to run it down.

Tommy was far too young for the birdsong languages and spicy aromas of his birth place to have left a lasting mark on his infant psyche, but his parents' love was surely reinforced by swaddling and cosseting by a nanny and the house staff, most of them Chinese, who were all ready to coo, cluck and spoil at the drop of a rattle or the scrabbling of a salamander lizard trying to nose its way under the mosquito netting.

When he was two, he had to suffer the emotional relegation pangs experienced by most first born when a sister, Joan, was born in 1911, also given Argyll as her second name. But harder blows were to fall.

Notes
1. Personal papers.
2. See for instance, *The New York Times*, Letters to the Editor, 6 June 1905.
3. Since 1969 one of the twin pillars of the Standard Chartered Group.
4. Wilson, James 1805–60. Oxford DNB, www.oforddnb.com/view/article/ 29660.
5. See Bhageria, P and Mahotra, P.
6. Norman Holmes Pearson's Introduction to *Double-cross System in the War of 1939 to 1945* by J. C. Masterman.
7. Personal papers.

4

From a View to a Death

In 1913 there was a spell of home leave and the family, with Lilian pregnant again, came back to the UK. They rented a house in Richmond in Surrey, (unaware of the rôle that charming and, as yet uncongested riverside town was to play in Tar's later adventures with the tricky Welshman SNOW), where a second son Ian[1] was born in July. He must literally have been in swaddling clothes, fussed over by the amah, or nanny, his parents had brought with them across the world from Medan, when sometime in September, the family travelled north to Scotland. They had rented a fishing lodge close to Dulnain Bridge, even today little more than a dot of a village framed by the Cairngorm Mountains, miles of pine forests and glacial screes, and straddling one of the Spey's main tributaries, the river Dulnain. It had family resonance, set just two hours' drive north of their honeymoon hotel at Pitlochry and a little less than forty miles south of Elgin where John Hutchinson Robertson first practised. The river's name is said to be a corruption of the Gaelic for 'flood' or 'spate' and it is notorious for the speed at which it rises after rain. A much misquoted version of an ancient Greek aphorism warns that 'Those whom the Gods wish to destroy, they first make happy'. What happened at that time of holiday happiness is lost in the waters and in time but its destructive force will be icily clear to any parent. The notice in *The Times* 'Deaths' column, with its original capital letters, was terse. 'ROBERTSON: On the 21st September 1913, at Dulnain Bridge, Scotland. Joan Argyll, the only daughter of Mr. and Mrs. JOHN ARGYLL ROBERTSON, aged two years.'

Tommy's brother Ian remembered only that she 'drowned in the river . . .' Did she tumble from the eighteenth century stone bridge that carries the B939 road through the village? Were the family fishing or just picking their way happily through the pebbles along the river? If she simply slipped, what was the amah doing? Did Tommy see his sister swept away? Later family memories suggest that the terrified amah sobbed to his shattered parents that it was somehow Tommy's fault, not hers. Whatever scene the mind conjures up, the blow must have been frightful, air and light sucked out of the family, a weight of grief perhaps compounded in Tommy's case with a lacerating sense of responsibility, even guilt. But for Tommy the incomprehension of the loss, the black mourning clothes, the sad hush punctuated by quiet sobbing were to be followed by a parting which may have been even more searing.

The Chartered Bank respected sorrow, but had a business to run.[2] It needed a new man in Kuala Lumpur, then the capital of an agglomeration of territories – Selangor, Perak, Negeri Semblan and Pahang – put together by Britain in 1895 (and now a major constituent of modern Malaysia). John Argyll accepted the post. Maybe he and Lilian wanted to put distance between them and their loss. But though they took baby Ian with them, Tommy was left behind, a decision ostensibly based on the calculation that by the time their next spell of home leave was due, he would be past the benchmark age of eight. Children look inward, with only a blurry barrier between reality and imagination, and find it hard to talk about the shadows that haunt their nursery nights, but it is no great feat of imagination to conclude that whatever he was told, Tommy felt that he was somehow being punished, ostracised, cut out of the family because of whatever he may have done or failed to do, on the river bank. Instead of the heat, excitement and Colonial comforts of Kuala Lumpur, and the deeper warmth of the family embrace, he found himself in the architecturally gracious but staid spa of Tunbridge Wells. It had long shed the raffish glamour of its Regency heyday and since 1909, the year Tommy was born, had been allowed to add the designation 'Royal' to its name. It was now largely a genteel enclave for retired Army officers and overseas Civil Servants, crusty conservatives of the kind who have been collectively – though mythically – caricatured as writers of letters to the *Daily Telegraph* lamenting the decline of modern Britain, and signing themselves 'Disgusted, of Tunbridge Wells.'

If the death of his sister and the rupture from his parents left a scar, it was one he concealed beneath a genial exterior for the rest of his life. As one of his close family remarked, 'he always wanted to be liked'.

Notes
1. Robertson, Major-General Ian Argyll Robertson of Bracla, CB, MBE, MA, DL, 1913–2010, Seaforth Highlanders and later Commandant of the 8th Highland Division.
2. It was running it quite well. In 1913 it reported another rise in profit, and an 18% dividend for shareholders, despite a string of banking failures in India and a near meltdown in the silver market there. Only joint intervention by Hong Kong and Shanghai Bank and Chartered Bank saved it from collapse.

5

Lost and Found

Tommy was sent to live with Mim Healing's sister Margaret Hurst, 'Aunt Peg' and her husband Bertram, a vicar in Tunbridge Wells.

As Tommy's brother Ian later remembered, their aunt and uncle 'did their very best against all odds'. But they were long odds. Aunt Peg 'had none of the good looks of the rest of her family, nor the spirit, was older [than Mim] and very deaf. Uncle Bertram was dull, holy and older still. It was little short of cruelty to leave a small boy with a couple he hardly knew . . . Tommy felt deserted. How can one judge the subjective effect this might have had?' One who could, and captured it in his largely autobiographical novel *Of Human Bondage*, was Somerset Maugham, who spent several miserable boyhood years under the fusty wing of his mean-spirited uncle and a kindlier aunt in their claustrophobic Kentish parsonage.[1]

To compound the sense of alienation, Tommy was soon sent to board at what would nowadays be called a 'pre-school' at Crowborough. The two middle-aged spinsters who ran 'Brackenwood' were 'a delightful pair and ran a very happy school' for the twenty or so young boys in their care. Even so, being away from what he had briefly known as his new home, going back to the Hursts only for holidays, must have been wrenching, although cricket, and rounders, and playing soldiers around a bracken-covered Roman camp on the Common, were exciting diversions. Perhaps less so the twice daily prayers and the ritual Sunday walk in file to the local church, dressed in a child's version of a sailor's suit topped by a jaunty cap.

From Brackenwood Tommy moved to a preparatory school, 'Sunnydown', on the Hogs Back outside Guildford, where the headmaster, Mr. How, and his wife had some 60 boys in their care.

The dates are blurred but somewhere in the background, the First World War, that savage real-life version of those soldier games was being fought out, and even young boys would have been given pep talks about patriotism, sacrifice and the callousness and savagery of the Huns. Folk memories of the time tell us that the rumble of gunfire and trench-mining in France could sometimes be heard in the South of England; whether it disturbed the tranquillity of Sunnydown we do not know.

We do know that on the other side of the world, in Kuala Lumpur, Robertson family life went on, centred on the bank, their home in a large bungalow high up on Maxwell Road, and the Royal Selangor Club, another characteristic Imperial export in its mock-Tudor style reminiscent of the Surrey hills, and its racially-restricted membership. It was popularly known as 'the Spotted Dog', an evocation of its early days when, legend has it, the wife of one of its founder members would tether her two Dalmatians to the gateposts when she and her husband were in the Club.

Though the First World War itself never reached the Malay States, John Argyll was commissioned in the local Defence Volunteers, and the Chartered and other banks stretched themselves to supply the credit needed as Britain clamoured for ever increasing quantities of the essential raw materials – notably rubber and tin – that the Far East produced. When it was over he and Lilian went back to England, mainly to leave their second son Ian, first at Brackenwood and then to join Tommy at Sunnydown, a reunion that relieved Tommy's loneliness and gave Ian a mentor as he faced the odd and often cruel rituals that define the world of a collective of small boys or even, as in the case of Army life, grown men.

When not hunched over schoolbooks, reciting by rote, or trying to tease Mr. How into a spasm of anger which would make him bite through the fountain-pen he had the habit of clenching absent-mindedly in his teeth, the boys' school life was a happy mix of sport, swimming, bird-nesting, and picking fruit in the school garden. Visits by small groups (Ian missed out on the opportunity) to take tea with Sir Arthur Conan Doyle, in his house nearby, when he would entertain the awed boys with fairy stories, rather than

Sherlock Holmes' adventures, were an occasional extra-curricular high point, as were summer holidays in the care of a Governess, building sandcastles and playing cricket on beaches which, as in most memories of that time, were always sunny and never crowded.

On 3 June 1919 John Argyll was appointed to the Order of the British Empire (OBE) for 'services in connection with finance and war charities in the Malay States'. Though in later years the story grew that he had been personally invested by Edward, Prince of Wales, the records show that he received the honour from the High Commissioner for the Malay States on 20 March 1920.[2] The Prince did make a Far East tour around his Royal father's far flung Dominions on the battle cruiser HMS *Renown* for several months from October 1921, and John Argyll would certainly have been on the guest list for one or more of the glittering receptions; in all likelihood the two memories have been conflated. The Prince went on to a short-lived reign and the high drama of his Abdication, a drama in whose denouement as we shall see, Tommy, by then Tar claimed to have played a sensitive rôle for MI5.

In 1923 John Argyll brought the family back to Britain, settling down at 14 Hanover Terrace, a colonnaded Nash façade fronting onto the greenery of Regents Park. Seen through the prism of today prices and fashionable addresses, this seems a 'high-end' home even for a senior commercial banker. But though the house, with a mews cottage at the back, was large, in those distant days the Terrace, with its then unwhitewashed, smoke and fog-grimed façade did not have the social cachet of Belgravia or Mayfair. To judge from the directories of that time, the best it could boast amongst its residents were two minor MPs. Moreover, as part of the Crown Estate, until as recently as the 1960s its houses and flats were only available on short leases, so that living there did not entail the same jaw-dropping financial commitment needed today; a house a few doors along the Terrace from the Robertsons was recently for sale at £20 million. Even so, and allowing for the relatively low cost of maintaining a domestic staff, John Argyll's lifestyle was some way beyond the 'many a mickle makes a muckle' philosophy of his forebears. A chauffeur who lived in the mews cottage drove him to and from the

City of London in an impressively high bodied seven-seater Minerva saloon, the Belgian built challenge to the Rolls Royce and Hispano Suiza. Its dashboard was an art deco delight of burr-walnut, silver dials and knobs, whose rôle in operating the six-cylinder engine modern motorists can only guess at. For weekends there was a Riley, though which of the sporty, even rakish models of that much-missed marque – 'As old as the industry, as modern as the hour' – we do not know. The Lynx, the Gamecock, the Ascot, the Monaco, the Kestrel, among many others, conjure up images of country house parties, or a quick dash down the A4 to Skindles Hotel in Maidenhead.

The Robertsons also had a full-time cook, and the support staff needed to run a house with five bedrooms, three receptions rooms and what estate agents term 'the usual offices'. In that now vanished world *The Times* carried daily columns of advertisements seeking domestic help, carefully graduated by 'below stairs' status. Governesses, Companions and Lady Nurses topped the list, followed by Private Secretaries, Housekeepers and Cooks. Bobbing respectfully in the wake of these domestic battleships came a flotilla of Parlour Maids, House, Kitchen and Scullery Maids, the nicely styled Between Maids, and Gardeners. The high-rolling lifestyle may be explained by another family memory that at some point John Argyll gave up the relatively staid world of commercial banking and moved into stockbroking, then a happily unregulated hunting ground, where the well-informed and well-connected could make a good living. Punitive tax rates, levies on capital gains and cadres of 'Compliance Officers' grimly determined to uncover the smallest breach of an ever swelling book of rules, were not even clouds on the horizon of the brokers' world in Throgmorton Street. Tommy was also on the move, from the small world of Sunnydown to the uncharted acres of a British public school, as dangerously unfamiliar in its way as the hinterland of Medan.

Notes
1. See Hastings, p. 12.
2. Courtesy the Central Chancellery of The Orders of Knighthood.

6

An Unsentimental Education

Charterhouse had been founded in London in 1611 but moved in 1872 to the Surrey hills near Godalming. Its Victorian buildings and towers dominated the skyline like a vast medieval abbey, or a super-sized version of the Carthusian monastery which had been its original home. He had to learn its inwardnesses, its vernacular, its topography, even its calendar. What Mr. How would have called, prosaically, the Autumn Term of 1923, when Tommy arrived with his tuckbox and suitcase, Charterhouse knew as The Orations' Quarter. The School had four 'old houses' Saunderites, Verites, Gownboys (historically the scholars' house) and Girdlestoneites. Seven more were added later. Tommy was to join Girdlestoneites. It would have taken all of five minutes for the anxious new boy to be told by a patronising senior in a silver striped blazer that whatever the official name, his House was always referred to as 'Duckites'. The blameless Mr. Girdlestone had walked with a splay-footed waddle, earning him the nickname 'Duck' from his malicious pupils. Saunderites was to be pronounced 'Sarnderites' and one of the 'new' Houses, Bodeites, had originally been Buissonites, in honour of a one time Head of Languages. It had to be hastily renamed after he decamped with the School Matron.

Where was the Wilderness? How did you get to Big Field? What are Verites blazer colours? What does a brown tie signify? How do new boys know these things, unless they have been passed on by a brusque father or condescending elder brother who have crossed the same minefields? Even the academic ladder was idiosyncratic. Boys did not move up automatically from class to class as each new school year began, but according to their progress and prowess. That meant not all boys reached the top form and that some senior classes included boys who were younger but brighter than those a level or two below them. Tommy was a quick learner and soon found his feet.

In the 1980s a maverick British second hand book dealer, published a guide to British bookshops in which he classified their proprietors by a series of acronyms, as arcane in their way as Charterhouse's naming of Houses. One he awarded only sparingly – he found most other dealers tiresome, a view they reciprocated – is probably quite apt for Tommy as a schoolboy, and indeed for the rest of his life. 'ETGOW' stood for 'Easy to Get On With', an amiable all-rounder. To judge from his annual examination results Tommy was somewhere in the middle of the pack academically, but made his mark across the variegated spectrum of school life, a contribution probably more appreciated by peers and masters than brainpower. He played football (a game Charterhouse and its competitor Westminster both claim to have invented) for his House and several times for the school itself. Cricket too, which would have pleased his mother; the school score books suggest he was a deft bowler. He played Fives, sang in the choir and appeared as a Trojan Guard in an ambitious musical production of Gilbert Murray's rendition of the classic Greek drama 'Rhesus', described by the reviewer in the school magazine as 'astonishingly good'. The reviewer was an anonymous academic who, observing that Murray's version was a revival, could not resist the donnish quip that it was a 'rhesuscitation'. Tommy was even a stalwart member of the school Fire Brigade, though there is no record of its having had to cope with any serious conflagrations during his time. In his first year he played the piano for Duckites in an inter-House music competition, contributing 'Poupèe Valsante' by the Hungarian born composer Poldini, the piano squatting incongruously in the centre of the School's boxing ring. Further down the same bill came Chopin's Nocturne in F Minor, played by one J G Kell, son of the then Director of MI5 and as we shall see later, the source of the suggestion, several years later that Tommy should join his father's service. The Kells were devoted parents and would certainly have been there.

Holidays were a time to enjoy Hanover Terrace, rowing a boat on the lake in Regents Park, visiting Madame Tussauds with Ian, eating ice-cream in the American style, white tile and chrome Parlour at Selfridges, learning to drive under the chauffeur's watchful eye and beginning to cope with the frustrations of golf on summer breaks in Ballater and Turnberry. Much as the First World War had rumbled in the background during his time at prep school, so Britain's socially divisive General Strike in 1926 does not seem to have clouded the tranquillity of his life, other than with memories of John Argyll1 fulminating in fine 'Disgusted, Tunbridge Wells' style that the Trades Unions would ruin the country.

We who live in a different era need to remind ourselves that even though we see on television screens the daily tally of young people's deaths in distant lands, for Tommy's generation world war, the almost unimaginable scale of the human sacrifices and its wounds, both real and psychological, were a visible and devastating reality, not the stuff of history books, films and anniversary celebrations on windswept beaches. In 1927, the year he left Charterhouse, the school opened its Chapel designed by Giles Gilbert Scott and consecrated to the memory of the close to 700 former pupils who, as barely grown young men had died in the First World War. It must have been a sobering background to his final term when, already a monitor or senior boy in his House, he began to work in the Vth Form Special Science class, where boys prepared for the entrance examinations for the Royal Military College at Sandhurst.

For Tommy, joining the College (nowadays the 'Academy') a crucible memorably described by one of the thousands of young men forged in it, as 'Hogwarts with guns'[1] was like a game of Snakes and Ladders in the Hanover Terrace nursery on a wet afternoon.

Notes
1. Patrick Hennessy Literary Review, 2007.

7

'Bags of Swank'

As the canvas-roofed Commer truck rattled through the College's Town Gates from the station, carrying Tommy and fellow new entrants, all trying to look nonchalant rather than nervous, he slid back down the Ladder from being a senior boy at Charterhouse who knew his way around, and was liked and respected by his peers, to a bemused new arrival on a foreign landscape whose layout and customs had to be learned in double-quick time, and where he was under far more pressure to conform and perform. Another nickname for Sandhurst, 'the Factory', must have seemed well-deserved. Though he was now styled a 'Gentleman Cadet' it was made brutally clear to him and his fellows, as it was to their predecessors and successors, that for now they were the lowest of the low. A more polite formulation was that a Cadet was 'not quite a Gentleman and not quite an officer' summed up in the menacing growl with which the Sandhurst Drill Instructors greeted Tommy and other apprehensive new arrivals: 'I'll call you 'Sir', and you'll call me 'Sir'. The difference is, you mean it'. (For John Argyll Robertson, proud though he and Mim certainly were, one thing had not changed – he was still having to dip into his pocket. Back then, the Course alone cost some £300 to £400 (depending on what one uses as the basis for calculation, somewhere between £20,000 and as much as £50,000 today) and John Argyll would also have paid handsomely for Tommy's expensively tailored mess kit as well as his mess bills, which given the Sandhurst lifestyle, were no doubt at wince-inducing levels.)

An old joke had it that on a clear day a newly-arrived Cadet standing on the roof of the Old College building could see the landmarks of his Army future spread out around him. Sandhurst itself, the military garrison and training grounds of Aldershot, the Staff College at Camberley and 'finally, Broadmoor Lunatic Asylum'.

We do not have Tommy's own memories of his spell there (his parents had meanwhile moved to a large and, again, well staffed house outside Woking, exchanging the Minerva for an American Buick V8). But those of his contemporaries such as David Niven and the author John Masters suggest that in those first few months, cadets might have felt the Commer truck had trundled them straight to Broadmoor. Harried and bullied, they stomped the parade ground, sweating, bellowed at by moustachioed drill instructors, spent long, mindless hours polishing brass cap badges and belt buckles, rubbing down the goose-pimpled leather of their boots with a toothbrush handle till the toe caps took on a mirror-like shine, even buffing the steel studs on the soles, and ironing the spare set of laces. Once burnished to glossy coal black perfection, one pair of 'best boots' would be carefully stowed in the bedside locker, only to be worn on the most important parades. Every wooden and metal component of the standard issue Lee-Enfield .303 rifle had to be burnished or waxed, every screw loosened until the weapon rattled impressively when it thudded from bruised shoulder to parade ground asphalt and back. The 'Sir' from the instructors was delivered with matchless, withering contempt but with a delicate regard for social niceties. 'Mr Lord Greenleaf, you look like a bloody monkey on a stick, . . . SIR', the imprecation preceded and followed by a torrent of oaths and abuse, gives a flavour. Or 'Mr Robertson, Sir, you're trying – very trying. My wife is ugly, I've got salad for my tea, so we can keep this going as long as you like'. 'Idle' was a favourite shriek, not in its usual sense of lazy, but applied to anything that caught the Instructor's eye: 'idle hair', 'idle boots' even an 'idle bicycle'. As John Masters remembered, the word alone was often enough. 'When a sergeant put his face an inch from mine and screamed 'Mr. Masters, Sir, IDLE', he was saved the trouble of more exact definition and I was thrown into panicky speculation as to the nature of my sin.' One martinet had allegedly been seen wheeling his baby in a pram through the Married Quarters and when he reached the corner of the street, jerking it into a sharp right-angled turn in fine parade ground style. Nor were the instructors politically correct. As they lined up on the drill square, a contingent of Egyptian Cadets sent all the way to England to be moulded into potential leaders was discomfited by the brusque bark: 'Stand still, the gyppo number four in the front rank!' In Tommy's time each cadet was issued with a bicycle. It was the most practical way to get around, but like almost every other human activity, Sandhurst had to turn cycling into a military art form. This mystified a group of Chinese cadets who found it hard to respond to the College's archaic insistence that bicycles were to be mounted and ridden as if they were horses. The exercise involved a series of orders incomprehensible to anyone who had not served in the cavalry, and prolonged maladroit hopping on one leg, with the other poised on the pedal until the order 'mount' was barked. It took the new arrivals some time to get the hang of things, and their attempts provided much light relief to the crowd of cadets who gathered to watch 'The Chinese Bicycle Lessons'.

Eventually, the Cadets became inured to Brasso, blanco, and bawling, and classroom work overtook the pell-mell rush of inspections and parades, marching up and down like automata urged on by their drill sergeants to display 'bags of swank'. They had time now to explore the delights of a wider world, clad in loudly checked tweed hacking jackets and grey flannel trousers. In Hugh Thomas' words 'The twenties were wild at Sandhurst, as elsewhere'. Like all young men, cadets got drunk from time to time, sometimes spectacularly. They trashed the rooms of those they found uncongenial or pushy, and if an unpopular cadet left his bicycle unchained it might well be hurled off the roof to a background of baying and jeers or the young man himself could be tossed in the lake. There were occasional brawls, madcap driving, fumbling forays to the two 'two weary tarts in Camberley' and many evenings roaring to London in sports cars, roistering from pub to club until dawn broke. Some bills were paid after visits to 'Ma Hart's', the Camberley pawnbroker, where gold watches or silver-backed hairbrushes were proffered with shame and met with disdain. Many more were met through overdrafts from long-suffering bank managers and by cheques wrung from even longer-suffering parents. It is hardly surprising to see the claim that while himself a Cadet, Ian Fleming, creator of James Bond and a year older than Tommy, fell victim to an uncomfortable infection of the kind which imprudence can often visit on young men (known in Sandhurst argot of the time as 'picking up a nail'), and left early.

But there was elegance too, especially the June Ball, the Cadets in their blue 'patrols', the ladies shimmering, and senior officers in 'nearly every mess kit of the British Empire', an exquisitely tailored, gold braided Imperial mélange of styles, among them the tartan trews which Tommy was to wear after he left Sandhurst. It must have had something of the flavour of the Duchess of Richmond's famous Ball in Brussels on the eve of Waterloo, a victory evoked by the brass cannon captured from the French in the battle which stood on display outside the Old College Building. In Tommy's time the cavalry traditions were still kept up, although already being pushed into history by the petrol-engined roar of the tank. We get a glimpse of it from a verbal portrait drawn by Lord Belhaven, thoughtful winner of the Sword of Honour, Sandhurst's ultimate accolade. 'Frosty air sharp with the scent of stables, the ring of hooves on cobbles; horses led from lamplight, their breath pluming the air, arching their necks, turning their heads to the tightening girths, stamping, blowing their nostrils, shocked by the nervous dance of hooves and tucking in of bellies by the bright sharp cold . . .'

Tommy did his parents credit. As at Charterhouse he was not at the top of the academic ladder – he passed out just below the midpoint of his intake of 171 – but he was again a leader and an all-rounder – promoted steadily to Lance Corporal, Corporal and Junior Under Officer, turning out for football and donning white flannels and a striped cap to play cricket for the Sandhurst Wanderers. It was not that serious. On one cricket tour during summer leave in the Isle of Wight, he told his brother 'as much time seems to have been spent ineffectively shooting at seagulls with revolvers as playing . . . and drinking beer'. Though we cannot now connect the dots, the Isle of Wight was a family home of another dashing Gentleman Cadet, later debonair film star, David Niven,

who arrived at Sandhurst from his school at Stowe a few months
after Tommy. Though Tommy does not figure in Niven's delightful
if perhaps 'spit and polished' memoirs they were friends, and
Tommy's brother Ian remembered that Niven was one of a handful
of Tommy's contemporaries for whom John Argyll had any time.
Niven 'greatly amused' him.

Tommy's Passing Out Parade, in which his No. 1 Company
carried the Champion Banner, was taken by the First World War
hero, Field Marshal Lord Allenby, who told the proud young men
and their even prouder parents to remember that 'concentration and
preparation' were the two 'great things' that mattered. He obviously
had in mind military leaders, but it was a maxim as relevant to
Tommy's subsequent career in MI5 as to more straightforward
soldiering. Allenby added the advice that in war 'they had to do not
what they thought Napoleon would have done, but what Napoleon
would not have found fault with', a rather ambiguous tribute which,
had he been alive to hear it, would have brought a wry smile to the
lips of the diminutive Corsican who for so many years had been
Britain's Public Enemy No. 1.

Tommy and his friends marched briskly away to their various
destinies with heads and hopes high.

Lord Belhaven again, 'It was a good education for young men and
soldiers, our two years at Sandhurst, the best that could have been
devised, wide in scope, not too worldly, a harmonious discipline of
character, mind and body. It served us well in our later years, with
its memories of sharp happiness and rough humour.'

The next step in Tommy's Snakes and Ladders progress lay in
Dover Castle, then the UK depot of the 1st or Home Battalion of
the Seaforth Highlanders; the 2nd Battalion was in India. Ronnie
Mackintosh Walker, a Seaforth officer on the Sandhurst staff, who
in another milieu would have been called a 'talent spotter' for his
Regiment, thought the gregarious, sporting young Scot would make
a good Mess companion. Quite rightly – originally raised by the Earl
of Seaforth in 1778, and later absorbing the Ross-Shire Buffs and the
Duke of Albany's, the Seaforth had recruited its rank and file from
the northern Highlands and its officers from well-connected young

men with similar roots and the right style and background. He was following in the boot steps of a contemporary whose trajectory would take him to Maidstone Prison, rather than the Staff College, a sad story to be told later and again one in which Tommy, by then Tar, would play an undercover rôle.

8

Trews, Top Hat and Truncheon

In August 1929 Tommy's 'batman' or soldier servant – a perk that came with his new officer status, but a factotum surely more in the mould of Blackadder's Baldrick than Wooster's Jeeves – unpacked his bags in the Citadel, part of a range of crenulated fortifications built around Dover Castle in the mid nineteenth century as a bulwark against a renewed threat of French invasion. The Citadel was a warren of damp brickwork, subterranean stone corridors and stair wells, vaulted ceilings and heavy wooden doors, much like a Piranesi vision of a Roman prison. (What is left of it became a Young Offenders Centre, and later a holding pen for illegal immigrants). Kitting his son out in the several sets of uniform that he needed – including a kilt (an 'unrivalled garment for fornication and diarrhoea' as a drunken Scots officer once counselled John Masters) and trews in Mackenzie tartan, a sporran, a beribboned 'fore and aft' Glengarry bonnet, white spats and a sword – must yet again have cost John Argyll the equivalent of several thousand pounds in today's money. But however expensively impressive he may have looked to awe-struck civilians gawping at the parades, Tommy had again slid back down a Ladder from being a master of his own portion of the universe, a Sandhurst 'Brahmin', to something approaching 'Untouchable' status. He and the other young officers were herded off to drill on the barrack square as though Sandhurst had never happened, once again yelped at and insulted by instructors much like those glimpsed at a different place and time by the author Anthony Powell: '. . . staff sergeants left over from the Matabele campaign with Harry Lauder accents and eyes like poached eggs'. There were yet more unwritten codes to be mastered, what one manual for young officers called the 'numerous and intricate rules' of behaviour in the Officers' Mess. There were rituals for passing the port and offering the Loyal Toast, rules for when surnames could be used instead of ranks; in any event junior officers were not permitted to address their seniors unless the latter spoke first. Women's names were never to be mentioned ; politics, 'talking shop' and religion were taboo. While such formalities and niceties were usually observed with the exquisite precision of a Japanese geisha house, dinners marking some special occasion or the anniversary of a distant but never to be forgotten Regimental victory might see a temporary lifting of the pall of etiquette. After the pomp and circumstance of the Pipe Major skirling as he circled the table, a particularly bibulous evening might end with the spectacle of grown, not to say overgrown men briefly casting all thought of rank aside to roar around the candlelit dining room in their red mess jackets playing childish games. Some of them, such as 'High Cockalorum', in which the officers grunted and heaved into a perspiring pyramid, so often ended in broken bones that they were later banned.

A few weeks later Tommy found himself, head reeling with map references, rendezvous and complicated movement orders, leading his men across the dark Downs between Dover and Folkestone, a night exercise conceived by its planners as a battle between the notional 'warring kingdoms' of Kent and Thanet. It was taken seriously, and reported by *The Times* in the play by play detail then reserved for Test matches. But the essentially artificial nature of the manoeuvres – imaginary Divisions, no bullets, no deaths and 'points' for each side based on scorecards handed in to the 'umpires' by reconnoitering officers on bicycles – may have been a source of subconscious inspiration when as Tar, Tommy planned his Second World War deception schemes.

But John Argyll's wallet and cheque book were much in demand, inevitably leading to father-son problems and for Tommy another move on the Snakes and Ladders board.

Mim Robertson had always insisted he should be well turned out, and he did not let her down. His suits came from Meyer and Mortimer, then in Conduit Street on the site of what is now the Westbury Hotel, and a firm almost as old as the Seaforth

Highlanders, his shoes from Jermyn Street and his hats from Lock & Co in St. James's. There was no point in dressing up just to delight the damsels of Dover. Tommy bought an MG Midget sports car, burbling off for a round of golf at Worplesdon or up the A2 to London. So many theatres, so many restaurants, so many nightclubs. A directory of the time lists hundreds, from the Berkeley Buttery, and the Café de Paris to the Bag o' Nails, the 400, even a dive which briefly flourished as the Charterhouse, before an abrupt closure; it reopened as the London Sports Club. So many girls, so many bands, so many bottles, so much dancing. And so many bills. But regrettably, so little money. One of the girls, the pretty daughter of an officer who had been killed in the First World War, became, in Ian Robertson's words 'rather special' but John Argyll, who thought she was the main reason Tommy was living stratospherically above his means, did all he could to stand in the way and in short order she married someone else.[1]

Though his lifestyle suggests a car crash was a persistent risk, the big collision when it came was with his father. Tommy was faced with a debt he could not settle, and when he asked John Argyll for money, the latter reacted with fury. Internecine conflicts are impossible for outsiders to fathom, even more for outsiders looking back almost eighty years. Any sympathies should probably be with John Argyll; spendthrift sons have to be brought to heel. Though he did not stint on his own lifestyle, he was at least earning money. Tommy was not but was still spending it with carefree disregard. Like countless others, John Argyll had seen his capital depleted by the Wall Street Crash, a cataclysm of the kind now familiar to a new generation of investors, and he was about to see his income cut by retirement. Not the best of times for a young man to ask for still more money. Something snapped. Quite what happened, who shouted at whom, whether that lost love was an issue, we do not know other than the laconic comment that there was 'some trouble in the family.'[2]

It is impossible to tell at a distance how their personalities may have meshed or clashed. Tommy's brother Ian remembered[3] John Argyll as 'more serious than jolly but he was certainly not dour. He knew nothing of the Arts and hardly read anything besides the newspaper, but he liked a good joke and a good laugh and he enjoyed the music halls. At times he could let his hair down.'

'He was a Scotsman through and through; he wore the kilt at home and abroad and put on his dress tartan for any social occasion. He never lost his Scottish accent. He made a fine collection of Malayan butterflies and a valuable collection of Commonwealth stamps. In later years he did some very good embroidery for chair covers.'

John Argyll must have paid up in the end since in those days the only realistic alternative for a young man with money worries lay with the West End moneylenders, whose capacity for bleeding debtors dry was legendary. Beyond that we know only that John Argyll complained to Tommy's Commanding Officer that his son obviously had too much free time; would the CO make sure he was fully occupied. The crescendo came in December 1930 when Tommy resigned his commission, to the Regiment's regret. They felt he had 'the makings of a really good officer'. While it seems likely that the row led directly to the resignation, Tommy also had to face the reality that if he remained with the Seaforth Highlanders the next posting would be to India where it was hot, sporadically dangerous as bouts of tribal or Nationalist conflict erupted, and otherwise a barren cycle of drinking, drill, dysentery, and dalliance with fellow-officers' frustrated wives. And in those inter-war years, promotion in the Army was a long and often disappointing road. The leather armchairs in the Mess sagged under the frustrated weight of Captains and Majors sliding into middle age with nothing much to look forward to beyond a meagre pension and a job trying to teach congenitally insolent boys at a prep school like Sunnydown, or putting on a front of false bonhomie as secretary of a Home Counties golf club.

Tommy's brother Ian meanwhile kept on a steadier course, to Winchester, Trinity College, Oxford, and a successful Army career beginning in the Second World War; the world turned full circle, and in a sense he finished what Tommy had started, when from 1942 to 1945 he commanded the 1st Battalion of the Seaforth

Highlanders. A third brother Sandy, who inherited his mother's artistic and musical talents, served in the Cameron Highlanders, and was captured in the second Battle of Tobruk in 1942. He spent the rest of the war as a POW and predeceased his brothers.

In a few years the Seaforth's loss would be the secret world's gain, but meanwhile Tommy had to earn a living. Depression and recession might blight the British economic landscape, unemployment might soar, and worries might multiply about sterling's decline against the US dollar and gold, but in the 1930s, the City of London still held its ground as the epicentre of the world's money flow. John Argyll used his City connections to find a place for his congenial if worrisome son. Fairfax & Co., the small 'discount house' based in now vanished offices near Mansion House, suited Tommy to a 'T'. The 'right background', a good appearance, conviviality, a keen interest in cricket and a low golf handicap were far more important than the ability to calculate discount and exchange rates, or assess creditworthiness. That was what managers and clerks were employed to do.

The discount houses – the smaller ones were also known as "bill brokers" – are now part of City folklore, much like starched collars fixed to the shirt by gold and ivory studs, hand-cranked adding machines, leather bound ledgers with their columns of copperplate entries, and any sense of propriety in financial dealings. But in Tommy's day, and indeed into the 1970s, the discount houses were still the cornerstone of the London money and Government securities markets.

While the telephone had sometimes to be used for business, as distinct from calls to girlfriends or bookmakers, it was essentially a market dependent on the personal touch. The bill brokers stood out in a drab world as they strolled with studied nonchalance from bank to bank along the City's narrow streets, twirling a neatly furled umbrella, their working dress an already archaic combination of a glossy silk top hat, a neatly knotted necktie either in a muted mix of silver and grey, or perhaps with coloured stripes proclaiming to the initiated where the languid wearer had been to school, framed by a stiff shirt collar, black jacket and crisply pressed grey and black pinstriped trousers, and shoes, their toe caps gleaming like a Sandhurst cadet's boots. 'Bags of swank' again, though of a different kind.

These might be depressing times for the City – though the larger discount houses were reporting excellent profits – but the front had to be kept up. Depending on the time of day each call on a bank might involve a ritual crystal glass of Amontillado and before any mention of something as tedious as business, the conversation would perambulate agreeably through ritual English exchanges about the weather, the Test match, last weekend's round of golf or the follies of government. In 1932 Tommy would have carried with him on his rounds the aura of 'the man who did a hole in one at Worplesdon', a feat on the 13th hole for which the Club gave him a trophy made up of miniature silver golf clubs and balls.

Oversimplifying several centuries of hallowed tradition, the essence of the work was a form of virtuous money-laundering – collecting short term funds from banks who found themselves with a temporary surplus, and reinvesting it wherever a fleeting profit could be found; with other banks who needed cash to balance their own books, in the commercial IOUs known as Bills of Exchange or in British Government securities. We know Tommy found it boring, as the description above may suggest, even though he later claimed the City had given him a facility for quick arithmetic from the task of squaring his own firm's ledgers when the working day ended at 3.30pm. Tommy's youthful casualness about spending money sat oddly with a studied indifference, unusual in the City, towards making it; his family remembers that in later life, he was never that interested in money, as long as he had enough to live on. It was an attitude rather different from Anthony Powell's portrayal of thrusting young men about the City in the 1930s, anxious to 'get on' and 'make a killing', typified by the bill broker . . . 'Scarcely aware even how pictures were produced, who could at the same time enter any gallery and pick out the most expensively priced work there from Masaccio to Matisse simply through the mystic power of his own respect for money'.[4]

In Tommy's version passed on to his family, he grew bored and made a career change which even Powell's fertile imagination would have been hard put to it to contrive as fate spun his characters through the foxtrot of life. He joined the police.

Notes
1. Private papers.
2. Private papers.
3. Private papers.
4. Powell, Anthony, *A Buyer's Market*, p. 201.

9

Through The Looking Glass

As Tommy later told the story, with the assistance of another introduction by his long-suffering father, he swapped his pinstriped pants and polished shoes for blue serge and black boots to plod the cobblestones of Birmingham as a rank and file 'copper'. A nice tale, but one which reflects either a certain ingrained economy with the truth or a burnishing of the facts to make an entertaining story. In reality the move was part of his induction into MI5.

Appropriately for a life so full of secrets, how and when Tar became involved with MI5, is a puzzle. We know that it was a personal recruitment by Vernon Kell, the Service's creator, builder, and hands-on Director,[1] at the suggestion of his son John, Tar's piano playing school friend. The official record shows that Tar joined on 31 March 1933. But two stories need first to be told, both relating to British *causes célèbres* of the time, the Invergordon Mutiny and the high profile trial of 'the Officer in the Tower'. Tar's involvement in both is woven into the tartan of family memory. His rôle in the second is confirmed by the direct recollection of one of the very few people in a position to know.[2] Taken together they suggest that Tar may have been working unofficially for Vernon Kell even before his formal appointment. Extrapolating from contemporary practice, one modern MI5 watcher is inclined to discount this, while accepting that at this distance in time there is no evidence either way. Since the Service was so much Kell's personal fiefdom, and Tar was a 'known quantity', and above all because Tar is unlikely to have conjured up the stories from thin air, we are inclined to give him the benefit of the doubt. The common thread is Kell's son John.

The Mutiny shook the country badly in 1931, two years before

Tar joined MI5. Britain's then 'Government of Cooperation', usually remembered as 'the National Government' was a fractious, fragile political alliance hastily cobbled together in the economic aftershocks that followed the General Strike, the Wall Street Crash and the Depression – the depreciation of sterling, a gaping Budget deficit and then, as now, foreign fears that London's banking system might fail. The new government's knee jerk response was an Emergency Budget. Up went taxes. Down went the salaries of everyone employed by the State, from Cabinet Ministers (most of whom could stand the pain) to teachers and crucially, servicemen (most of whom could not). Strident Labour opposition further weakened the Government's position. The final blow to confidence and credibility came on 15 September when garbled newspaper reports of how the cuts would affect the already badly paid ordinary seamen, not least young men with families, reached the Atlantic Fleet, majestically at anchor at Invergordon on Cromarty Firth.

Though what happened has come down to us as 'the Invergordon Mutiny', MI5's first attempt at an official history, written at the end of the Second World War by a 57-year-old MI5 officer, John Curry,[3] (but not published until 1999), refers to it in inverted commas as the 'incident' and at the time the Admiralty used 'spin-doctored' euphemisms such as 'unrest' and 'occurrences'. It was a non-violent affair – excited speechmaking, cheering, rallying cries echoing from ship to ship, choruses of 'The Red Flag' and, less aggressively, 'The More We are Together', but the crews of several ships refused to put to sea for scheduled exercises, despite warnings from their officers, in the style of Captain Bligh, that the troublemakers would 'get no further than the end of a rope'. The Royal Navy had for centuries been the bulwark of the British nation. In a way, it was the nation personified. So to the Admiralty and the rest of Whitehall, Invergordon was an alarm call. Only ten years had passed since the cataclysms of the Russian Revolution and the subsequent Civil War, and Eisenstein's dramatisation of the bloody insurrection on the Tsarist battleship, *Potemkin*, ramming home where a naval mutiny might lead, had reached British 'art house' cinemas as recently as 1925. The British censors had been wary of allowing it to be broadly released. The Government followed a standard 'playbook'. It set up a Committee to investigate, rolled back the pay cuts for the lower decks, promised there would be no 'penalisation' and censured Rear Admiral Wilfred Tomkinson, (who had the misfortune to find himself as the senior officer while the Commander in Chief was in a Portsmouth hospital), for not disciplining the dissidents at the first signs of trouble. The Fleet soon settled back into its normal routine though not without some further rumbling. In the background MI5 and the Special Branch of the Metropolitan Police began 'quiet investigations' to identify the ringleaders and to determine whether what had occurred was part of the perceived 'Bolshevik menace'. It was too little, too late. Four days after Invergordon, the Bank of England told the Government that foreign credits were exhausted, and two days later Britain abandoned the gold standard. Sterling lost a quarter of its value – the first of the long line of twentieth century financial surrenders and currency devaluations.[4]

But what does this have to do with Tar, whom we had assumed was strolling the City pavements? The relevance for us is those 'quiet investigations'. Reminiscing with his family decades later, Tar said he had been sent up to Invergordon to 'take the temperature', which translated as having a drink with any sailors he found propping up the bars in the local pubs. He had the charm, and the Scottish credentials – John Hutchinson Robertson's first medical post at Elgin lay just the other side of the Firth – to carry this off, though on the face of it a dashing young 'officer type' chatting up seamen in a dockside 'snug', heavy with the smoke of Wills' 'Woodbine' cigarettes had the potential to lead to embarrassing misunderstandings. But who sent him there?

Though the Admiralty had promised there would be no 'penalisation', by November those 'investigations' were followed by another bland announcement that twenty-four men had been discharged for continuing 'conduct subversive of discipline'. The scope of MI5's unpublicised involvement is hinted at in a letter to the War Office in which the Lords Commissioners of the Admiralty, expressing their 'high appreciation' to Kell and his staff for their efforts, all the more since they recognised that MI5 was 'not organised to deal with unrest in such circumstances or on so extensive a scale', the latter phrase perhaps a hint that extra men like Tar had been called in to cover the task. Though the latest History repeats the story of Tar's rôle, its source is his Obituary in *The Times* rather than archival, which does not help to pin the anecdote down. We are left with the assumption that Kell, master in his own house, beholden to none for how he ran his 'firm' and who knew Tar through his son John, might have plucked him from the City for a brief spell, on the one hand as a young man who could get people to talk, and on the other as a prospective candidate whom he wanted to test in action. If so, we can see it as forerunner of the 'Icebreaker' exercise used to test the mettle and panache of present day SIS trainees by setting them the task of wheedling personal information from strangers in pubs. We met John when he and Tar followed one another, frowning in competitive concentration, to show off their skills at the school piano. They remained close, partying and nightclubbing together and music of a different kind, a little night music, also figures in a glimpse remembered by someone who knew them both at the time.[5] It is of a party, in Kensington or Mayfair, young debutantes crowded around a piano, giggling, humming, singing along, as John, who clearly had more talent on the keyboard than his schoolmate, tinkled away at 'Stormy Weather' or 'I'm Getting Sentimental Over You'. But it would be quite wrong to leave the impression of John as a playboy. Newspaper archives of the 1920s and 1930s have many references in the then extensive and discursive sports pages, to his appearances for Charterhouse and New College, Oxford on tennis, squash and Fives courts or on the running track. While still at school he had been marked by *The Times* as 'one of the three outstanding all-round young runners' of the year.

Much as he would have liked to, and much as this all too brief sketch suggests that he had many of the right attributes, John Kell had not joined his father's Service. When it came to recruiting, the 'old boy net' was one thing but Kell senior was sensitive to the risk of being attacked politically for nepotism.[6] But that did not stop

John suggesting likely candidates, or being asked by his father what he thought of one or other potential recruits, and even if Tar had been the only recommendation he made to his father, it would have been enough to earn him a mention in the history books.

Notes

1. Kell, Sir Vernon George Waldegrave, CB, KBE, 1873–1942, Oxford DNB 2004.
2. Personal papers.
3. Curry John: *The Security Service, 1908–45: The Official History*, London 1999, (Introduction by Christopher Andrew).
4. See e.g. Taylor A. J. P., p. 297.
5. Personal papers.
6. Personal papers.

10

The Bloody Tower

The case known as 'the mystery of the Officer in the Tower', hit the headlines early in 1933, just before Tar's official entry into MI5. It was a sad and now strangely forgotten affair and it goes unmentioned in both Curry's work and the more recent History.

The year had begun ominously with Hitler's appointment as German Chancellor. In February the fire that destroyed the Reichstag building in Berlin gave the Nazis, who had probably orchestrated it, the opportunity they had long sought to step up their witch hunt against Communists and anyone else who might get in their way. (Lily Sergueiew, who a decade later would become Tar's agent TREASURE, was hauled in by the Gestapo in Berlin who suspected her motives as a Russian émigré claiming to be a journalist who wanted to cover the alleged plotter's trial). In May 1933, President Hindenburg's shaky signature on the so called Enabling Act essentially swept away Germany's Constitution and handed Hitler dictatorial power.

Back in London, the hapless young officer of the headlines, Norman Baillie Stewart, faced a Court Martial on charges of passing relatively trivial military information to the German Army. He had been a fellow Cadet of Tar's at Sandhurst, though on a different intake, and they had briefly overlapped as subalterns when the Seaforth's home battalion was stationed at Dover Castle. Family memories suggest that Tar played a part in Baillie Stewart's unmasking by passing on 'to some agent' that Baillie Stewart was a Nazi sympathiser and had collected photographs of British military equipment; another account has it that Tar even gave evidence in camera at the Court Martial. Yet again a fragment of first hand memory tells us that Tar was brought into the affair at the suggestion of John Kell and reinforced the positive impression already held by Sir Vernon Kell, leading to his formal recruitment shortly afterwards.

Baillie Stewart and Tar had more in common than Sandhurst. Both were children of the Imperial Diaspora, (as was Kim Philby, who will make frequent appearances in this story).[1]

Both had felt the misery of being left parentless in Edwardian England in their fragile early years. Norman's father, Colonel Hope Baillie Wright was an Indian Army officer, his paternal grandfather had commanded the Hyderabad Cavalry and on his mother's side, the family tree was garlanded with admirals and senior officers. She was a Stewart, a lineage of which Norman was so proud that while at Sandhurst he dropped 'Wright' from his name and became Baillie Stewart. According to the Army List, Baillie Stewart was commissioned into the Seaforth Highlanders on 31 January 1929 and Tar on 29 August in the same year. Given the background they shared, it is remarkable that their lives took such different paths.

The Baillie Stewart story describes the inexorable downward spiral of a once-promising, self-pitying 'Odd Man Out', rather than a traitor seduced away from his allegiance by money or idealism, though he later claimed that the fact that his father had some aristocratic German relatives had given him pro-German sympathies.

Based on his early career trajectory, he should have ended up reasonably well and certainly not in Maidstone Prison. From Bedford School, he passed with high marks into the Royal Naval College at Dartmouth (which a lung problem forced him to leave), and earned a Prize Cadetship to Sandhurst where he worked hard, standing out both on the parade ground and in his studies. He became a Cadet Under Officer – a significant recognition in that tough and élitist world – before taking his commission and serving with the Seaforth in India. With the benefit of hindsight and a sense of how to burnish a good anecdote, David Niven remembered Baillie Stewart as 'a shifty looking customer with a broken nose . . . a singularly unattractive piece of work',[2] though contemporary photographs actually show him to have been a tall, rather distinguished young officer. *The New York Times*, which carried many reports as the drama unfolded, described him as a 'good-looking Scots youth'.

In his own account of his progress and downfall, Baillie Stewart portrays himself as bullied, hard done by, misunderstood, the butt of jokes and insults, (often about his change of name), and socially out of place, despite his effort and achievements. Even his first contact with the Germans while on holiday in Berlin had been misinterpreted. It had been what Goethe might have called his elective affinity for Germany and a respect for protocol, which led him to ask his hotel head porter how to get in touch with the German General Staff. All he wanted was to get a ticket to the bristling Prussian version of the Changing of the Guard in Potsdam and also, like a courteous fellow officer, 'leave his calling card'. He had no intention of offering his services as a spy. The porter provided the introduction and Baillie Stewart found himself chatting with a monocled major, anxious for information on the British Army and equally anxious to press cash on a young officer who said he was short of funds. Nothing if not even-handed, the head porter was also a tipster for SIS, to whom he promptly passed on this exotic nugget via the British Air Attaché. Then came reports from the British Military Attaché in Rumania that the Germans were peddling the plans of a new British tank; where had they got them? Back in London, M15 began to poke into Baillie Stewart's bank account and intercept his correspondence with the major, each using improbable pen names and trying to create the impression they were a lovelorn couple discreetly settling debts incurred in the course of a trans-continental affair.

By January 1933, when MI5 pounced, Baillie Stewart had resigned his Seaforth commission after a minor spat with his colonel over, of all things, whether cabbage was too plebian a dish to be served in the Officers' Mess. He transferred to the Royal Army Service Corps. Thus when he was arrested he could have been left in its rather subfusc uniform, and the whole affair handled out of sight by a discreet military tribunal in an anonymous building in Aldershot. All the more since from what was said at the hearing, the information he was alleged to have passed over, or been asked to pass over to Berlin at that stage does not seem to have been of much strategic or intelligence import. Any foreign Military Attaché worth his spurs would have picked up far more about British tactics and equipment from careful observation, or even the fulsome *Times* reporting of the exercises around Folkestone, described earlier, than anything Baillie Stewart could have provided.

But MI5 opted for maximum exposure. Baillie Stewart was told to put on his eye-catching Seaforth trews and Glengarry bonnet, and was locked up to wait for his Court Martial, not in the crowded anonymity of a London jail or a military prison deep in the countryside, but in the Tower of London. That the Tower was engraved in blood in British folk memory as a place where, as the historian Lord Macaulay wrote 'the captains of armies, the leaders of parties, the oracles of senates, and the ornaments of courts', two Queens among them, had been beheaded, added a gruesome fascination to the case. And since much of the Tower was open to the public, who could gawp at Baillie Stewart on his daily exercise walks along the gravelled parapets, the spotlight of press and political attention glared even more brightly, intensified by the Government's initial refusal to identify the 'secret prisoner'. Though its reporting bore the paw marks of heavy MI5 briefing, even *The Times* complained of the 'almost melodramatic publicity'.

All of this, the Court Martial in the draughty Drill Hall of the Duke of York's Headquarters on Kings Road in Chelsea, the foreign witnesses who could not be identified because their lives might allegedly be put at risk, the evidence given by Victor Sylvester, celebrity bandleader and doyen of British ballroom dancing, seems rather clumsily stage-managed, designed to send a fortissimo message to the new régime in Germany that MI5 had sensitive antennae and could detect even the earliest stages of any attempt to get military intelligence or suborn the Armed Forces. Any hostile intelligence service could have picked up and learned from the published witness list the main tools MI5 had used to gather evidence; no fewer than five Post Office inspectors gave evidence, along with the manager of Lloyds Bank, Pall Mall. If they did not know him already for his work in military intelligence in the First World War, the Germans would certainly have been able to identify the MI5 officer who led the investigation – and later many others – even though he was described on the witness list as representing 'The War Office'. Then Major later Lt. Colonel W.E. Hinchley Cooke, spoke fluent German – his mother was German. He was known to the MI5 junior staff as 'Hinch', though not to his face, and remembered many years later by one of the office girls as 'a fat, Prussian-looking man, going bald, with a very thick neck and bulging eyes behind thick glasses.' (A German description of the time painted him as 'robust, fresh-faced, appears to be good natured, speaks German fluently in a variety of dialects from Saxony to Hamburg'.)

After a seven day hearing Baillie Stewart was jailed for five years and cashiered. Throughout his time in Maidstone Prison, as the files show, MI5 kept a close eye on his correspondence and visitors and even dictated to the Home Office the conditions of his eventual release. Kell's Service had a long reach. They were right to be suspicious. Baillie Stewart could not brake his self-destructive slide and resurfaced in the Second World War broadcasting propaganda for the Nazis from Berlin. Only the fact that he had earlier applied for German citizenship and even registered for service with the German Army saved him from the hangman's noose which awaited his fellow broadcaster William Joyce. With his nemesis 'Hinch'[3] watching balefully from the well of the Old Bailey courtroom, Baillie Stewart was jailed again for another five years. He died in Dublin in 1966. An alternative to all the publicity which according to the New York Times, was briefly considered, was to use Baillie Stewart to penetrate what was clearly the rebuilding of the German intelligence service, but double agents lay in MI5's future as a strategic weapon and the fatal fault line in his character would have made him a weak and unreliable candidate, though as we shall discover, many of Tar's wartime agents had personal flaws, the exploration of which would have kept a college of psychiatrists busy for years.

But as with Invergordon, what was Tar's rôle? We may not have every last fact, but we have a great many; press reports, the list of the Court Martial witnesses, (though the names of those who gave evidence 'in camera' cannot now be found, they seem all to have been foreigners), papers from the MI5 file including a long hand written confession, the self justifying autobiography Baillie Stewart had written and which was published in 1967, when he presumably had no reason not to name names, even extracts from his prison records. None of them mention Tar.

Though Tar resigned his commission in 1930 and Baillie Stewart's first visit to Germany was in the autumn of 1932, he and Tar could well have kept in touch. What we know based on a direct family memory is that John Kell, making the Seaforth connection, suggested to his father that Tar could help. Quite how he helped can only be guessed at. Given Invergordon and Tar's personality, Vernon Kell probably suggested he should chat to Baillie Stewart as a sympathetic brother officer and persuade him to see the error of his ways. Gaining confidence through camaraderie was one of Tar's strengths.

If so, he was very likely the unidentified officer claiming to represent the War Office who, Baillie Stewart later alleged, had duped him, after the guilty verdict but before sentence was passed, into admitting his 'irregularities'. The officer assured him that if he did, he would be cashiered, thrown out of the Army in ignominy but would not go to jail. As Baillie Stewart lamented in a letter to his father, in agreeing to a deal on which MI5 renèged, he was 'a poor, blind fool'. If this was indeed Tar's rôle, it would have to remain unseen. The rather theatrical police-style ploy was not something MI5 would want to have aired. Tar was at the start of his underground career and it would have been common sense and good tradecraft to keep his name out of the limelight, like T. S. Elliot's poetic cat 'Macavity', the epitome of 'deceitfulness and suavity'. And whatever Baillie Stewart might or might not have done, the unwritten code of the Seaforth would have brought furrowed brows in the Mess at the thought of one officer hoodwinking another, guilty or not. Another timing puzzle, which again suggests Kell may have been running Tar as, what his sister-service SIS called an

'Unofficial Assistant' before actually signing him up, is that while the records show Tar joined MI5 at the end of March 1933, Baillie Stewart had been arrested two months earlier, and the Court Martial opened a little more than a week before Tar's first day of service.

Kell would have extended the formal invitation over a discreet Clubland lunch with an apologetic indication of the measly salary, partly compensated for by it being paid in cash and without any tiresome taxes, and more than outweighed by the national importance of the task. Any formal vetting in the depth and detail brought to bear today, the multi-ethnic interview panels, with a watchful psychiatrist in discreet attendance, the probing into family life, relationships, sexual preferences, bank accounts, political sympathies, even internet habits, would have struck Kell as intrusive and irrelevant. It was his Service and his judgement, his 'nose', that sniffed out what lay behind Tommy's urbane façade. When we come to look back on Tommy's career we can speculate about what Kell saw, or thought he saw, in him and what made Tommy such a good, though far from obvious choice.

It is possible that even the spell in the City may have been engineered. What fragments remain of the Fairfax files after its Blitz-related closure in the 1940s are said by their official custodian to show no trace of Tar, but they are not open to public access on the rather odd grounds that even after some 75 years, the customer information they contain is confidential.

Whatever the preliminaries, on 31 March 1933, Tar stepped into a world which, at times in his many years of service must indeed have seemed as if *Alice in Wonderland* had been adapted for the screen by Graham Greene. In the normal world outside it was a rather English day; readers' letters to *The Times* gave detailed instructions on how best to brew 'a good cup of tea', debated whether a statue by Admiralty Arch was holding a sextant or a quadrant, and complained that coke-fired boilers in Government buildings were adding to London's permanent pall of smoke.

If London was smoky, how much more so Birmingham, which is where the police episode comes in. It was not, as Tar later claimed, a move arranged by his long-suffering father, rather improbably a friend of the City's Chief Constable, Cecil Moriarty.[4] Nor was it an early version of a bored young man's 'gap year'.

In fact, as Emily Jane Wilson's pioneering research reveals, his three months' stint in Birmingham was part of his induction into MI5, and he spent most of the time at the city's Police Training School, one of the biggest such schools in Britain. As well as local trainees it took in officers from the Military and War Office police, and what was then the Empire and MI5 as well. The Moriarty connection is simply explained by the fact that as Deputy Chief Constable, (he did not take over the top job until 1935), Cecil Moriarty was directly responsible for training.[5]

Even though Tar knew he was there for only a short spell, it must have struck him as a long way from the Mayfair marriage mart and merry go round. True, unlike many other areas of the country, which were still ravaged by the Black Death of the Depression, Birmingham's motor industry, a major employer, was flourishing. And it was unrecognisable as the urban mess and traffic nightmare we know today. Writing at the time Tar moved there, the author J B Priestley could still reflect on the as yet unblitzed and unreconstructed Birmingham that 'For a moment . . . you believe that at last you have found an English provincial city that has the air and dignity that a great city should have . . .' But behind the imposing Victorian façades there were dole queues, grimy slums, poverty, a rude awakening for a man more used to café society than steamy 'caffs' and police canteens. At least as the product of the sweat-scented changing rooms and noisy corridors of a public school and the 'bullshit baffles brains' culture of Sandhurst, Tar would easily have found his bearings in the semi-military régime of the school, its dormitories and communal washrooms, the heavy boots and the thick serge uniforms, the geometrical disciplines of bed making, the heavy china mugs of tea which braced the bleary-eyed young men for the morning parades and which, so myth had it, were also laced with bromide to keep their alluvial instincts in check. In any event he could take comfort in the thought that he would soon be back in South Kensington.

So much has been written about MI5 that to recap its history at any length would be a waste of space; the bibliography notes some of the many books, some excellent, some less so, which give a fuller picture of its successes and its failures. We will focus on the organisation as Tar knew it when he joined, and papers that do not seem to have been tapped by others.

When he joined Tar was given one instruction, and one avuncular admonition. The instruction spelled out to all MI5 entrants of the era the cloak of anonymity and ambiguity in which they had chosen to wrap themselves, and underscored the point that it was Vernon Kell's own Service, not just a clandestine cog in the Whitehall machine. With the original capital letters and italics retained, they were told that '. . . in all their relations with British Officials, Police and Government Departments they are authorised to describe themselves only as representing SIR VERNON KELL personally and not as representing any Government Office or Department.'

'In official dealings with private persons they are authorised to describe themselves if necessary as representing the Government Department appropriate to the nature of the work in hand. In cases of doubt they will say they are representing the War Office.'

Beyond that Tar had no specific training. In those days new officers learned 'on the job' from watching, talking to and listening to their peers, reading files, acquiring the 'house style' for the memoranda which had to be dictated at each twist and turn of a case, making mistakes and with luck, drawing the right conclusions from them.[6]

In Whitehall terms MI5 was what twenty-first century financiers would call 'off Balance Sheet', even a 'Special Purpose Vehicle'. Its existence, like that of its sister service SIS would not be officially avowed for another 60 years and its funding was buried in the so-called Secret Vote.[7] It was Vernon Kell's creation, born out of the Special Intelligence Bureau he had been chosen to set up in 1909. He was then 33 years old, the asthmatic son of an Army officer from a regiment less grand than the Seaforth. He was a gifted linguist who had qualified as an interpreter in French, Russian, German and Chinese. He was a devout churchgoer, a keen fisherman and a kind father.

Vernon Kell had seen his Service grow in the First World War, and shrink again after the Armistice to a small group in which no-one on Whitehall took much interest in the inter-war years. 'The pay was small, and the prospects such as make no appeal except to a certain number of officers with private incomes . . .' Nevertheless Kell's reputation and his ability to win friends and influence people in the corridors of power helped him fend off attempts to close MI5 down and steadily rebuild its reputation. The turn came in 1931, after a Whitehall row, the first of many squabbles over 'turf' with the Secret Intelligence Service, SIS or MI6, created at the same time as MI5 whose rôle was supposed to be as an overseas espionage service confined to working outside the country's 'Three Mile Limit'.

In loose harness with the Metropolitan Police Special Branch, SIS had been running a network of 'Casuals' in the UK targeting the Communist Party of Great Britain (CPGB); its rôle came to light when SIS fumbled and passed some of its intelligence to MI5 and awkward questions were asked about its source. The resulting rather fretful examination of demarcation lines led to a concordat with the Police and SIS, in which Kell broadened his mandate to take over from Scotland Yard counter-intelligence work against the CPGB, and its perceived rôle as the UK arm of the Moscow based Communist International, or Comintern. The latter's global spider's web of undercover agents supported with money, exhortation and background guidance any disaffection which would bring about the goal of world revolution; many were also involved directly in espionage. This proved to be a growth industry and also the catalyst for a rejuvenation of his Service, as it brought in from Scotland Yard the small team headed by Guy Liddell.[8]

His team had been tackling the CPGB target in its various manifestations shading from the gullible, the earnestly idealistic, through militant and revolutionary to those prepared to serve the Soviets directly. Ironically, the Scotland Yard unit had itself been 'targeted' by a clandestine Soviet network set up in London in 1919 by William Ewer, foreign editor of the Trades Union newspaper the *Daily Herald*. Operating as 'the Federated Press Agency of America' and supported by a parallel 'front' masquerading as the 'Vigilance

Detective Agency' Ewer's task was to identify the Special Branch's surveillance targets, and report on British counter-measures against espionage. His task was made easier when he succeeded in suborning two Special Branch officers, but his network was unravelled in 1929.

Liddell's unit would form the nucleus of MI5's counter-espionage success in general, and the Double Cross schemes in particular.[9]

In another element of the reorganisation, the SIS set up Section V, one of whose tasks was to channel to MI5 the intelligence its agents collected about the Communist International's activities overseas. To complete the reshuffle, the SIS agency, known as the M Organisation from the initial of Maxwell Knight[10] who ran it, was also folded into MI5. In the late 1930s Knight ran several noteworthy penetration operations against Communist espionage, the burgeoning British Union of Fascists (he had been an enthusiastic member of one of its antecedent organisations) and foreign embassies in London.

Notes

1. Philby, Harold Adrian Russell, 'Kim', born in the Punjab in 1912, died Moscow 1988. An ideological convert recruited by Moscow and manoeuvred by them into a correspondent's rôle on *The Times* and increasingly important rôles in SIS. He was the archetypical double agent. He claimed that his favourite song was Frank Sinatra's 'I Did It My Way'. Some might have thought the Platters' 1955 hit 'The Great Pretender' suited him better.

2. See e.g. Niven, David and Lord, Graham.

3. By 1943 Hinchley Cooke had been officially designated as 'Officer in charge of Prosecutions' with the acronym SLB.

4. Moriarty, C. C. H., CBE, 1877–1958, Irish born career policeman, author of what were to become the standard textbooks on police law.

5. Courtesy of Dave Cross of the West Midlands Police Museum.

6. Much as in the 1960s the present author, unencumbered by any professional qualifications, picked up whatever skills it took to become a London merchant banker, a now vanished species.

7. The Service has had several names in its near-century of tackling subversion, sabotage and spies and terrorists of many different stripes from anarchists and the IRA through to today's new breed. It is now the Security Service or in Government shorthand, SyS. For consistency and to match popular usage, we will stick with 'MI5'.

8. Liddell, Guy Maynard, MC, 1892–1958, one of the counter-intelligence world's underestimated grandmasters. We saw a parallel earlier between the

world Tar had entered and that of Lewis Carroll's Alice. It is irrelevant but of passing interest that Liddell was the great nephew of Alice Liddell, Carroll's inspiration if not obsession for the rôle.

9. Writing at the end of the Second World War from memory, to help John Curry with his History, Liddell listed many of the now forgotten but clearly sensitive operations he ran in this period, not least tracking the channelling of Moscow cash and proceeds from the sale of former Tsarist Crown jewels to militant British unions and the bankrupt Labour newspaper, the Daily Herald. The latter case in August 1920 may be the first time the British Government had disclosed to the press the text of intercepted diplomatic messages.

10. Knight, Maxwell, 1900–68, briefly a British Fascist, later deft agent-runner, naturalist, broadcaster, author.

11

'Secret Service, Next Stop'

MI5 finds itself nowadays squirming uncomfortably in the media crosshairs on issues thankfully outside our scope and timeframe, though some of the sharp focus may be a consequence of its own efforts to make itself more visible and accountable, and in the process, to shape its image. Vernon Kell would have blanched at the thought of the British TV drama series portraying its Millbank headquarters as a high-tech temple of mystery and glamour. The all-seeing, all-knowing, all-condemning officers, recruited with an eye to Equal Opportunity principles, and who evidently spend more on one visit to the barber or the hair stylist than Tar would have earned in a month, peer through hooded eyes at a dystopian world through banks of screens onto which, with the touch of a button they can bring up the inwardness and interconnections of anyone's life, evildoer or innocent, and watch their every movement. The script-writers' thumbnail sketches of some of the main characters in the series describe them variously as 'uncompromising and ruthless', 'unpredictable and reckless', or 'perceptive and stealthy', balanced by the 'calm and collected' Harry.

But even the conservative Kell was not averse to some image building of his own, though confined to a very small circle of trusted contacts who were on his Christmas card list. The 1918 card, shows Britannia striking down a ferocious, slavering beast with her trident, straddling a logo proclaiming 'The Hidden Hand'. Using the Roman numeral for 'five', MI5's initials are transmuted into the slogan 'Mankind's Immortal Victory'; a later card tells us that 'Malevolence Imposes Vigilance'.

In contrast to the TV image it is comforting that in the 1930s at least, MI5 was rather a nice place to work, almost like a family firm, though one whose stock in trade was suspicion, rather than anti-quarian books or fine wines. When Tar joined it was housed in a five-storey late Victorian building at 35 Cromwell Road, opposite the Natural History Museum in South Kensington, on the site where the Lycée Française and its cultural bulwark at the Institute Française now fight the good fight for everything French. Though the houses were terraced, with tiny gardens, they had been built for prosperous Galsworthian families – dowagers, City merchants, surgeons, bankers and barristers with a flourishing practice. As the traffic on Cromwell Road increased over the years, they had moved away to quieter Kensington enclaves, and the family homes gradually shrivelled into shabbily genteel hotels, warrens of bed sitting rooms each with its lonely occupant, and offices. Though even into the mid 1930s the stretch either side of MI5 still had several private homes, notably that of Winston Churchill's brother John at number 41.

It was already socially kaleidoscopic, accommodating among others the Indian Students Hostel, whose staff and guests may not have known it numbered amongst its neighbours not only MI5 but the London office of Indian Political Intelligence Service, from whose ranks had come many officers of MI5 and SIS. The 'India hands' were later moved into the MI5 office, where they complained bitterly about being accommodated in an unheated attic. The Post Office directory of the period does not list an occupier for number 35 but since other addresses are also skipped, this may not reflect subterfuge. It was hardly a well-kept secret. Legend has it that when the red double-decker buses trundled towards the junction of Cromwell and Exhibition Roads, their conductors had been known to bellow out, 'Secret Service, next stop'.

It was a tiny organisation by any Whitehall standard. Though it grew marginally over the 1930s to tackle new targets such as the German, Italian and British versions of Fascism, even by 1938, its history tells us, there were only 30 officers, and 103 secretaries and clerical staff. Vernon Kell was the patriarch of the family firm, supported by his wife Constance, his confidante, and his unbounded admirer. Kell's own diaries are the epitome of discretion, noting little or nothing beyond his social engagements and his regular church attendance. Her own unpublished account of his career is equally restrained[1], though it does show that from time to time, Kell played a personal rôle in investigations and told her with pride about 'birds' he had caught, and with concern about a *News of the World* exposé of his work 'some of its contents were true enough, some were very much off the mark'.

The feeling of 'family' was underscored once more on 17 December 1935 when John Kell married Dorothy 'Bobby' Walsh at Chelsea Old Church. Tar, listed by *The Times* as 'Mr. Tom Robertson' was best man.[2] Sir Vernon's Deputy Eric Holt-Wilson is the only other MI5 name identifiable among the guests at the wedding and the later reception at the Kells' home in Evelyn Gardens, South Kensington.

The novels of Graham Greene, Eric Ambler and Alan Furst provide fascinating images of the world of 1930s' espionage which Tar had signed up to fight. To the public at the time the threat was real, not the stuff of novels. *The Times*' archives for 1933 list reports of espionage trials and arrests from France to Finland, and Austria, Rumania and Italy. In the wake of the Baillie Stewart court martial the *New York Times* headlined a full page story from its London correspondent 'ONCE MORE SPY-FEVER GROWS EPIDEMIC – Suspicions and Fears Grip the People of Europe as Secret Agents push their Most Explosive Industry.' It went far beyond the Tower of London. In Moscow, Stalin orchestrated a show trial of six British engineers accused of spying and sabotage. In a Belgrade jail, a retired Colonel was hanged for selling military secrets to the Hungarians and Italians. Three men were executed in Danzig for taking an over-keen interest in Polish military preparations, and a German woman tried to crash through a French frontier barrier with components of a new French machine gun hidden in her car. Enthralled American readers were told that '. . . the thing that distinguishes spying . . . is its secrecy, and the infamy and intrigue, the dingy romance and tawdry heroism which flourish under cover of this secrecy'. What they did not know was that America itself was being targeted by a ring of German spies, led by the officer we saw earlier, flying out over the North Sea, who would later become Tar's first adversary.

As the world drew near to war and the level of anxiety rose in the office, Constance Kell made sure that there was an office Christmas tree and that there were 'presents all round' at the Christmas dinner. She even helped out for a time in the canteen MI5 shared with 'another Government department'. The Kells did not live in anonymity, 'minders' hidden in the hedgerows, CCTV cameras tucked under the eaves, but had an active social life, seen at Court, at concert halls, and at Cowes. All of this was 'networking' as an art form, reinforced by dinners with a group of UK Chief Constables, with 'the International Police Association' (the forerunner to Interpol) and Government receptions for the many foreign military attachés in London. There can have been no-one in what later became known as 'the Establishment' that he could not reach. Sir Vernon was chauffeured around London in a high-powered, hand built Invicta saloon, that John Argyll Robertson might have envied, a pennant on its bonnet displaying his personal motto 'Safe But Sure'.[3] Kell even shone a light from under his bushel to write to *The Times* from his home address to decry the dangers for passengers of the gas lighting still a feature of European trains. He also sought to arrange a reunion of British officers who like him, had been decorated by the Manchu Dynasty for their service in China during the 'Boxer Uprising' in 1900-01. It is hard to envisage that at the height of the Cold War, the Director of MI5 would have been invited to, let alone actually turned up for, a reception at the Soviet Embassy. Yet in 1938, as Constance Kell recalls, she and her husband were guests of the German Military Attaché. It is not surprising that she remembered the atmosphere as one of 'forced gaiety', with their hosts wearing 'strained, forbidding expressions'. It is possible that her strong presence was behind one of the mild surprises that comes from a search for Tar in an organisation chart from around 1935. Reflecting Britain as it was then, one would expect to find that the higher echelons of MI5 were populated by men only. It makes sense that Miss Dicker, described by one of her charges as 'rather terrifying', should be in charge of 'Records and

Women Staff but it is intriguing to note that Finance, an important responsibility, was in the hands of a Miss Masterton and that two key sections in the Investigative Division, 'Defence Security – Russia' and 'Civil Security – Home', were also in female hands, the first run by the redoubtable Jane Sissmore (later Archer), and the second a Miss D Saunders. It may be a modern reflection of that early 'age of enlightenment' that since the Second World War, MI5 has had two women Directors.

It has been claimed that until Dick White[4] joined in 1935, MI5 had no university graduates on its staff. Though it was hardly an intellectual hotbed, to Kell's credit the files show that in 1931, he did actually have on his team one H L Smith, a BSc and Fellow of Imperial College, in a section called 'Security Research,' and later the 'Scientific Section'; a bland catchall which covered anything from bombs to secret inks. A brief sighting of him in a 1942 file shows him offering expert advice on how purloined documents might have been typed and photographed.[5] His lone presence does not dilute the force of the point made by Christopher Andrew,[6] that with its recruitment of 'The Cambridge Five', Soviet intelligence had for several years, more British graduates working for it than MI5 and SIS combined.

To judge from their names the MI5 secretaries and Registry clerks were drawn from a rather narrow social universe – diversity had not yet entered the national consciousness – and had to be utterly trustworthy, vouched for by personal contact, a reliable headmistress or the eagle-eyed owner of some discreet employment agency, as likely as not a former employee of the service.[7] Trust only went so far. Until the institutional mindset mellowed with the build up for the Second World War, Kell was disinclined to employ more than one girl from the same family on the grounds that if two sisters lived at home, or shared a bedsitter, they might be inclined to chat to each other or their parents about what they had been doing all day. One of the secretaries remembered[8] that until the demands of the Second World War forced the doors open to all talents and backgrounds, the Service did not recruit Jews or Catholics. The proscription against Catholics, if true, is at first sight a fascinating throwback to earlier centuries when they were regarded with deep suspicion. More pragmatically it probably reflected a neurosis about Britain's long-standing conflict with the Irish Republican Army.

It is tempting to dismiss the whiff of anti-Semitism as no more than a sad reflection of 1930s' British prejudices. But as Christopher Andrew has found[9] the attitude prevailed for many years after the Second World War.

In Tar's early days the all-female secretarial and Registry staff (all of them single, or at least styling themselves 'Miss' in the rosters) were classed as temporary Civil Servants, with no pension rights, and no regular pay reviews. A young secretary earning £192 a year in the 1930s felt underpaid compared to her friends in the commercial world outside, though with the slight consolation that, like the officers, her salary was untaxed, and the major morale boost of involvement in something secret and important. Quirky too. As one recalled years later[10] 'We all queued up for our buff envelopes at the end of each month outside the office of . . . Miss Dicker and her equally terrifying assistant, Miss Constant, who wore a monocle.'

Though the officers could and often did find themselves working odd hours in odd places, for staff the day began at 9.00am and ended at 6.00pm on weekdays, and at noon on Saturdays, with occasional overtime operating the telephone switchboard at night and over public holidays. Computers and electronics lay in the future. The institutional memory of MI5, all those names, addresses, telephone numbers, facts, allegations, suspicions and connections, was captured not on encrypted hard drives but in ever-multiplying rows of dark green cabinets crammed with meticulously cross-referenced card indices and buff cardboard files. Their endless pages, threaded with a metal-tagged purple string, recorded the details and connections of anyone who, rightly or wrongly, had come to MI5's obsessive attention.

Unlike today, there was no gym, no bar with a view of the Thames in which to unwind after hours with a glass of beer. When not at their desks, the officers usually went to their Clubs for lunch or prowled the pubs on their secret errands. Most of the staff brought in sandwiches for lunch, sometimes crossing Cromwell Road for a mid-morning currant bun and a cup of 'coffee' made from Camp bottled essence in the cafeteria of the Natural History Museum. No British institution of the time could ignore the ritual of afternoon tea. Looking up potential spies and saboteurs in the files and entering the names of new suspects, was briefly interrupted when the Registry girls put down their pens and pencils and trilled down to the basement where a Miss Avison provided tea and biscuits for a penny. Meanwhile the officers, Tar remembered, would meet upstairs, often joined by Kell, for 'tea parties', to talk over the cases on which they were working, (an exchange probably barred in today's security conscious world by stringent 'need to know' principles) and in the process get to know one another better. 'It was a very friendly outfit', he recalled. Nor did MI5 then have at its disposal the battery of pervasive electronic surveillance and monitoring gadgetry which has become an accepted part of the fabric of our modern life. If it wanted to read a suspect's mail – its main tactic and one hallowed by use by British Governments since the 18th century though apparently without much of a basis in law – it had to ask a libertarian and often reluctant Home Office for a warrant, (though getting a phone tapped seems to have been a more straightforward exercise), and it had only a small team of 'watchers', though the Special Branch was a valuable extra resource. The detail in a note on a wartime meeting of the Communist Party's 'Cadres Class' at 'Gas Industries House' suggests that the audience included an undercover Branch officer with a retentive memory.

Though Kell – 'a small, quiet man' in one girl's eyes, 'a really splendid man' in Tar's – was rarely seen by the junior staff, they were aware that both he and Constance were especially protective of their girls, hence the admonition mentioned earlier, when on joining Kell advised Tar 'not to get too friendly' with the female staff. This may have been standard counsel for new entrants, reflecting Kell's traditionalist sense that officers and staff should not fraternise, or perhaps more pointedly targeted at a handsome young man with a twinkle in his eye and a sports car, whose gadding about town with John Kell would not have escaped Constance Kell's watchful eye.

Until the Second World War changed the social landscape[11] MI5 staff addressed the officers by their rank and name, 'Captain Smith' or 'Major Jones' and civilians, as Tar was at the time, as 'Mr. Robertson'. The men were always punctilious in calling the girls 'Miss So-and-So', while the girls themselves called each other by their surnames. 'I did not know the Christian names of most of my colleagues for years', one remembered.

This did not stop them tagging their seniors with irreverent nicknames, much as the unfortunate Mr. Girdlestone at Charterhouse had become 'The Duck'. When the start of the Second World War put Tar back in his Seaforth uniform, his tailored tartan trews (compounded perhaps by his debonair charm) saw him nicknamed 'Passion Pants', and notwithstanding Colonel Eric Holt Wilson's iconic status as an MI5 officer since 1912, his devout Anglicanism earned him the tearoom tag of 'Holy Willie'. O. A. Harker,[12] known to close colleagues as 'Jasper', was remembered by one girl as 'a dapper man with smooth silver hair and a curious rolling walk which, rumour had it, was because he had no toes! He did wear very small shoes.'[13] The 1930s' designations of MI5's frontline investigative sections – 'Internal Security in Army', 'Internal Security in Navy', 'CE [Counter Espionage] Germany Italy France', 'Fascists and Nazis in UK', 'Arms Traffic', 'CE Minor Countries, Miscellaneous', 'Civil Security Foreign', 'Civil Security Home', 'CE Russia', 'Enquiries and Special Enquiries' – give a perhaps misleading impression of its scope; many of the sections were staffed by just one or two officers. It was certainly worried about the Communist menace. This may have provided Tar's first glimpse of MI5's work since by one account when he first joined he shared a small office with Guy Liddell and Millicent Bagot,[14] who had targeted the Communist threat when they worked under the Special Branch umbrella. Tar's first official appearance in the MI5 staff lists is in March 1934 where his job is shown as 'CE [Counter-Espionage] – Germany, France, Italy and Miscellaneous', under Baillie Stewart's nemesis Edward Hinchley Cooke.

A 1933 memorandum which from its context appears to be part of a study of what MI5 would face in time of war, and what its powers of arrest might be, cites another internal paper, with a pronounced, almost apocalyptic whiff of 'Reds under the Bed', which maintains that 'supporters of subversive and seditious societies would probably be found to exceed 100,000'. According to a survey of election figures 'a conservative estimate of Communist sympathisers in the UK of varying degrees of activity might be around 350,000 to 500,000'. Dealing with them in an emergency would require 'one steepish step to begin with. The movement, deprived of its heads – some 5,000 to 10,000 – by early action, would be largely disorganised and the number of individuals to be actually dealt with [by MI5] at one time would after the first few weeks, gradually diminish. Most of the heads of the Communist organisation would by that time be rounded up or at worse, working under difficulties as fugitives.' 'All Communists are potential saboteurs', another note declares.

Even given the real apprehensions of the time that seems a rather bood-curdling view. Even though 'supporters' is a broad definition, and no doubt there were many of them outside the Party's ranks, the latter's declared membership usually hovered around the 5,000 mark, peaking briefly above 10,000 in the aftermath of the 1926 general Strike. But there is no doubt the Soviets and their UK Communist disciples were hard at work spying and subverting and MI5 scored some major successes against Soviet inspired intelligence operations, notably in rolling up a Soviet spy ring at Woolwich Arsenal.

There were also failures, despite the fact that Special Branch and later MI5 thought they were keeping a close eye on Communists and sympathisers, through penetration and surveillance; a 1936 file entry lists the dates some of their targets (among them the Left Wing publisher Victor Gollancz) passed through the English Channel ports. For instance, it was not until 1942 that the arrest of a North London printer, Oliver Green, for forging petrol coupons led to the discovery that he was a central player in a Soviet espionage ring created in 1937, whose nucleus had been a dozen veterans of the International Brigade who had fought against Franco in the Spanish Civil War.

But the glaring lapse was that in common with SIS, the Foreign

Office and other pillars of what later became known as the British 'Establishment', MI5 was dangerously blind to the idea that men of the same school and social background as its own officers could be seduced by the cross-currents of the era and the ideological siren songs of Moscow, into penetrating Whitehall and passing secrets to Moscow based on the Jesuitical argument that they were not betraying their country but protecting the world against Fascism. (The adjective is not out of place: one of the most effective Soviet agent runners, the Hungarian Teodor Maloi[15] had been a Catholic priest until the horrors of existence in a First World War POW camp brought him to Bolshevism). Nor did MI5 or Special Branch pick up traces of Maloi or the other Soviet agent runners, the 'Great Illegals', flitting unobtrusively to and fro across the North Sea from the Continent as businessmen, journalists or commercial photographers. The British academics at Cambridge and Oxford who acted as the advance guard of Soviet talent-spotters also flew beneath their radar. Viktor Popov, Soviet Ambassador in London in the 1980s, when his Embassy housed more KGB officers than diplomats, wrote that 'the British security service looked for Soviet spies primarily amongst middle class men and women who made no secret of their Communist views. British snobbery meant that the service simply could not comprehend that anyone in the corridors of power could be a Soviet agent . . . [it] believed 'Top People' thought of the Soviet Union as an enemy and could never bring themselves to work for it.'[16] It was 1933, the year of the Reichstag Fire, of TREASURE's chilling brush with the Gestapo, of Baillie-Stewart's disgrace, and the year Tar joined MI5, that Kim Philby, newly graduated from Cambridge, drove a motorcycle to Vienna and in a fatal flush of youthful idealism and puppy love for a girl called Litzi, was excitedly sucked in to underground work for the Kremlin, the start of a career of duplicity without precedent in espionage history. It was a trajectory along which he would come to know perilously much not just about the Secret Intelligence Service which employed, promoted and protected him but also about many of Tar's Double Cross cases, the Most Secret Sources which supported them, and SOE. His name crops up in so many different contexts in Tar's story alone that even after so much has been written about him, the feeling remains that even now there are details of his treachery which may not have been fully explored.

In 1935 Tar's job description changed to 'CE Minor Countries – Miscellaneous' and a year later to 'CE – Japan, Italy, France, USA', the latter at first sight a rather surprising target area, though perhaps explained by America's Irish and German communities and the presence of other ethnic groups latently hostile to the British Empire. It was a period in which, he later told his family deprecatingly, that he spent a lot of time 'trailing around after the Japanese Military Attaché'. Neither suggest the career path of a high-flyer.

Notes

1. Imperial War Museum Archives.
2. Tar was a compromise candidate for the rôle. John Kell had two even closer friends, each of whom would have been much offended had the other been asked. So the choice fell on Tar.
3. Kell was a keen fisherman, Lady Constance much less so, so his driver Maclean often doubled as his ghillie.
4. White, Sir Dick Goldsmith, 1906–93, Director MI5 1953–56 and Chief of SIS 1956–72.
5. Smith later moved across to SIS.
6. Introduction to Curry, *History*, p. 8.
7. Legend has it, that in later years, MI5 and SIS had a demarcation line much as in their professional spheres when it came to recruiting female support staff. An agency in London supplied 'Home Counties' girls in twinset and pearls to MI5, while up in Derbyshire a reliable lady kept her eye out for sensible types from further north for SIS.
8. Personal papers.
9. Andrew, *Defence of the Realm*, p. 285.
10. Personal papers.
11. Only to some extent: a random glance at *The Times* in 1943 shows casualties listed as 'Officers' killed, wounded or taken prisoner, followed by a separate tabulation for 'Soldiers'. And as Professor Richard Aldrich discovered, when the US Army took over a British intelligence base in Germany in the 1960s, they were amused to find that while they were used to a democratic demarcation of toilets between ' Men' and 'Women', the British had three, dividing 'Men' into 'Officers' and 'Other Ranks'.
12. Harker, Brigadier Oswald Alan, 1886–1968. Personal papers.

13. Their German opposite numbers in the Abwehr had a curiously similar penchant for nicknames. Its Head, Admiral Canaris, was known – behind his back – as 'The Greek', Captain Moll in Hamburg was 'Skipper' while the agent-recruiting skills of Dr. Praetorius had earned him the soubriquet of 'The Ratcatcher'.

14. Bagot, Millicent Jessie Eleanor, CBE, 1907–2006. Her encyclopaedic knowledge of Communism and Soviet intelligence is said to have suggested her to John le Carre, whose first steps in the intelligence world were with MI5, as the model for Connie Sachs in the George Smiley novels.

15. Though the name is usually spelt Maly in intelligence literature, V. V. Popov spells it in Russian as 'Maloi' and is more likely to be correct.

16. Popov, V. V.

12

'That Was The Year, That Was . . .'

Even by the standards of that dangerous decade, 1936 had more than its fair share of events that would send the newspaper sub-editors searching for bold type and dramatic words. Some were on an international scale. Some were more narrowly British. Some went unheeded by the wider world but sowed the seeds of the Double Cross adventures ahead.

Some were happy. For Tar the happiest was one which merited only a low key entry in the Marriages column of *The Times*. It recorded that on April 18th he married Joan Grice-Hutchinson. It fits nicely with the thread and tone of our story that they had first met at one of the Healing family's cricket games. It conjures up a picture of racing-green Rileys and MGs lining the gravelled driveway. Girls in summer frocks and wide-brimmed hats watch admiringly as the handsome Tar, his grass-stained white flannel trousers held up by a carelessly knotted navy, pink and maroon Old Carthusian tie, runs a few paces to the crease and bowls, left-handed, a cunningly spun, deceptively slow ball. The batsman swings but finds only empty air as it tweaks off the grass past him. The shouts of 'Owzat' and the umpire's pointing finger are key elements in the ritual, but unnecessary here; the splayed stumps speak for themselves. Manly murmurs of 'well bowled' mix with genteel handclapping. Mim Robertson in the scorer's chair makes a careful note that another wicket has fallen to Tar's artifice, and turns to fuss over the jugs of iced Robinson's Lemon Barley Water. Joan's father Charlie, like Tar an Old Carthusian, a golfer and a cricket lover, had been a soldier. He was awarded a Military Cross for his bravery in the many months of carnage which entered the First World War history books as the Battle of Gallipoli. Earlier branches of the Grice and Hutchinson family trees had sprouted other soldiers, an MP, a clergyman, engineers, a clergyman, explosives experts and a clergyman. Back in the 18th century the Grices had been Birmingham gun makers specialising in flintlock pistols and muskets.[1] When Tommy soldiered at the Seaforth Highlanders' depot he would not have known that in 1843, a Lt. George Hutchinson had been given a gold watch by the South Eastern Railway Company for his 'services in blasting the Round Down Cliff at Dover'. He was more fortunate than another family member who was fatally hoist by his own petard in 1851.

Joan, an only child, was still recovering from the shock of seeing her first love killed as he rode in a point to point, but the tranquil, quintessentially English, family setting and Tar's charm and good looks worked their magic and they were married on a chilly Saturday, in her parent's home village of Upton-upon-Severn, a dozen miles from Worcester and in the heart of Healing country. Mim Healing played the violin in one of the musical ensembles encouraged and often conducted by the rising Worcester-born composer Edward Elgar,[2] some of his music no doubt enhanced the wedding.

To be poor or unemployed in London in those inter war years was unremittingly grim. To be a clerk or a shop assistant on a small wage, rattling into London by train or tram for a long working day, was drudgery. To be rich was bliss. To be like the Robertsons, a young London couple with a modest income and lively lifestyle, was not all plain sailing; even if there were families in the background with some capital. Indeed though Curry's History describes the salary of an MI5 officer as 'small' this is perhaps rather subjective. Tar began on a salary of £350 per year. Translating past money values is a difficult and potentially misleading exercise, but that salary might equate to some £17,500 today. But that is not necessarily a measure of real purchasing power; in the 1930s each pound bought a great deal more than it does today. Certainly not generous but it was free of tax, and until the Second World War, paid in crisp white £5 notes. An MP's salary in the same era was only £400 a year. By contrast as a junior partner in the family publishing house, future Prime Minister Harold Macmillan had to 'make do' with an annual income of £6,000. As we know from novels of the period – Denis Mackail's charming *Greenery Street* is a fine proxy – well-bred but not well-heeled urban newly weds tended to be 'romantic, unpractical, sensitive, improvident, fundamentally un-businesslike and constitutionally incapable of seeing anything as it really is . . .' They expected, and their circle expected of them, that until the first high-wheeled Silver Cross pram arrived in the hall, life meant a bustle of dinner parties, evenings at the theatre, charity balls and weekends in the country. But though money was always short – there were tradesmen's bills to pay, the credit account at Peter Jones to be kept under control, and pained sermons from the bank manager to be endured – a short lease on a small house in Chelsea could be had for a down-payment of few hundred pounds, and despite or because of the bank manager and with a discreet touch of parental help, there was always enough cash around to meet the meagre wages of a cook and parlour maid.

But there was more to the year than one happy marriage. Germany's troops marched back into the Rhineland unopposed, and reclaimed territory lost under the terms of the post First World War Treaty of Versailles. Hitler's pride was temporarily dented at the Berlin Olympics when his obsession, that strength and beauty were exclusively Aryan preserves, was confounded by the black US athlete Jesse Owens, who won four Gold medals. Italy annexed Ethiopia. In Spain, Franco and his military co-conspirators launched an assault on the Republican government and began a civil war which engaged the military attention of Germany and Russia and the ideological commitment of thousands of young people. Spanish peasants and poets from around the world lost their lives and illusions, while the Soviet Government stole the Republic's gold reserves. Juan Pujol a young Catalan hid in a friend's house for two years to avoid conscription. In the end he was caught but he would later emerge as GARBO, one of the greatest double agents.

As a freelance correspondent for *The Times* on the Spanish

battlefront, attached to Franco's HQ, Kim Philby took the first step into the heart of the 'Establishment'. At the same time the chess players in Moscow were moving Guy Burgess into the BBC, the opening gambit towards the same goal; they had placed Donald MacLean in the Foreign Office just the year before.

Back, awed, from a visit to the Soviet Union, Anthony Blunt was close to recruitment as a Soviet agent by Burgess, while beginning to make his name as an art historian, a long march which would take him through the heart of MI5 into Buckingham Palace and eventually out again to exposure and disgrace.[3] Another of Tar's star line-up, Dusko Popov, later to become famous as TRICYCLE, was at university, expressing risky ant-Nazi sentiments and striking a friendship with Johnny Jebsen, later an Abwehr officer who recruited him and later still became a double agent down in Tar's books as ARTIST. Niklaus Ritter, the German intelligence officer whom we last saw out at sea, had just arrived in Hamburg from the US to take up a new job with the Abwehr. Arthur Owens the double, or perhaps triple agent whom Ritter knew as JOHNNY and Tar as SNOW, was starting on his personal odyssey of deception. MI5 had begun to open his mail and watch his movements, but just where his real loyalties lay was a question which would baffle the British Admiralty, SIS, and later Tar, until the end. Another double agent, the dashing Eddie Chapman, later agent ZIGZAG, was leading the high and low life up and down England as a member of 'the Jelly [for gelignite] Gang' of safecrackers, 'nightclubbing in London on the proceeds and day-tripping to Brighton with an ingénue on either arm', as one admirer later wrote. The restless future double agent TREASURE was on a fact-finding mission in Czechoslovakia, a country already under threat of dismemberment by Germany, perhaps posing as a journalist, but perhaps unwittingly doing the bidding of a German Abwehr Officer.

Notes
1. US internet shopping sites catering to the esoteric hobbies of black powder firearms buffs, such as Track of The Wolf and Dixie Gun Works, still offer replacement 'Grice 1762' mainsprings for Brown Bess muskets.

2. Elgar, Sir Edward, 1857–1934, 1st Baronet, OM, GCVO.
3. Blunt, Anthony Frederick, 1907–83, traitor, art historian, quondam Professor of the History of Art, University of London, MI5 officer in the Second World War, later Director of the Courtauld Institute and Keeper of the Royal Pictures, a Soviet agent from the 1930s into the 1950s. Known as Sir Anthony Blunt, KCVO until stripped of his knighthood in 1979.

13

For King and Country

With the Second World War just three years ahead, MI5 found itself in 'absolute darkness' about the Abwehr. It had just one officer dealing with 'the German aspect' and even in 1938 just two, for whom it was not even a fulltime job. It would take the intricate triumphs of Double Cross to remedy this. Meantime there were other tasks for it and for Tar, notably an episode which had nothing to do with counter-intelligence or subversion, and for which his then job title of 'Miscellaneous' would be an understatement.

Another headline event of 1936 had been the death in January of King George V. His heir, Edward, Prince of Wales acceded to the throne as Edward VIII. The new king's infatuation with Mrs. Wallis Simpson, an American divorcée with an ambiguous background, and his determination to marry her posed a Constitutional conundrum. How would such a marriage square with his dignity as king and his position as head of the Established Church? Could she become queen? The questions set politicians, Empire and Dominion leaders and eventually newspaper proprietors (whose initial stance had been to muzzle their papers) into partisan frenzies. These were exacerbated by the feeling in some key quarters that the new king, unkindly nicknamed by some 'Edward the Caresser', was simply not up to his responsibilities.[1]

The controversy, long kept out of the British press began to escalate into 'the Abdication Crisis'. Robertson family memories[2] of what Tar told them offer an insight into Delphic comments in Jack Curry's early official history about MI5's rôle. He writes that as the temperature rose 'certain delicate enquiries were made [by MI5] under the Prime Minister's directions. These were matters touching on the Constitution and on ultimate issues of sovereignty and were very far removed from any question of guarding the King's realm. They involved its innermost integrity.' He suggests[3] that Prime Minister Stanley Baldwin[4] ordered MI5 to conduct these 'enquiries' because 'no other suitable machinery existed', and because of the trust which Vernon Kell had inspired in high quarters over years of discreet service. The most obvious area for probing would have been Mrs. Simpson's cosmopolitan and allegedly promiscuous background, though since that lay buried in musky Shanghai bedrooms it would have been more a job for SIS. We know that MI5's sources inside the German Embassy were keeping them well informed on Ambassador von Ribbentrop's characteristically misguided views that the king was 'a certain winner'. We also know from the memoirs of the eminent historian Professor M. R. D. Foot, who saw the underlying correspondence, that Geoffrey Dawson, then editor of *The Times*, was involved with several 'Establishment' luminaries in taking discreet soundings of opinion from the Dominions, on Mrs. Simpson's acceptability; the response was negative.[5]

The new authorised History[6] tells us that although Special Branch did build up a file of surveillance reports on Mrs Simpson's parallel involvement with Guy Trundle, a Mayfair car salesman, MI5 itself has no dossier on her or the Abdication drama. But given the risks of the task, one would hardly have expected the canny Kell to leave a paper trail. The story Tar told his family suggests just how potentially explosive these delecate enquiries were. The new king's brother, and next in line to the throne, was then the Duke of York, father of the present Queen Elizabeth. His London home was 145 Piccadilly, just across Hyde Park Corner from Buckingham Palace. Then as now, MI5's repertoire included telephone tapping and Tar claimed[7] that to help the Government keep abreast of 'how the situation was moving' he had been directed to slip into Green Park by night, to tap into the telephone line on which the harassed and confused king, and his brother, appalled at the burden he was likely to have to take on should abdication became a reality, talked about the day's developments. It was not a task for which MI5 could seek official sanction. Nor could it have risked involving the Post Office, which then operated the telephone service.

In those early years, long before MI5 acquired its own 'in house' capability, tapping involved labelling the target line at the local Exchange as one which needed to be checked for 'technical reasons'. When the unsuspecting caller dialled the target number, the call went through in the normal way but it was simultaneously diverted through the Central Checking Exchange, where another plug would route the call to ear-phoned note takers at the Orwellian-style 'Central Observation Panel'. The process necessarily involved putting several Post Office operators and engineers 'in the know' and could lead to unusual clicks and echoes on the line, quickly alerting even an innocent ear.

Taking Tar's story at face value, his stroll in the park would still have needed the help of at least one trusted engineer to find the junction box in the bushes, and pick out the line to tap amid the spider's web of coloured wires. He would then either have used ear-phones and taken notes, or if he had a bag of batteries, he might even have used the 'Telecord' machine proudly launched a year or so earlier by the Dictaphone Company. But techniques aside, what are we to make of the story? There are no MI5 files to confirm or contradict his account. Nor is there anyone left with a direct recollection of events. In the absence of any other evidence we can at least accept that Tar's account puts some flesh on Curry's very bare bones and that he had no reason whatever to invent it.

In 1937 Tar was switched to 'Arms Traffic', a minefield we might well call it, for a country which was on the one hand bracing itself for war and on the other still hoping that, with conciliation and concession it would be avoided. What is now euphemistically called 'the defence industry' plays an important rôle in the modern British economy. So too in the 1930s though back then the blunter term 'armaments' was used and there were far more companies involved, in aggregate a significant factor in British industry, employment, exports and Stock Exchange investment. Fairy, Handley Page, de Havilland and Hawker produced a wide range of aircraft. Imperial Chemical Industries' product catalogue included explosives and the constituents of mustard gas, red-hot armour plate rolled out of the mills of Hadfields and Beardmore. Ship builders Cammell-Laird,

Thorneycroft and Yarrow competed for contracts while the industry's giant Vickers Armstrong, made everything from warships to aircraft, including tanks, artillery and machine guns. But like twenty-first century bankers the industry was the target of what one company chairman delicately called 'opprobrium'.[8] Stirred by Left Wing politicians and the liberal press, heavyweight Commissions of Enquiry in the USA and UK stigmatised the industry's principal figures more directly as 'Merchants of Death', who played off potential belligerents against one another and then supplied both sides, handing out lavish bribes to politicians and colluding to fix prices. But those sensitive areas were not ones in which M15 would have been encouraged to focus its inquisitive attention. A more obvious rôle for the Service and its informers would have been to monitor Left Wing trouble-making or Irish Republican sabotage efforts in the workplace.

However the inclusion of the pejorative word 'Traffic' in Tar's job description suggests a more likely target area. Since the end of the First World War, Europe had been awash with surplus, surrendered and stockpiled guns and ammunition. As new conflicts erupted, notably the Spanish Civil War, and Italy's invasion of Abyssinia, now called Ethiopia, and new nations and their new armies arose from the rubble of the First World War and the muddle of Versailles, demand grew to match the supply. They were private buyers too, among them the well financed French Fascist 'Cagoule' organisation, who stockpiled weapons on a substantial scale.

A business which later generations know as BSA, a maker of bicycles, motorcycles and innocuous airguns, was then trading as Birmingham Small Arms, and alongside its bicycles, manufactured an array of weapons from rifles to machine guns.

After the First World War BSA had been appointed the agent of the British War Office to dispose of surplus or supposedly unserviceable rifles and pistols. By 1930, it was all too aware that this lucrative but murky market flourished behind the curtains of luxury hotels, and in anonymous offices overlooking Lake Leman in Geneva, and that the use of 'front men' in Greece or Mexico, bribes and 'commissions' were the order of the day. So it passed its rights on to the 'swashbuckling' and qualm-free Captain John Ball, once of the Royal Flying Corps, and his Belgian partner Grimard, who brought to the venture the engineering capacity to remake and rebore weapons long rejected as 'obsolete'. Tracking the large scale shipments by their Soley Company (based not far from his parents' Regents Park home) and its cosmopolitan competitors, such as Marcus Wolf and Willi Daugs, would have been interesting work for Tar, all the more since much of the Soviet Union's support for the Republicans in the Spanish Civil War was in the form of clandestine arms purchases orchestrated by Stalin's secret police emissary Walter Krivitzky and paid for in bullion from the Spanish National vaults.[9]

Notes

1. Though the British press remained mute until the last moment, newspapers overseas were gloriously indiscreet. When a court in out of the way Ipswich granted Mrs Simpson the divorce which would free her to marry the king, a US newspaper is said to have headlined the news with an irreverence matched by its unexpected sense of British history, 'King's Moll Reno'd in Wolsey's Home Town.'(*Oxford Dictionary of Quotations*, p. 544.
2. Personal papers.
3. Curry, p. 60.
4. Baldwin, The Rt. Hon Stanley, 1st Earl of Bewdley, KG, PC, 1867–1947, politician and statesman.
5. Foot, p. 108.
6. Andrew, *Defence of the Realm*, Note 76 on p. 898.
7. Personal papers.
8. West and Anderson.
9. See for instance http://www.carbinesforcollectors.com/spaintable.htm

14

'A Palace and a Prison'

It is somehow reassuring and humanising to take another look at the contrast between these glimpses of a world of subterfuge and dark dealings and some more scenes from the more mundane side of life at MI5, 'an everyday story of counter-intelligence folk'. In what the film industry would call a 'prequel' to the early twenty-first century, MI5 moved for a short period to the top floor of Thames House, on the north side of the Embankment, by Lambeth Bridge, then a speculative office development in an area 'off the beaten track' for businesses, and later the impressively grand Head Office, designed by Sir Frank Baines in the 'Imperial Neo-Classical' style, of Imperial Chemical Industries, once British industry's standard bearer. The wheel has turned full circle and today much of the complex is the headquarters of an MI5 or Security Service, vastly grown, infinitely more sophisticated, unrecognisable by Tar or his colleagues if they were around to attend one of the regular curry lunches arranged to keep in touch with retired staff, and certainly not as much fun to work for.

In September 1938, Hitler's demands for the territory of what was then Czechoslovakia, brought Europe still closer to the brink of war. Without bothering to consult the hapless Czechs, Britain, France and Italy allowed the Nazis to swallow its German – speaking area, and gave them de facto control of the rest of the country. It was a concession which was famously and foolishly trumpeted by British Prime Minister Neville Chamberlain as 'peace for our time' though it only put off the inevitable conflict for a year. The 'Munich Crisis' must have had MI5 officers working their sources in London embassies or elsewhere, but as Chamberlain flew twice to Munich in the last fortnight of the month – an early exercise in 'shuttle diplomacy' – they were faced with a more prosaic task. Whispers rustled from girl to girl and desk to desk that the Registry was to be evacuated. Where to, those who knew didn't say, and those who did not, speculated uselessly. Officers and staff all pitched in to pack the institutional memory into large cardboard boxes, a massive transplant of the bureaucratic brain. The next morning the chattering staff assembled in Horseferry Road and clambered into red double-decker STL buses. The files followed in Army trucks, some of the officers in cars. Still no one knew where the caravan of secrets was headed; nor did they ever find out. At a lunchtime stop at a pub in West London, word reached them that the crisis was over and back they lumbered to Thames House. The 'what if?' school of history would have a field day conjecturing about the consequences, had there been a bad accident somewhere on the Great West Road, the files spilling all over the road, or if any one of many hostile groups from the IRA to the Abwehr, had got wind of the plans.

In 1939 there was a more conventional move, to Romney House, a new building near the Whitehall end of Great Smith Street. From anecdotal accounts the work still had its lighter moments; one girl remembers leaning over a balcony to drop a paper clip on 'Hinch's' bald head as he left the building. But security still mattered; a girl who joined at the time recalled being inducted by Miss Dicker 'with some severity and little enlightenment. I still did not know what this job was about.' But again underscoring the 'family business' she was later taken to be introduced to Vernon Kell himself, finding him 'kind and encouraging'.

By this time the Registry had grown, as if feeding on itself. It was still one long room, divided by subject into four or five sections, each physically separated by cupboards housing its particular files. The Registry girl remembers: 'In the centre of these dark green enclaves were our desks, tightly grouped and equipped with elderly type-writers and not much else but a variety of pencils. Here two or three of us worked cheek by jowl with our Head of Section and I soon learned that her encyclopaedic knowledge of the files – ours dealt with Fascist and pro-German sympathisers and activities – kept us and the papers moving briskly. On [my] first day, as on many others,

I scurried round our cupboards manhandling files and struggled to grasp their extraordinary system of numbering. Handed a lot of old papers to file away, I can still remember the laborious unpicking of files and threading them up on those purple tags and the mess I made of a Minute Sheet. More enjoyable was my last job that day, making new covers for battered files. One could be quite artistic with a broad nib and a lot of Indian ink.'

'Because of close quarters in this room, supervision was constant and we were all under the eagle eye of the Head of Registry, Miss Paton Smith, who sat at one end and missed nothing. It was nice to be promoted to go off to the Card Index room, armed with a sharp pencil and some new reports to be "looked up" or new cards to be put away. It was a quiet room where we walked up and down the rows peering through the cards, drawer on drawer of them in wooden cases . . . Biros, electric typewriters, photocopiers, computers were undreamed of, at any rate by us. Telephones in the Registry were few and not much used, certainly never for private calls.'

Around this time, Tar played a part in nailing a venal 'mole' in the Foreign Office Communications Department, a communications clerk who had fed code secrets to the Russians. There are various versions of how Captain John King was induced to confess. Each involves a different West End pub, many drinks, and Tar; one even has him purloining the drunken King's safe keys to get his hands on incriminating evidence. The most reliable account suggests King was first softened up under heavy but inconclusive questioning by Jasper Harker and Valentine Vivian of SIS and then finally confessed 'after further interrogation' which is most likely the rôle Tar played; a smoke-filled saloon bar would been an ideal venue to play the 'good cop' after his colleagues' 'bad cop' routine. A search of the King archive throws up no mention of Tar or the whisky-fuelled 'confessional' but that signifies nothing either way.

Unlike the relaxed days in Cromwell Road '. . . there was no basement canteen, no coffee or tea breaks but a Thermos flask lurked under a desk here and there. At lunch time I went with another new girl into Horseferry Road, not a gourmet's paradise, and found a dairy that served baked beans on toast for eight pence. This became our usual lunch and suited our purses . . . Keen shoppers sped to the Army & Navy Stores. A rare treat was a dash to Vincent Square to see a Flower Show.'[1] When war broke out the Registry and many of the officers moved to Wormwood Scrubs; though their letterhead continued to give 'PO Box 500 Parliament Street, SW1' as the address, the telephone numbers on the 'Shepherds Bush' and 'Acorn' exchanges were rather easily identifiable as West London. The telegraphic address, 'SNUFFBOX' was perhaps some wag's idea of a joke. The prison had been emptied of most of its usual guests when the Home Office fretted that while its walls were thick, its roof was not, and a bombing raid might send hordes of hardened criminals rampaging across the suburbs.

The high prison walls might have been escape proof but were no barrier to romance. Peggy Harmer met her future husband Christopher, a peacetime lawyer and one of Tar's colleagues and closest friends, while she was working there as a secretary. Like most who were recruited she had no idea what she was joining – perhaps some humdrum section of the War Office – when a 'Most Secret and Confidential' letter to her family's country home invited her to report to Wormwood Scrubs. Her final lap was on a number 15 bus. 'I walked in and these great big iron gates clanged behind me. It was quite daunting. Then I was taken up an iron staircase to a cell. It was just like being in "Porridge"', she told the writer Ben Macintyre. (All the more since a small group of prisoners remained in another wing; the warders warned the girls to be careful, 'some of them haven't seen a woman for years.') As Trevor-Roper later remembered mischievously, Vernon Kell 'could be seen . . . after lunch expatiating in the area normally used for prisoners' exercise: a fine figure of a man; casting an appreciative eye on the secretaries, who tended to have elegant figures and aristocratic surnames . . . chosen, like racehorses, for their legs and their breeding.' As he paced and pronounced, he could have had no idea that despite so many years of discreet and loyal service, his career was hanging by a thread.

(Another account tells us that though secretaries shared cells, the officers each had one to themselves. The girls' modesty was offended by the wooden toilet doors which prison security rules mandated should only cover the midsection of the cubicle doorway, leaving head and legs in full view.)

Much aggravation arose from forgetting that once shut, the cell doors could only be unlocked from outside. Since the cells were virtually soundproof, calls for release could only be made through the slot in the door through which the prisoners had been handed their food. Anthony Blunt who had recently joined the Service fared better than most. As personal Assistant to one of the Directors, he shared the former Deputy Governor's roomy office, with a view over the muddy Common beyond the walls. A handy base for his first betrayals of MI5 secrets to his Soviet controllers, to whom he was known at various times as 'TONI', (hardly the most secure codename), 'JOHNSON' and 'JAN'.

A German 'tip and run' raid proved the Home Office right. The prison walls and gates were strongly built. No one had worried about the roof.

The Registry, with the bulk of its files stored not in the prison itself but in an outbuilding which had served as the prison laundry, was especially exposed. When the German incendiaries burst overhead, scattering a shower of 2 kg phosphorus packed 'bomblets', many of its precious files were scorched, scattered, or saturated by the firemen's hoses into a sodden mass. Neither history nor family memory tell us whether Tar's schoolboy experience with the Charterhouse Fire Brigade proved of any practical benefit.

New quarters were urgently needed. Tar and his fast-growing team were re-housed at 58 St James's Street, a bland office building, in Regency days the site of Jordan's Hotel. It was handily around the corner from SIS Counter-intelligence Section V in Ryder Street, and equally conveniently, just a few steps from clubs such as Whites, Brooks's, Boodles and Pratts, and the distinguished shops which had served their members for centuries – Lewis for fine tobacco and Turkish cigarettes, Berry Brothers for wine, Locks the hatters, Lobb for bespoke footwear and Truefitt & Hill, a haven of discreet barbering since 1805.

The Registry's new home was an even starker contrast. It swapped the clanging doors, white-washed cells, tiny barred windows and echoing landings of Wormwood Scrubs for the magnificence of Blenheim, created in the early 1700s for the great Duke of Marlborough, by Sir John Vanburgh and Nicholas Hawksmoor. It is the only non-Episcopal country house in England to be styled a 'Palace'. Winston Churchill who is said to have ordered the move, had been born there as a grandson of the seventh Duke; he must have been amused to think that all those secrets, Britain's now rather battered and tattered repository of knowledge of the potential spies and saboteurs ranged against his country, was stored in his ancestral home and in huts scattered on the once hallowed lawns.

Those who dealt with the Post Office and later British Telecom, when they were monopoly providers of telephone services will sympathise with Liddell's complaint after the move that even in the midst of war, only two telephone lines linked the body and brain of MI5, and officers in London in urgent need of Registry data were snippily told their call was in a queue and might take two hours to go through. The catch phrase 'Don't you know there's a war on' did not apply only to surly butchers and grocers as they told their hungry customers what was not available. But while those banks of cabinets grew by the day, they still contained little hard information about MI5's German opponents. As Dick White admitted[2] London had at the time only a 'vague idea of how the German system worked [and] what its objectives were in time of war'. It was a gap that the skill and cunning of Tar and his colleagues, and a barrage of intellectual firepower drafted into MI5 at the outbreak of war, would fill with panache.

Notes
1. Personal papers.
2. White lecture, National Archives.

15

Out With The Old . . .

Though there are no hints of it in the Double Cross case archives, those early nerve–wracking months of the war were a period of turmoil within MI5. It is a tribute to the leadership of Guy Liddell and the cool professionalism of Tar and his colleagues that, though they could hardly ignore the threat to the stability of their organisation, they just got on with their jobs.

Churchill knew that MI5 was floundering. Kell was old, his Service was underfunded and though he had done well in encouraging the recruitment of new talent to meet the challenges, the Service's organisational and administrative structure had not kept up with the demands of the times; 'unfit for purpose' would be the modern jargon. (MI5 was hardly the only organisation unprepared for hostilities. Reviewing the sorry state of affairs not only in the Armed Forces but also in key civilian ministries such as Supply and Food as 1940 began, historian A. J. P. Taylor described the Government as 'still moving into war backwards with their eyes tightly closed'.)[1]

Even as the Armistice bugle sounded in November 1918 sage men had warned of the heavy burdens which would fall on M15 again if and when another war came. September 1939 found it struggling to cope and even before the Wormwood Scrubs fire, the Registry, on which all else depended, had come close to imploding under the strain. The self-reinforcing anxieties of press, politicians and public had fuelled the almost hysterical conviction that Hitler's conquests had been much helped by 'the enemy within', the much-trumpeted 'Fifth Column' of traitors and secret agents inside his target countries. If it had happened on the Continent it would surely happen here.

An avalanche of calls and letters brought rumours of jackbooted nuns parachuting down near Nuneaton, puzzling lights that spinsters and retired Generals with time on their hands were convinced were German signals. Homing pigeons flapping high over nearby coppices brought nervous birdwatchers to conclude they were carrying Gestapo messages. Anxious callers noted cabbalistic symbols chalked on country telegraph poles, strange patterns ploughed into remote fields, and denounced as agents the German, Italian or other foreign neighbours, supposedly hunched in their parlours listening to overseas broadcasts. One old lady reported that her neighbour was signalling to the Germans by arranging her washing on the clothes line in a sequence of short and long garments that she was convinced was a crude form of Morse code.

Government itself needed to make sure men and women engaged on secret work had no security 'black marks'; this alone generated some 40,000 enquiries a month to MI5 in those early days. Every enemy alien in the land needed to be screened to determine whether he or she merited internment – even if they were elderly Jewish violinists or doctors who had fled from the Nazis, or Italians waiters who had lived and worked in Britain all their lives, a policy pursued by MI5 with a zeal which did not help its standing in Whitehall when well-connected targets were vigorously supported by their MPs and lawyers.[2]

Factories across the country handling or hoping to handle government contracts clamoured to have their personnel screened. The factories themselves had to be checked for vulnerability to sabotage. The armed forces needed to be put on guard against 'subversives' in their ranks. Controls were stepped up on travellers arriving and departing by sea and air; merchant seamen were put under scrutiny. Lord Hankey,[3] now Minister without Portfolio in the War Cabinet after many years at the epicentre of Whitehall power, twenty-two of them as Cabinet Secretary was sent in to take a look. His report, though seen by some as pulling punches, was enough to convince Churchill that more was needed. The first 'more' was the creation of a new over-arching body, the Security Executive, to co-ordinate intelligence and counter-espionage across

Government and the armed forces, thus making it in theory the political 'overlord' of the secret world. Its Chairman, charged with seeking out and sorting out 'overlaps and underlaps' wherever they might be, was the abrasive, wealthy career politician Lord Swinton.[4] It was a step with repercussions.

The second 'more' was Kell's abrupt dismissal in June 1940 after thirty-one years' service to the State. It might have been anticipated, if only in the wake of the Registry collapse but his temporary replacement by Jasper Harker, he of the 'very small shoes' ushered in a time of turbulence. Harker had not wanted the job, and was not up to it. One of MI5's bevy of brilliant wartime recruits, the late Sir Ashton Roskill QC told the historian Christopher Andrew in a 1984 interview that Harker was 'a sort of highly polished barrel which if tapped would sound hollow, because it was'. Nonetheless Swinton's claim a month later that he held 'executive control' over the Service undermined whatever authority Harker might have claimed and early unilateral initiatives by Swinton, described below, were bound to rankle. To the point that Liddell and several colleagues – Tar amongst them – thought seriously of resigning, but decided that given the grave burden of the war, they had to stay. But it was clear that Harker was not the answer.

The eyes of Whitehall soon fell on [Sir] David Petrie, Banffshire-born son of a master millwright.[6] Like the Robertsons, he too looked East finding adventure and success in the thrusting Scottish Diaspora. At the age of twenty-one he signed up as a constable in the Indian Police, surviving a nasty taste of life 'at the sharp end' when he was badly wounded in 1914 in a shootout with Sikh militants. As part of the machinery of Empire the Indian police had far more to do with thwarting nationalist and Communist underground movements than bullock cart traffic jams and burglary in the major cities, and Petrie's flair for the work took him to the top as Head of the Indian Intelligence Bureau. It is not hard to trace the hand of Sir Stewart Menzies, Chief of SIS, in the choice, since as Keith Jeffrey's History of SIS reveals, Petrie was then serving in Cairo as 'General Manager' of SIS' Middle East stations.

Summoned back to London, he cannily decided that before

accepting the responsibility, he wanted to take a look for himself, and arranged for Swinton to commission him to review MI5's 'system of intelligence and administration'. Petrie, a solidly built, rather formal and taciturn figure, went about it thoroughly, talking not just across the Service, but to SIS, and the three armed forces, to get their views. When he reported in February 1941 Petrie rejected as 'grossly overstated', the harsh comment of one informed outsider that MI5 was 'a rabble', (it would be unfounded but not improbable to attribute this to Menzies). But, he went on, the epithet 'does reflect the idea of a loosely linked assemblage', a concept he then proceeded to develop with brio. It was an organisation suffering from 'a lack of direction and a weakness of control', its officers 'dispirited and not in good heart . . . not 'on their toes'. . . not led and supported as they should be . . .'

Petrie was especially scathing about the Service's heart and mind, the Registry. It was no longer 'a going concern'. Masses of paper lay unsorted; the Registry was too large and burdened by 'elaborate and cumbersome procedures' which had caused it to seize up and at the same time had created for the girls exiled down to Oxfordshire an atmosphere of 'deadly dullness'.

Petrie was equally critical of Kell for recruiting officers from a narrow base of his and his senior colleagues' 'social contacts', focused on 'likely people . . . with the requisite character and outlook and if possible, some experience' rather than the other way around. Job descriptions were tailored to fit the recruit, rather than looking for the right person for the job. Potential recruits in the academic world and the professions were deterred by low salaries and the possibility of being fired at a months' notice, with the result that many recruits tended to be drawn from the ranks of the retired or 'those out of work'. There was no proper training and no devolution of responsibility. When the resources needed to conduct the war became apparent, officers 'rushed around' among their contacts and friends of friends and some men were even recruited without the knowledge of the central administration, their presence coming to light only when they were stopped at the door for having no official pass, or when 'a crowd of hungry people presented themselves for pay'.

Petrie's figures show that in September 1938, the time of the Munich crisis, MI5 had 33 officers and 119 'other staff'. A year later the comparable totals were 83 and 253, and by January 1941, 234 and 676 respectively, (of the latter 634 were women). He found the staff as a whole dispirited, complaining of a lack of direction, pressure of work, disorganisation and interference from outside. Though he did not mention the mooted resignations of Liddell and his colleagues, Petrie did point out that in B Division, whose counter-espionage work was the 'very core and centre of the raison d'être' of MI5, morale was poor. It too was not well organised with six controlling officers trying to run twenty-nine different sections, and a pyramid of sub-sections, some of these in fact consisting of just one man. Petrie was describing B Division as it was before the Double Cross initiative was in full swing, backed by the brainpower imported from the outside world, but the mismatch between his views and what we know of the real work of B Division suggests two possibilities. Either Petrie wanted to create a bleak baseline against which, as the presumptive next Director, he would be able to demonstrate how much things had improved, or the cautious Liddell and his colleagues were not ready to share their 'crown jewels' with a man who was for the time being an outsider, even though an experienced one, with no 'need to know'. An outsider, moreover, who though wise in the ways of intelligence, was reporting to a politician, a class not renowned for its discretion. Both factors were probably at work. Given the sense of several commentators that the abrasive Swinton was a big mistake, we can note that John Masterman dedicated his ground-and-rule-breaking history 'To The Earl of Swinton PC, GBE, CH, MC, DL amongst whose many services to Great Britain the Chairmanship of The Security Executive 1940–42 was not the least' – words which suggest, albeit a touch ambiguously, that Swinton did indeed make a contribution. Swinton may not have been given enough credit for the diffuse but important rôle he played in bolstering MI5's bruised reputation in Whitehall, and above all in Downing Street, and making sure by what historians have called 'his drive and authority', that it had the resources it needed. He certainly left his mark in one critical area, the broken down Registry. Despite its obvious faults, old Service hands resisted the recommendation of one of Swinton's 'outside' experts that the records be converted to a Hollerith punched card system for recording and collating data.[8] But once he took full charge, first winning Whitehall acceptance that contrary to Swinton's view, the Director must be master in his own house, one of Petrie's first rulings was that this should be done. It is a strange testimony to the internationalism of business that the Hollerith was also used 'with success' by Himmler's Waffen SS and some sections of German military intelligence.[9]

Notes

1. Taylor, p. 466.
2. Among others swept into the net, sent first to jail in Liverpool and then to a camp on Ascot Racecourse, was St. John Bridger Philby, former Indian Civil Servant, explorer, Muslim and father of Kim. His vocal criticisms of British Middle East policy were proving too awkward for the Government. He was soon released.
3. Hankey, Maurice Pascal Alers, 1st Baron 1877–1963.
4. Cunliffe-Lister, Philip, 1st Baron Swinton, 1884–1972.
5. Curry, p. 18.
6. Petrie, Sir David, KCMG, CIE, CVO, CBE, 1879–1961.
7. Hinsley et al Vol. 4 p. 323.
8. Originally developed for the US Census Bureau by Herman Hollerith; in 1911 his Tabulating Machine Company was one of four corporations which merged and later became today's IBM.
9. Doerries, p. 140.

16

. . . In With The New

It was a trying summer nevertheless. MI5 and especially B Division saw the new Security Executive as unnecessarily duplicating many of its own functions in tracking supposed 'Fifth Column' activity and even counter-espionage, and Swinton's proposed creation of a new W Branch to tackle German intelligence communications, as yet another duplication of existing machinery. But Petrie singled out for special criticism Swinton's 'unfortunate mistake' of parachuting in as co-Head of B Division alongside Guy Liddell, a high profile City of London solicitor, William Charles Crocker. Crocker[1] evokes echoes of Antony Powell's Kenneth Widmerpool, always on the rise. Born in 'Pooterish' Upper Holloway, the son of a solicitor's clerk, Crocker won his Military Cross serving with the Artists Rifles in the First World War and built his legal career as a shrewd investigator of a rash of sometimes sophisticated, often clumsy attempts by small businesses, to submit fraudulent fire damage insurance claims often with the connivance of a senior Fire Brigade officer and a prominent claims adjustor. He thus had the aroma of larceny and deception in his nostrils, knew how to cultivate informants and had built up excellent contacts with the City, the Metropolitan Police and elements of the London underworld. On the face of it not that bad a choice.

Nonetheless Petrie, infelicitously adapting Shakespeare[2] remarked of Crocker's short-lived tenure – he seems to have arrived on the scene around May and left at the end of August – that 'the evil that this man did lives after him', though he does not tell us what those heinous offences were. Clearly those used to the old ways resented the fact that he was an 'intrusion' from outside into their closed world, a pinstriped cuckoo in their comfortable if tangled nest, as

well as a man with divided loyalties; Crocker had kept his seat on the
Security Executive so remained a 'Swinton man'. The lack of a
demarcation line between him and Liddell might be seen as at best
confusing and realistically as a demotion for Liddell. And Crocker
scored something of an 'own goal' by bringing in a team of Scotland
Yard detectives, ostensibly to give MI5 investigative expertise and
the power of arrest. It was a move which not only perturbed B
Division but also upset other detectives at Scotland Yard who felt
their career prospects had been blighted. But 'evil'? Was Petrie fair?
From Liddell's diary entry on 6 September 1940, Crocker's sudden
departure had evidently taken him by surprise. There is even a mild
touch of disappointment in his comment that 'I gather that he was
not prepared to accept the position which we had to find for him but
that he had a row with Lord Swinton as the result of which he had
retired not only from this office but from the [Security] Executive as
well. Personally I am very sorry in a great many ways that this has
happened as I am sure he could have done very useful work here.
The real mistake is that he was pitch-forked into this office on half-
baked information of the situation. For this I am afraid he was to
some extent to blame.' These are hardly the words he would have
used had Crocker really been a malign influence. Not that any of
this deterred Crocker who after the war, was President of the Law
Society for many years, and married, en secondes noces, into
American wealth.

Petrie's comments about the calibre of Kell's officers also seem
overdone, certainly as regards B Division.

Masterman makes the self-deprecating comment[3] that though the
talented outsiders, he among them, who were brought in at the start
of the war 'contributed some useful ideas', it was the professionals,
'who were responsible for the policy, for the plans and the execution,
and who provided the initiative and the leadership the rest of us
needed.' In a later memoir he pays particular tribute to Tar:

'Tar was in no sense an intellectual but he had certain qualities of
a high order. A born leader, gifted with independent judgement, he
had above all an extraordinary flair in all the intricate operations of
his profession. Time and again he would be proved to be right in his

judgements when others, following their intellectual assessments, proved to be wrong. To work under and with him was a privilege and a happy experience . . .'

But as Masterman also points out, while Tar is the centrepiece of our story, Double Cross, like the entire B Division of MI5, was a team effort, a small chamber orchestra under the baton of the avuncular Guy Liddell – not an entirely fanciful image since Liddell came from a musical background and was a talented cellist. His work was his life; his marriage foundered. He was remembered by John Masterman as 'a cultured man, primed with humour and friendliness. In a way he belied his appearance, for a stranger might have thought him a gentle and agreeable dilettante – but that was far from the truth. No man was better informed about the details of his profession than he and no one pursued his objective with more firmness and skill.' The laconic entries in the published version of Liddell's Diaries give a good sense of his attention to detail, his willingness to listen to and back his colleagues and give them considerable freedom of manoeuvre. On the lighter side, when Tar asked for advice on how to respond to a request the Abwehr had made to Tar's super-agent GARBO for details of British mainline railway timetables, Liddell noted drily: 'this means they probably contemplate shooting up our trains in the same way as we're shooting up theirs in occupied territory . . . there are so many trains and since they do not always run at the time that is scheduled, little harm can be done by giving the Germans the timetable.'[4]

But the genial exterior concealed a steeliness that perhaps not many saw and which may have helped Liddell gain his own Military Cross in the First World War. Recalling in his diary an internal debate about what to do with a mysterious German emissary nick-named 'The Infra Red Man', if he turned up at a Paddington rendezvous, Liddell noted: 'My inclination is to bump him off but there are many difficulties.' He used the same 'pulp fiction' terminology to record a debate with SIS about the problems a source named OSTRO was causing by peddling to the Germans confected but disturbingly accurate information about Allied plans in the run up to D-Day: '. . . the present suggestion is that we should try to buy him up or bump him off'.[5]

When he wrote about the 'rushing about' in search of recruits at the start of the war, Petrie may again be painting too black a picture since he does not mention or give any credit for the influx of academic and legal talent it generated.

Likewise no-one who has even skimmed the hundreds of pages of typewritten notes, many dictated by Tar, in MI5's archive on SNOW, let alone the records of the many other multi – facetted puppet shows whose strings he so deftly manipulated, can agree with Petrie's criticism about officers not maintaining files. They are meticulous, detailed, hour by hour accounts of nerve-wracking scheming, psychological boosting, thoughtful invention and manipulation, as well as leadership and teamwork.[6]

Once Petrie took over, a new era began. Despite the negative and questioning tone of his initial report, he turned out to be, in Masterman's words, 'a rock of integrity, the type of Scot whose reliability in all conditions was beyond question with strong and independent judgement but ready and willing to delegate and trust.'

Frayed nerves and wounded feelings were soothed, and much as Hollerith grew into IBM, the Kell 'family firm' was on its way to becoming a major multinational enterprise. It was around this time, according to Jack Curry that Tar, remembering those early 'tea parties' in Cromwell Road, instituted what he called 'Lower Deck' weekly meetings, run by Curry, to serve as a forum for swapping news and views, and co-ordinating cases.

In recounting Tar's experiences and those of his colleagues in the pages which follow, we need to bear in mind that though we are looking at a key initiative, we are only telling part of the overall story of MI5 and even of B Division itself in this crucial period. Even a listing of the other Divisions – A handled Administration including the all-important Registry, C dealt with Examination of Credentials, a euphemism for security vetting, E looked after Aliens Control and F kept a sharp eye out for Subversive Activities – gives just a glimpse of what else was going on, not just in the UK but across the whole of the British Empire.

But it was not all office politics and bureaucracy. There were cases to run, none trickier than SNOW, last seen out at sea. His story, which kick-started the whole Double Cross enterprise, is a powerful endorsement of the despairing counsel given to the present author by a Cold War intelligence officer that, 'Even when you have all the facts, you may still never know the truth.' It is also a reminder that the Double Cross narratives have many points at which the shadow of some other possible plot momentarily swims across our vision, not unlike the shapes known to the ophthalmic surgeon Douglas Moray Robertson as 'myodesopsia', or to ordinary folk as 'floaters', the blobs which drift distractingly across the retina in bright light, without shape or direction, usually not symptomatic of any deeper seated problem but almost impossible either to ignore or to eliminate. There are several not just in the tangled web of SNOW and CELERY but also in the TREASURE story; the blurred record of Rudolph Hess's bizarre flight to Scotland is another, as are the complexities of the HAMLET case. When these were tried out on him, the officer we have just quoted responded that at least in SIS: 'We don't do plots. We can only think linearly.'[7]

Notes

1. Crocker, (Sir) William Charles, MC, for many years President of the Law Society 1886–1973.
2. *Julius Caesar*, Act III, scene ii.
3. *On the Chariot Wheel: An Autobiography*, p. 219.
4. Liddell, 10 February 1943.
5. Liddell, 6 February 1941 and 16 February 1945.
6. Readers with an interest in the secular transmutation of language might note that the symbol @, which today we associate only with email addresses, was used extensively in the security world of the 1940s and even later, as shorthand for 'alias', as in Rantzau @ Ritter.
7. Tar and Joan would have been among the 30% of the British public who from 1941 on tuned in to the BBC's weekly panel discussion 'The Brains Trust'. One of the best known participants was Professor C. E. M. Joad, whose favourite response to questions, almost his catch-phrase, we can adopt as a comment here, 'It depends what you mean by plots.'

17

Snowflakes

'SNOW has one peculiar habit – he only wears his false teeth when eating and he has a sort of sleight of hand trick of slipping the dentures into his mouth under cover of a handkerchief before a meal.' The observation might have been penned by Somerset Maugham in one of the Ashenden stories he based on his own service as an SIS agent in Switzerland in the First World War. It actually came from a rather shocked young British Army officer, whom Tar had introduced to SNOW as a notional 'sub-agent'. Arthur George Owens, around 40 years old as our story opens, and rather simplistically code named SNOW is the only known spy to earn an entry in the 2008 edition of the *Encyclopedia of Wales*. An SIS undercover watcher once described the diminutive SNOW – various reports put his height at five feet, or a touch more – in terms which might have offended his fellow-countrymen as a 'typical Welsh underfed Cardiff type . . . soft-spoken and lacks assurance in manner . . ., very short, rather thin and bony face, ill shaped ears . . . a somewhat shifty look.' A British Special Branch watcher was more succinct, comparing him to 'an underfed rat'. Abwehr officers who met him later noted that he was 'very highly strung and jumpy . . . looked like a very poor class of merchant seaman. Drank a lot of brandy . . .'

A far cry from James Bond, and from Norman Holmes' portrait of him, as the 'W. G. Grace' of the Double Cross system's early period, though whatever else he may have been, SNOW was no coward. He knew all too well as he walked the tightrope between London and Berlin, that if he fell foul of the British he risked a long stretch behind bars, and once war started, even a dawn meeting with the hangman. If the Germans thought he was double-crossing them, their retribution was something he would not care to contemplate.

SNOW was a long way away from Ian Fleming's suave world, and much closer to the seedy milieu that was the working canvas of the novelist Patrick Hamilton. With his utterly self-centred personality, his rumpled raincoat and battered trilby hat, he might have slithered from between the pages of Hamilton's *The Gorse Trilogy*. Like Ernest Ralph Gorse, much of SNOW's time was spent warming a chilly heart in the instant camaraderie of the saloon bar. SNOW too was much taken with money-making schemes that somehow did not quite work out, dancing a furtive foxtrot to keep one step ahead of the bailiff and the debt collector. He shared Gorse's glibness under pressure, the ability to lie convincingly and for the moment believe every word of the falsehood, and above all, the burning desire to be liked. Before he came Tar's way he had been a baffling, exasperating and worrying presence around Whitehall, offering his services and hawking 'secrets' around many covert nooks and crannies, including the Admiralty's Naval Intelligence Department, SIS, the Special Branch and MI5. His story brings to mind the *New York Times* purple prose, cited earlier, about the 'infamy and intrigue, the dingy romance and tawdry heroism' of the 1930's spy world.

Owens was born in Swansea, and is said to have served in the Royal Flying Corps in the First World War. He emigrated to Canada but returned to Britain in the 1930s. After working as an electrical engineer for the Expanded Metal Company, a firm with many Government contracts, he went into partnership with them to exploit an idea of his for using a lead oxide paste in industrial and marine batteries. He sold to the Royal Navy and to German ship-yards and somewhere along the way began to pass to the Admiralty some of the technical data he picked up in Germany, and photographs of German ships. He also supplied batteries to the Metropolitan Police, a relationship which took him in and out of Scotland Yard, and which later he deftly used to explain away his visits there to the Germans, in case their own watchers had seen him there.

Reminding us of the old maxim that 'a journey of a thousand miles begins with but a single step', from being an occasional informant for the Navy he was passed on to SIS, who took him on as an agent through one of its 'front' companies, Indexes Ltd, coincidentally registered at the then new office development on the Embankment, known as Thames House, which has twice housed MI5 itself. He continued to give SIS snippets of Naval intelligence, including a report on German coastal motor boats which they noted was of 'distinct value'. Another foray ended less successfully when a UK Customs Officer asked about a camera SNOW had not declared. SNOW claimed it had been given to him by SIS, and Special Branch had to be brought in to smooth things over. It was probably over time, rather than as a sudden epiphany, that the idea of working 'both sides of the street' developed.

Intelligence folklore has it that when someone volunteers, or is persuaded to help an intelligence service, the motive can be found under one or more of the letters in the acronym MICE – 'Money, Ideology, Compromise, Ego.' The driving force for the diminutive Welshman was mainly M – he was always hungry for cash – though E came into it too, the not uncommon urge to prove he was smarter than the professionals with whom he dealt. Even though a later comment by John Masterman suggests that SNOW did harbour a degree of admiration for German 'efficiency' and at least at the outset, wanted to keep in with them because he thought they would win though this is conjecture and hardly qualifies him as ideologically motivated. Indeed the files record many protestations to his British contacts that he was unequivocally on their side. The British version is that he told SIS that on one of his many trips, all of them at SIS' expense, he had run into a Herr PIEPER, a German engineer, who had contacts in Germany and Italy and whom SNOW thought worth cultivating as a source of intelligence. SIS rose to the bait and SNOW made several more trips, armed with cash to pay PIEPER's own travel costs and expenses as he launched on his mythical intelligence mission around Europe; PIEPER even made at least one visit to London. But the flow of intelligence was curiously slow to start. In fact it was flowing the other way. PIEPER was an Abwehr officer, trained to spot M as a motive and SNOW had quickly accepted his suggestion that if he wanted to spy he should work for the Germans, as they 'paid better'. Every aspect of

SNOW's story has at least two versions. Traces in what little is left of the German files suggest that he actually came to their notice when he began to hang about a London 'club for German au pair girls' managed by an Abwehr talent spotter, making it clear he was anxious to contact German intelligence. This may be true. It smacks equally of a story confected to deflect pointed matrimonial questions about where he spent his evenings and why.

The SNOW material in the MI5 archives runs to many volumes, countless pages, already 'selected' and with names redacted. There is also a wealth of material on the fraudster known as CELERY and the other players, which mostly overlaps but quite often throw up facts missing from the SNOW account. We can also see SNOW through the eyes of TAR's opposite number, the Abwehr agent-runner and network builder, Nikolaus Ritter, alias Dr Rantzau, Dr Jantzen, Dr Reinhardt, Dr Renken, and Mr. Landing,[1] who thought, when we met him on his fruitless flight over the North Sea, that SNOW was his man, a suspicion that nagged at Tar constantly. Ritter's memoirs[2] were written in 1972. His memory was jogged by copies of some captured Abwehr records taken to the Washington archives after the war and shown to him by an American writer.

Though this was long before MI5 files were decanted into the public domain, Ritter also claims to have seen a British document, again unspecified, dealing with the SNOW case, which he argues reaches the wrong conclusion about SNOW's rôle. We shall see. His memories, which suggest he had no idea about the Most Secret Sources do not always coincide with the British account, and are annoyingly vague on dates, but his version is close enough to it in some respects to deserve a measure of credibility, though books by retired spies, be they British, German or Russian are written to be sold, and to show their authors in the best possible light, not as historical records. We also have the benefit of a postwar interrogation of Ritter by an MI5 officer. Through it all runs the one question: who was SNOW really working for?

When he joined the Hamburg office of the Abwehr, Ritter's mission was to cover aviation, though his experience of aircraft was limited to two test flights in a First World War biplane. He had served as a teenager in the Kaiser's army, trained as a textile engineer and as a restless young man heeded the call to 'Go west' and taken a boat to the US. There he worked for the Mallinson Silk Company in New York – 'The Complete Charm of Womanly Beauty is preserved and accentuated by the exquisite slenderizing texture of Mallinson's Silks and Fabrics de Luxe' – followed by a downward spiral of odd jobs as a parquet floor layer, a housepainter, a metal-worker and a dishwasher before setting off with friends, to criss-cross the country Kerouac-style in a beat up Dodge. Somewhere on his travels he met and married Mary Aurora Evans, an Irish American born in Alabama, who was working as a teacher in St. Louis. They had two children and seemed well settled in the US – he found a steadier job in textiles – until a cocktail of homesickness and Abwehr blandishments brought him back to Germany with his family. Tar was not alone in having an unsettled early career path and taking Ritter at his word in his memoirs, the principles which his Prussian father instilled in him were not too different from those of the Robertson household: 'Discipline, obedience, playing by the rules, courtesy and good manners'.

Berlin was the centre of Nazi power, and the Abwehr's head office. But Hamburg was even better as the base from which to run worldwide espionage networks. For centuries it had been a hub of international shipping, trade and finance, with connections spanning the globe and a major shipbuilding centre. The Elbe estuary and the crane-lined quays echoed to the blast of ships sirens as passenger liners and cargo vessels came and went. Their passengers, their polyglot crews, the shipping and cargo agents, the banks and insurance companies, the shipyard managers, provided the Abwehr with a unique combination of sophisticated resources, contacts, knowledge, plausible 'cover' and myriad ways of smuggling people, goods and messages.

As an Abwehr officer Ritter was extraordinarily busy, a 'White Rabbit' of espionage, scurrying not just around Europe trying to remember which identity and passport he was using for each trip, but also back to the US to set up what US newspapers later headlined as 'The Ritter Ring'. It produced significant intelligence, not least the technical drawings for the Norden bombsight and Sperry gyroscope, invaluable for a rapidly retooling Luftwaffe, though in the end an FBI 'mole' burrowed into his insecurely structured network and it was rolled up in a blaze of publicity.

In contrast to the Robertsons' happy domesticity, sometime after Ritter and his wife had returned to Germany they went through an acrimonious divorce. He claimed the main reason was the pressure of his work. He refused to let her take their two children back to the US and Mary stayed on in Germany throughout the war, surely facing community hostility and suspicion as an 'enemy alien' single mother. Ritter then married his Abwehr secretary, who to judge by her name was the German social equivalent of the well-bred girls in MI5. It was not until 1946 that Mary Ritter was able to return to the US with their two children.

Ritter was perhaps ten years older than Tar, and rather clinically described by one British source as '5' 8" or 5' 9" tall, round face, florid complexion, high cheek bones, clean shaven, fair hair parted on the right side, irregular teeth; has one tooth on the left side of his mouth which protrudes so that it forces his upper lip over the gum when he laughs or talks with emphasis . . .' He was solidly built, an attribute which in keeping with the Abwehr's penchant for nicknames, had led to colleagues in the Knockenhauer Strasse offices to dub him 'the Mini-Goering'. In his version of how it all began, he had barely found his desk when one of his colleagues, Naval Captain Hans Dierks handed him the file of a potential agent, a Welshman who had 'offered his services' when Dierks was serving in the German Embassy in Brussels. Dierk's brief was naval intelligence; the 'walk-in' was more likely to be someone Ritter could use. As Ritter read the file he 'grew more and more excited – my first spy!' SNOW, whom the Abwehr codenamed 'JOHNNY' had told them he was an electrical engineer who had a small factory. He was also a salesman for several foreign companies, among them Phillips of Eindhoven, which gave him good cover for travel on the Continent. He was prepared to offer the Germans information on the British aviation industry 'because as a Welshman he hated the British'. Coming from an IRA fanatic, hate was a claim anyone who knew

Ireland's bloody history might have taken seriously. But the Welsh? Welsh nationalists were long on the emotional rhetoric known as 'hwyl' but their only tangible act of defiance in the run-up to the war had been in 1936 when three firebrands torched a pair of huts at a new RAF base.

Ritter was too eager to stop to think about such things and dashed off a note to JOHNNY on the business letterhead of an Abwehr commercial 'front' company describing a dry-cell battery he was ostensibly interested to export to England; would JOHNNY care to come to Hamburg to talk business? He would and did, though he had no idea he was watched by the Gestapo from the moment he crossed the frontier. Ritter found himself faced by a blond-haired, intelligent looking man with an attractive laugh, a description which hardly tallies with the pen portraits we have just cited. He was small, a head shorter than the German, which led Ritter to give him his second, affectionate Abwehr nickname, 'The Little Man'. He was wearing a smart brown suit and as Ritter, who had an eye for such things, noted approvingly, 'matching' brown shoes, rather than black. 'My future success depended wholly on this meeting. This unusual man was the key to my work against England.' They began with a cover meeting with a battery manufacturer at which JOHNNY showed he knew the technical ins and outs of his business, and ordered two batteries as samples; the manufacturer appointed JOHNNY as his UK agent, giving him a plausible reason for travelling to Hamburg. Ritter took him to a private room at the Graf Moltke Hotel on Steindamm[3] where JOHNNY produced his first 'offering', a piece of a new alloy the British were using for a shell casing, and details of how the casing was assembled. Abwehr experts in Berlin were impressed; they had not heard of the new development. 'I was very proud' Ritter noted. Though he was convinced of JOHNNY's bona fides he wanted more proof of his reliability and JOHNNY was sent back to London armed with a set of questions about Northolt aerodrome on the A4 to the west of London, and the 'arsenal' at Wolverhampton. Unknown to JOHNNY, they were a test, since the Germans had the information already from aerial reconnaissance and 'other sources'. JOHNNY passed the test and even gave his new-found friends some 'other interesting details'. But Ritter was cautious. Was he making other surreptitious contacts in Germany? The Gestapo watchers said 'no'. Was he tempted by girls? Though the watchers reported that he had 'an eye for the ladies' it never went any further. Ritter tried this again himself, taking JOHNNY to a nightclub which had telephones at each numbered table so that men and women who liked the look of each other could call across, flirt, and suggest a dance. After JOHNNY had taken a chaste turn round the floor with a girl no doubt planted by Ritter he explained, rather primly, that he was married, and that in fact he would like to bring his wife on his next trip.

If girls did not tempt him, how was he with drink? Ritter took him to hotel bars and traditional beer halls where the bull-necked patrons linked arms, swaying from side to side in sweaty rhythm pounding their steins on the scrubbed tables as they roared out the choruses of traditional drinking songs. Or perhaps a nightclub, where a Marlene Dietrich lookalike – man or woman – strutted sultrily as ' Naughty Lola' offering a 'pianola upstairs in her salon'. JOHNNY drank his share, but kept his head.

The months passed. JOHNNY, who was now on the Abwehr's books as agent 3504, the first two digits identifying him as a Hamburg Air intelligence asset, the last two perhaps implying that there were not that many others. The intelligence he produced was good but not sensational, in Ritter's memory, copiously detailed and some 'bits and pieces we did not know'. Most of his reports, always on schedule, always detailed, and delivered in person were based on personal observation, though JOHNNY claimed to have developed useful contacts, one in the Air Ministry, others in RAF Depots. 'All were Welsh, like him', Ritter noted, his head doubtless spinning with apocalyptic visions of a burgeoning nationalist movement, a posse of armed Druids, ready to undermine Westminster's rule. JOHNNY was paid but not a lot. Ritter commented later with professional caution that agents whose standard of living suddenly blossomed attracted unwelcome attention.

Sometime in 1938 JOHNNY brought his wife, though it was not

a successful visit. Ritter noted that she was uninterested and did not join in the conversation. In the spring and summer of 1939 as the dogs of war bayed louder and it grew increasingly obvious that there would be no more easy travelling to Germany, JOHNNY was taught how to use a radio. His first schoolroom the apartment of the grandmother of Ritter's secretary; an address which had also served as a cover address for letters from JOHNNY. He then graduated to a new Abwehr radio station in a manor house in the Hamburg suburb of at Wohlsdorf. (The station soon grew into the Abwehr's largest communications hub. At the height of the Second World War its 120 operators hunched over the dials of their Hammerlund Superpro and Hallicrafter Skyrider radios were in 24 hour touch with agents from Teheran to South America. Known nowadays as the Kupferhof, or 'Copper House' probably from its red roof, it is an impressive three storey building serving twenty-first century Germany as the equivalent of a Sixth Form College. Sometime in the summer JOHNNY brought over his new girlfriend LILY, of whom Ritter remarked that her only resemblance to his first wife was that she too was blonde. LILY was cheerful, a head taller and several years younger than JOHNNY, bright and loaded with what Ritter, using the English phrase in his German text, clearly approved of as 'sex appeal.' (An archive note says she was of German extraction, a point not mentioned by Ritter). JOHNNY was obviously infatuated with her, but he still had to work, learning not only how to operate, but how to code and decode, how to take a Lorenz short wave set apart and put it back together, and where best to hide it. He was given Alice Hobart's novel *Oil For The Lamps Of China* as the basis for his personal book code; only he and Ritter would known that sequences of numbers sent to or by JOHNNY would enable the other to find the page, the line and the exact words of the underlying message.[4] The radio was shipped to Southampton in a German trawler, and deposited in the 'left luggage' office there. Whoever handled it mailed the claim ticket to JOHNNY in London. Though after war broke out it was still feasible to meet – for a while – in Belgium and Holland, so the radio was strictly a fallback. But JOHNNY still had to try it out and by Ritter's account there were whoops of triumph in Wohlsdorf when his first test transmission came through, right on time. '*Ein glas Bier*' (A glass of beer) was his cheery message, a phrase which was about all the German he knew. From that point on he boasted, JOHNNY supplied the Germans with information of 'incalculable value'—the radar system and the location of the larger sites, the build up of RAF aircraft in Britain and France, the strength of coastal defences, deployment of barrage balloons, cargo convoys, fuel depots and how they were camouflaged, aiming points for bombing raids, and in the middle of all this, weather reports for the Luftwaffe, often twice daily. His messages were 'outstanding for their precision and detail'. At this point JOHNNY was compiling the reports himself and 'took no one else into his confidence'. As Germany crumbled in 1945, the Abwehr records that were not deliberately burned or shredded, vanished in the vortex of fire and destruction so little of the German side of the story can be verified. One scrap which survived[5] is an early weather report datelined 'London Kingston' and sent by JOHNNY on the evening of 23 September 1939. He told Hamburg that visibility was 1,300 metres, wind strength 3, the temperature 57 degrees, cloud level 350 metres, and cloud cover 'total'. No British reader of the data would have been surprised though quite what value it had for German planning is open to question; British meteorological records show that while the month started dry and warm, there were sudden thunderstorms and just after SNOW's report the temperature began to plummet.

Ritter does not spare us his own reference to the Welshman's totemic teeth, telling us that at one of their early meetings he reprimanded him for a lack of security. He had brought over from England the answers to a number of detailed questions about British defences, and Ritter was taken aback when these turned out to be written on a small scrap of paper folded inside a strip of cellophane. What if he had been stopped and searched? SNOW laughed and said he kept the strip tucked under his upper dental plate, where not even the most suspicious Customs officer would think of looking.

Clearly a man with panache, and perhaps inspired by those spy novels which he once admitted had shaped his sense of the intelligence world, Ritter conceived the idea of meeting in the North

Sea, the episode with which our story opened. We know Ritter's version; he would come out in a seaplane to rendezvous with a trawler which he believed was owned, by happy chance by a chum of JOHNNY's, another of those maverick Welshmen. It did not work out and the Dornier 18, eventually had to turn tail and take a disappointed Ritter back to Sylt. If we left the story there we could share Ritter's self portrait as a capable, bold case officer running a trusted agent against a key target with good results. But he was deluding himself. The intelligence he passed on so proudly to Berlin was what Tar called 'chicken feed', hand-milled in St James's Street. But did SNOW also pass on other 'uncensored' information. And even if he was feeding the Germans at Tar's bidding, can we see SNOW as a loyal *British* agent? Ritter never saw the mirror image of his own version of events, in which images and reality faced the other way, handwriting ran backwards and in which the answer to the question recalls Tweedledee's impenetrable comment in *Through The Looking Glass* – '. . . if it was so, it might be, and if it were so, it would be, but as it isn't, it ain't. That's logic.'

Notes

1. According to an FBI file note he also used the name 'Frank Harris' the notoriously priapic Edwardian-era publisher and literateur.
2. Ritter, 'Deckname Dr Rantzau'.
3. Still operating today as a 3 star 'economically priced' hostelry.
4. Hobart, Alice 1882–1967, a now forgotten author, but by the time of her death four million copies of her various books were claimed to be in print.
5. Brammer, p. 173.

18

Hare And Hounds

The Germans had lost sight of the fact that the evidence used to nail Baillie Stewart for his sins, more venal than mortal, was based on interception of mail sent to addresses in Hamburg known to be linked to German intelligence. So it was with SNOW's letters to DR SANDERS, several sent from 'The Visitors' Writing Room' of Canada House in London, and larded with guarded comments about 'tests' and 'sets.' By November 1936, at MI5's instigation these were being steamed open, copied and resealed by deft Post Office scrutineers and he was trailed, not always successfully (he was fond of sliding into big office buildings with multiple entrances), by the Special Branch, whose reports again give off something of that raffish Hamilton aroma. After calling at the Admiralty and an unidentified business office SNOW '. . . met at the Regent Palace Hotel the two women, Dyer and Scott, with whom he spent most of the afternoon at different restaurants, and at 4.15pm they visited Grosvenor House, though they were not seen to leave.' Two days later he was scurrying in and out of various Westminster offices, and pacing around to Victoria Station to make a telephone call, after which he made a brief stop at the Regent Palace and then 'called at several public houses' rounding off the afternoon with a stop at the Army & Navy Stores 'without making [a] purchase'. His intercepted post also gives a sense of a life fraying at the edges; debt collectors, hire purchase companies, his bank and the Inland Revenue were all pressing him. His addresses too suggest a measure of downward or rather, outward, mobility – from Sloane Avenue to Streatham and then out to Morden.

MI5 passed all this to SIS and in November 1936, SNOW was called in by a disconcerted Lt. Colonel Edward Peal[1] and fired, after a stiff interview in which he admitted to his German contacts, but again claimed these were being cultivated for the benefit of SIS. To add insult to injury (not that SNOW was easily insulted) a month later he came under fire from the German side. Dr SANDERS was probably responding to photographs SNOW had sent of British armoured vehicles and light artillery taken from a War Office Handbook which was not only unclassified but actually on public sale at the Stationery Office. Addressing SNOW as 'Dear Sir' he wrote with heavy sarcasm '. . . the contents of your last letter were, I am sorry to say, not of the slightest use to me. The newspapers of your country and of ours are much quicker than your letters. Since a number of years [sic] I am also in possession of the magazine pictures you sent me and you no doubt will understand that all this is rather disappointing; I don't own a museum, you know.[2] Kindly take notice therefore that henceforth your letters will have to be a little more up to date . . .' It must have struck the Germans as rather reminiscent of the slim pickings offered up by Baillie Stewart.

Undeterred, SNOW kept going, as did MI5. In September 1937 SNOW got back in touch with SIS and after some shilly-shallying, was seen by Peal, Edward Hinchley Cooke and an MI5 colleague. What did he want, Hinchley Cooke demanded? He had been told clearly almost exactly a year earlier that his services were no longer required. His reports had been of little use and he was in touch with the Germans. He could not 'run with the hare and hunt with the hounds'. SNOW repeated his line that he had made good contacts in Germany in the area of submarine batteries and could be of great help to SIS. Peal was having none of it, and the session came to a chilly end with SNOW being presented with a brief statement to sign to the effect that he did not work 'for any British intelligence service' and had not done so since November 1936. This meant, Hinchley Cooke stressed, that if 'on his own account he chose to have dealings with the German Secret Service and got into difficulties', his dependants could not claim compensation from the British. SNOW signed without demur.

That did not stop him sending in another report to SIS after a trip to Germany, purporting to give sketchy details of where some

German army formations were based, and their unit badges, information sniffily dismissed by SIS as containing nothing that they did not know already. SNOW seemed to be aware of the mackintoshed watchers and of the built in delays to his mail and volunteered a statement to Special Branch, the centrepiece of which was a claim the Germans had appointed him '. . . chief operator in England with authority to travel to America with a special German Secret Service Code and I am to receive here in England a special secret transmitting set which will enable me to be in touch with secret German headquarters in the Rhine district.'

In April 1938 SNOW turned up at the Admiralty like the proverbial bad penny, offering a roll of undeveloped film he claimed showed German warships at Hamburg. It was rejected out of hand and so, again, was he. In the words of the file note 'He was reminded . . . that in September 1937 he had been warned that the British Intelligence Services did not wish to have any dealings with him . . . he was conducted out of the Admiralty by Mr. Bradford . . . and told not to return.'

Even the polite Admiralty version of "the bum's rush" did not deter him. Two months later Valentine Vivian, the India-trained counter-intelligence veteran SIS, received a 'Most Secret' report from Albert Canning of the Special Branch. SNOW had surpassed himself by gate-crashing Oswald Mosley's BUF headquarters, formerly the Church of England's Whiteland's Teacher Training College, in Cheltenham Terrace off the Kings Road in Chelsea. The dark brick building (long since replaced by a block of expensive flats) looking out on the Duke of York's Headquarters where Baillie Stewart had been court-martialled, was forbidding enough. The crop-haired Fascist guards outside, black boots and trousers topped by black polo-necked sweaters, added a touch of theatrical menace to any visit or even the morning milk delivery from the United Dairies cart. The Report, probably based on information from a Special Branch 'mole', said SNOW had boasted that he had worked for British intelligence, especially in Germany. He made knowing references to Indexes Ltd, Thames House, 'Kell Products', 'The St James's Park people' and the St. Ermin's Hotel (a watering hole much favoured by SIS which later took over several rooms there as offices). He told the BUF that SIS was 'run by Jews', a notion which played to the fantasies of his audience but which might have surprised those who knew the background of the Service's senior officers, and was 'a terrible racket'. His pitch to the BUF was that only clandestine propaganda within Britain could stir its people to avert an otherwise inevitable war, and he wanted them to find six men who could operate underground radios. He could get the funds from Germany. Even more recklessly he added that 'if more drastic measures' were needed and the BUF demonstrated that it had 'a reliable following which would stop at nothing, he could arrange for a cargo of arms for use in a bid to seize power. Switching deftly to what may have been the main aim behind this phantasmagoria, he said he would also welcome information on aircraft production, RAF stations, naval depots and anti-aircraft gun locations; he was especially keen to have data on aerodromes in Kent and Essex. Canning added that SNOW had told the BUF he was 'a direct personal agent of Hitler'. Displaying a judgement for which they were not generally renowned, the BUF leaders decided SNOW was either an agent provocateur or 'a knave and a fool' and refused to have anything to do with him. SNOW had gone from bad penny to dangerously loose cannon.

In September 1938, he was interviewed again, this time at Scotland Yard by Hinchley Cook and an unnamed Special Branch Superintendent and Inspector, with a diligent Constable taking shorthand notes. The record is a curious one for such a heavyweight encounter, which started with Hinchley Cook delivering the 'caution' which most watchers of British 'police procedural' TV shows of a certain vintage could recite by heart; SNOW was not obliged to say anything, but if he did it would be taken down and might be used in evidence. The overall impression left by the record is that SNOW got the better of the encounter. Yes, he again admitted working for the Germans, but all that was only in the British interest, even though he accepted he was acting entirely on his own, without any official sanction or authority. All he wanted to do was help his country. He had risked his life 'and at least I deserve a little thanks. You understand that I am one hundred percent with you. Over there [in Germany] I am pro-German and I have to be . . . If I make a slip over there I am not coming back.'

He got no thanks, and gave nothing much else to his questioners, since he claimed to be unable to remember the name of the German who had 'appointed' him, any details of the code he was to use, or much at all about the other six or eight contacts he had made. He claimed the Germans had instructed him to approach the BUF, because the Abwehr wanted to know more about it and because the Fascists had sources inside the British Communist Party, who could provide valuable insights. But he did not mention the other aspects of his dangerous conversation, nor did Hinchley Cook raise them, perhaps because he did not want to reveal there was a source inside the BUF or because Vivian had not told him the full details of the Special Branch report. It is not hard to sense Hinchley Cook's exasperation and bewilderment. How much was real, how much was embroidery? Did the Welshman belong behind bars or in a strait-jacket?

Since as far as the files show, nothing happened it must have been decided that 'watch and wait' was the best course. If the Germans had forgotten the risks of using the mail, SNOW seems not to have heeded the old adage about 'a woman scorned' since around this time the first Mrs. SNOW, upset at having been dumped in favour of LILY and left to fend for herself and their son, wrote to both the British and for good measure Dr Ritter, whom she had met in Hamburg, even-handedly denouncing her husband to both sides as a double agent. Presumably both German and British shoulders shrugged – one of those nasty domestic tiffs, no more, and nothing was done.

Alarm bells rang again in January 1939, when a retired RAF Squadron Leader told the Air Ministry, SNOW had been heard boasting of his SIS connections and had also claimed 'in his cups' that he worked for Germany as well and 'had an SS badge' to prove it. Before this could be followed up, a series of strange encounters was to lead MI5 and Tar to the real prize.

Notes

1. Peal, Edward Raymond, CBE, 1884–1967.
2. Probably a reference to the 'posed' style of the photographs which did indeed look as though they were taken in the Imperial War Museum.

19

Prize Giving

It was handed to them by SNOW himself, a gesture which must have thrown some of his doubters and detractors off their stride, at least momentarily. What was he really up to? For the moment it did not matter.

The encounters were period-pieces. The first, between SNOW and a phlegmatic Special Branch detective, was at a Lyons Tea Shop in Westminster, with its hissing tea urns, potted palms and its trademark black and white tiled walls matched by the waitresses – known as 'Nippies' – in black dresses, crisp white linen aprons and matching linen mobcaps. The second was the same evening, at the George Inn, on Epsom Road in the South London sprawl of Morden. Our opening description of Tar as 'Hollywood's concept of a dashing military type' brings to mind another Hollywood comparison, physically and socially wide of the mark, but not entirely far-fetched. Alfred Hitchcock, master of film suspense[1] was not a good-looking young officer but the corpulent, Catholic, introverted son of an East London greengrocer. But as we follow Tar's complex plot lines – in one of which Hitchcock actually has a cameo rôle in his trademark filmmaker's style – it is tempting to see them as Hitchcock-genre movies, each with its own surprise twists and turns, heavily freighted with psychological complexities, with Tar as the director.

Hitchcock would have shot these scenes in black, white and shadow, tightening his camera focus to close in on the diminutive, nattily dressed Welshman and the stolid detective in a blue serge suit, shiny at the elbows, and black boots, heads conspiratorially together, slipping scraps of paper to one another, while the George's saloon bar regulars babble obliviously in the smoky background. We then jump two days, to a small office in Westminster and then the Left Luggage Office at Victoria Station, to a background of guards' whistles shrilling and Southern Railway trains puffing and clanking. The two-man cast is the same. Later the same day we see the detective tapping out on a black Underwood typewriter his summary of what it was all about, or ostensibly about; with SNOW one never knew. (After SNOW had given him a complex and evasive account of a later series of events another slightly bemused questioner observed: 'This dialogue sounds incredible but I have always found . . . that any incident related by SNOW has a basis in fact, however much he may misinterpret or distort its implications.')

Apparently without attracting the attention of Special Branch's port watchers, SNOW had gone to Hamburg on 1 January, where he had been shown (not for the first time, if we believe Ritter's account) how to operate a short-wave transmitter, had been given a code grid to use in sending his first priority, weather reports to guide the Luftwaffe, and a detailed list of questions on British military and air force dispositions, and arms manufacturing, on which the Abwehr wanted information. These he gave to the detective with the eagerness of one whose only desire was to help, capping that by producing three photo-stats giving details of how the set worked, and as a final flourish a Left Luggage receipt No. K7845 which, when handed over at Victoria Station would produce the set itself, deposited there by some unseen German intermediary. He even handed over the key to the suitcase in which the set was concealed. SIS and MI5 took a careful and no doubt gleeful look at it. The chronology is difficult to follow but from the archive account it seems that although SNOW tried to operate the set, he could not get it to work, seemingly because it was under-powered. As the last pre-war months slipped away, SNOW continued his active – and in large part intercepted – correspondence with German 'front' companies using business terminology from which as MI5 remarked 'it is wholly impossible for us and even for SNOW himself to disentangle . . . the genuine business content and the phrases or paragraphs which referred to espionage.'

In August SNOW and LILY went back to Hamburg, returning at

the end of the month, and then going to ground until 4 September, the day after war was declared, when he contacted Special Branch, arranging to meet at Waterloo Station. Quite what the complicated Welshman was expecting we have no idea but what he got was a Detention Order under the newly-introduced Defence Regulations and a mind-concentrating trip in a Black Maria to Wandsworth Prison. Tar now enters 'stage right', or rather, in Morden, in the evening of 6 September, where he, another MI5 officer and two Special Branch men banged on the door of the flat where SNOW and LILY were temporarily living with friends. It was a turning point for Tar and indeed MI5.

At that stage Tar was not an agent runner, but had emerged from his rather 'Jack of All Trades' career in the Service as its specialist in clandestine wireless. He was responsible for handling all reports of illicit wireless communications and co-ordinating the work of the Radio Security Service or RSS, (whose 'cuckoo in the nest' irruption into the intelligence community will get a well deserved chapter of its own), the Post Office, which had its own intercept stations, and Scotland Yard's long-standing clandestine listening post, tucked away discreetly in the gardens of the Police Nursing Home in Grove Park, Camberwell. Known as 'Camberwell Yard' it targeted mainly diplomatic traffic under SIS guidance, but also helped in detecting illicit transmitters.

In Morden, SNOW's bemused hosts said they knew nothing about any wireless. A brisk rummage revealed in the bathroom cupboard a small receiving set SNOW had built himself; but where was the non-functioning German transmitter, which SNOW had told Tar he had 'disposed of'? The file note describes what follows as 'sharp questioning', which elicited the information that LILY had indeed asked her hosts to hide a parcel which they believed was something to with SNOW's domestic travails. They took Tar to the corner of the small garden where a shallow layer of earth covered a paper bag with that elusive prize, the German transmitter. It was carried off to SNOW's prison cell. But yet again there were problems with the set, and before the game of blind man's bluff could begin in earnest, SNOW needed to be rehoused; Wandsworth was hardly a congenial home for a man who was on the face of it collaborating, and by 14 September we find Tar as his file note puts it rather domestically, 'flat hunting' in Kingston with SNOW and a Special Branch 'minder'.

Quite what the landlady of the top-floor flat at 9 Norbiton Avenue made of this ill-assorted trio, and what yarn they spun her, we can only guess, but for her, rent was rent and for Tar the attic above was ideal space in which to stretch out the aerial. Contradicting Ritter's account – though this may well refer to an earlier transmission of which MI5 were unaware – SNOW's first message to the Abwehr read, 'Must meet you Holland at once. Bring weather code. Radio time and hotel Wales ready.' He readily explained what it meant, but, as always, the real question was whether he was telling the truth? He told Tar that one of his main tasks would be to send weather reports. He had also been instructed – Ritter was still fixated on the myth of the Welsh Nationalists as a force for sabotage in South Wales – to identify a reliable member of the Party with whom the Germans could work.

According to Tar's file notes – which also show how well he understood the technicalities of his subject – the code was a transposition and substitution grid based on the key word 'CONGRATULATIONS'. But we recall Ritter's post-war memory that the code was based on the book *Oil For the Lamps of China*. And at some point in 1940, (perhaps in the process revealing a hint of a sense of humour), he says he gave SNOW a new source book *The Dead Don't Care* by Jonathan Latimer, a near-classic in the hardboiled 'pulp fiction' genre. So might there have been another code, another set, a back channel? There is no hint of it in the files and given the care with which the twists and turns of the story were sifted during and after the war, we have to assume that if there was, it was never used.

At the end of September, Tar agreed that SNOW could go over to see Ritter in Rotterdam, for the moment still neutral territory. As Tar commented cautiously to SIS, 'If by any chance at this juncture he decides to play straight with us and to return to this country, he should be in possession of very valuable data.' He did return, though whether he was playing straight remained as ever an open question. But Tar's detailed notes show that Ritter briefed SNOW at considerable length on the intelligence he wanted, especially the build up of aircraft production. Wales was still much in his mind. Maybe the Nationalists could blow up munitions dumps and the Port Talbot Steel Works, even the Milford Haven seaplane base. The Germans could put explosives and guns ashore for a potential insurgency. On a more sinister note, he also asked SNOW to pinpoint the location of the main UK reservoirs, especially those around London; 'apparently as a last resort', Tar wrote, 'they had in mind targeting them with bacteria-laden bombs.'

It did not take Tar long to find a candidate who was a plausible fit for Ritter's Welsh template. A fortnight later SNOW was back in Holland introducing the gullible German to 'GW', Gwillym Williams, a massively built retired Swansea Police Inspector, by happy chance a (non-rabid) member of the Welsh Nationalist Party, with a gift for languages, and a talent to deceive, since he was actually a Tar 'plant'. As SNOW knew this, he could have given the game away there and then. He did not probably less out of loyalty than a shrewd sense that there was more to play for, and more to be paid for. Ritter brought along another Abwehr officer, introduced as the COMMANDER, who spent much time talking to GW about using a submarine to land explosives and weapons on the South Wales coast, and actually handed him to carry home two wooden blocks in which detonators had been concealed. Could the Welsh Nationalists carry out sabotage outside Wales, he wanted to know, say in Bristol, Manchester, Glasgow or Liverpool. The targets would be dockyards, ships, warehouses, aerodromes, power stations and munitions factories. The Germans wanted to cause 'internal disruption' in Britain, hoping that 'the people' would then prevail on Churchill's Government to bring an early end to the war.

GW was yet another hard to handle asset. After a separate clandestine foray in London when he collected from a German 'cut-out' in the Spanish Embassy a talcum powder tin stuffed with cash for the fictitious expenses of SNOW's fictitious network, he complained to Tar about MI5's stinginess with expenses for its own agents, and threatened to stop work. Tar minuted savagely 'I succeeded in pacifying him. but he is an opinionated, mercenary Welshman and needs to be thoroughly frightened. I think he is a dangerous man, potentially, as he is no fool.'

Note
1. Hitchcock, Sir Alfred Joseph, KBE, 1899–1980, filmmaker of genius.

20

'It's Good To Listen'

The radio, the codes, the frequencies, an understanding of what Ritter was up to and his ambitions for penetrating Britain, were strong cards in Tar's hands. To understand how they were played we leave SNOW for a moment, and turn to the key rôles of the Radio Security Service (RSS) and the code breakers of GC&CS. Our main source for the former is an archival note, classified 'Most Secret', and headed 'RSS and MI6', written in September 1942. We also have a post-war reminiscence by the historian Hugh Trevor-Roper, an important figure in RSS and who, to judge by its style, probably wrote the first note as well. E D R Harrison's study[1] is another important analysis, not least for its dissection of the MI5 and MI6 'infighting' over this key resource and its output .

The story is one example, (the difficult history of the Special Operations Executive is another), that while the war itself was being fought with bullets and bombs, Whitehall's secret world was not immune from, indeed relished, its own battles, even though, fortunately, these involved sweat, tears and character assassinations rather than blood. As we have seen MI5 went into the war armed only with scant information on what the German intelligence service was, let alone what schemes it might have hatched in the run-up to hostilities. Maybe they had planted agents under deep cover, tapping out secret messages to their Berlin controllers from remote Scottish castles or modest maisonettes in Maida Vale. Or the Germans might have hidden radio beacons near strategic targets around the country to beam homing signals to Luftwaffe bombers. The only way to find out was to watch the airwaves for suspicious traffic. This was the mission given to RSS in 1938. It is always easy looking back to see the first misstep in a chain of events. Early in its life it had been suggested, with some organisational logic, that responsibility for it should be vested in MI5. Kell declined; his small Service could not accept the administrative and financial burden. So it was placed under the wing of the War Office, who would fund and run the organisation though it was understood its main 'customer' was to be MI5. It was an uneasy compromise with consequences, in Curry's words 'recalling the principles of Greek tragedy'.

Under the enthusiastic leadership of Lord Sandhurst, a brave eccentric in the best British tradition,[2] Post Office radio operators and around 1,000 amateur 'hams' known as Voluntary Interceptors twirled the dials and strained their ears day and night, listening for secret German operators, whom they nicknamed 'foxes' . . . RSS had fixed stations, at Lands End, John O'Groats and on the white cliffs of Dover, but most of the interceptors worked from their suburban sitting rooms, earphones tight on their heads, pencils clenched, while their wives tried to keep the children quiet, sustaining their husbands with periodic cups of tea. One interceptor was even raided by the local police after a suspicious neighbour reported hearing the chirruping of Morse Code late at night. But capturing faint signals of unknown origin and meaning was just the first step. Someone had to identify whether they were being produced by German transmitters or hidden beacons. If not, what were they? If they were, how could they be decoded? In December 1939 the first task, determining what traffic was commercial and what was clandestine, was given to Major E. W. B. Gill.[3] Since he was at the time the Bursar of Merton College, Oxford, he was at first sight an improbable choice, but Gill had served in signals intelligence in the First World War in Egypt and Salonika and left his mark on the history of the secret world by mounting an intercept aerial on the apex of the Great Pyramid. One of the College's Junior Research Fellows, then simply Mr. Hugh Trevor-Roper did not think twice about accepting Gill's invitation to join him. In later years Trevor-Roper was to prove himself a redoubtable academic infighter and intriguer, and his description of Gill as 'a genial Philistine with very little respect for red tape, hierarchy, convention or tradition' suggests that the two of them in combination may have relished, and may well have stoked, the bureaucratic bonfires which were about to flare up.

Gill soon concluded that the notion of Boche beacons buried around the countryside was a 'mare's nest'; the Luftwaffe followed beams sent out from Germany, rather than homing in on signals from Britain. But even so, the ionosphere was a Tower of Babel babble of commercial, military, merchant marine and other traffic. How could the interceptors discriminate the wheat from the chaff, the hens from the 'foxes'. There followed one of those Eureka moments which change the course of events, perhaps history. A moment made even more distinctive as it occurred inside Wormwood Scrubs, where RSS and MI5 initially shared 'very old fashioned and insalubrious' cell spaces, when Tar gave Gill SNOW's radio and codes. Gill now had a far better idea of what he was looking for, and had some idea of the code system. Fate, or rather, another bout of infighting in the secret world, would determine that he got little or no credit for what he later accomplished.

RSS began to 'discriminate', i.e. pick out, and log the traffic which fitted the SNOW matrix, sending the records to GC&CS at Bletchley Park for decryption, alerting them that they believed this to be German Abwehr material. There followed not plaudits but complaints. GC&CS was already overloaded, short of staff and anyway there was no confirmation that the traffic was what RSS claimed it to be. Would Gill kindly not send any more. From SIS in Broadway Buildings came a more bureaucratic barb. It claimed RSS had strayed way beyond its core mandate. According to that Most Secret note, the armed services, and the Foreign Office had long established systems in place for intercepting the traffic of their adversaries and opposite numbers. But SIS had not done so, the note claims sarcastically, 'it being assumed evidently that the [Abwehr] did not use wireless telegraph communications'. SIS now found itself upstaged by the intervention of an interloper, an interloper which was amateurish, insecure, and not the least of its crimes, was working hand in glove with MI5. In any case there was no team assigned at GC&CS to handle the decryption of the traffic even if it was what RSS claimed it to be.

RSS was still logging the traffic. But given the GC&CS response, what were they to do with it? The note gives credit to Gill for the next initiative; Trevor-Roper remembers it as a joint effort. Gill knew something about cryptography from his First World War days, and Trevor-Roper had a good knowledge of German. They were sharing a flat in nearby Ealing while working at Wormwood Scrubs and on 29 January 1940 they had cracked the first code over the dining room table; at this stage these were Abwehr hand ciphers, and not the more complex machine-generated Enigma traffic. The note tells us this 'caused some stir' in the form of an official rebuke to RSS for dabbling in GC&CS work and at the same time a belated if positive reaction from GC&CS, which delegated one of its senior officers, Oliver Strachey, to handle the RSS output. The decrypts he and his small team generated were code-named ISOS, standing for 'Intelligence Service Oliver Strachey,' or in another view 'Illicit Sources, Oliver Strachey.'

Strachey, Old Etonian, and elder brother of the Bloomsbury luminary Lytton Strachey (whose approach to historical fishing we have followed) was neatly drawn by Trevor-Roper as 'a long-serving epicurean professional cryptographer, not easily ruffled by such passing inconveniences as the outbreak of war'.[4]

Strachey and Gill co-operated closely and amicably, a relatively unusual dynamic in this high-voltage exchange, but Strachey's team was too small for the volume of work, and the next four ciphers were all broken by RSS. In the background the institutional fretting continued; who should be responsible, and as a corollary, take credit for, RSS. There was another crisis in December 1940 when RSS circulated what it perhaps rather provocatively called an Intelligence Note written by Trevor-Roper. Though the file describes this as summarising what RSS had learned about the Abwehr in Morocco, Trevor-Roper later amplified this considerably, claiming that he and Gill had in fact built up a picture of Abwehr traffic from Madrid and Hamburg, the former communicating with substations in Spain and Spanish Morocco, the latter in touch with outposts on the Baltic and North Sea coasts. There was also a station in Wiesbaden which trained potential agents in radio work whose 'laborious initiation of its pupils gave us some valuable hints.'

SIS reacted angrily to what it saw as another overstepping of bounds as well as gross insecurity in giving the note extensive Whitehall circulation. Its Felix Cowgill apparently demanded – happily for history, unsuccessfully – that Trevor-Roper should be court-martialled. RSS were given another stinging rebuke, told to stay out of GC&CS work, and for a while even denied access to ISOS decrypts. In Whitehall meanwhile the negotiations continued. RSS was clearly doing valuable work, but if it and GC&CS were to expand to cover the volume of traffic, the scale of which was now becoming apparent, on whose budget would it be borne? Even before the Intelligence Note incident, David Petrie, called on to arbitrate, had recommended transferring RSS to the control of SIS, a decision taken in March 1941 which the History implies MI5 did not resist since their main technical expert, a former Marconi Director had left them, and SIS had more powerful resources in the form of the Foreign Office radio station at Hanslope Park.

Writing after the war, Trevor-Roper, always quick to see intrigue, thought the SIS takeover was a bid to restore its Whitehall prestige after its networks in Western Europe had been 'rolled up' following the German's brazen kidnapping of two of its officers in the so-called 'Venlo incident' on the Dutch-German border in 1939. Whether or not he was right, by 1942, RSS was flourishing on a budget of £360,000 a year – many millions in today's money – had extended its network of stations to Cairo and Gibraltar, and had worked out that the best method of attack was to intercept the German's home stations, crack their messages and to alert MI5 as these began to reveal planning for agent training and landings, and the movements of Abwehr officers across Europe.

All controversies need their ritual scapegoats. Usually those who least deserve the rôle. Gill, who had been temporarily transferred while these machinations played out, and knew nothing about them, returned to find himself dismissed, demoted and transferred to a signals training unit in the windy wastes of North Yorkshire.

The Curry History comments ruefully, if naively, that no one could have foreseen how Felix Cowgill, once he had control, would use those old arguments about demarcation lines and the security of SIS' own agents in a 'narrow, selfish and incompetent' attempt to keep any Abwehr traffic not directly bearing on Double Cross operations in Britain out of MI5's hands (though most accounts agree that at a sub-Cowgill level, relations between Tar's teams and their counterparts in SIS Section V were amiable and co-operative and even Cowgill was eventually won over, or more likely saw the writing on the wall). MI5 fought back successfully but Guy Liddell sensibly kept Tar largely out of the welter of meetings and memoranda, wheeling in Dick White and even Sir David Petrie when necessary. Little did Cowgill know that while he was doing his crabbed best to keep ISOS secrets out of MI5 hands, in May 1943 his trusted colleague Philby would give Moscow Centre a detailed picture of the ISOS organisation and the names of those involved.[5] The RSS/MI6 note concludes that though in principle there was much to be said about the change of control 'RSS itself which was the sole competent judge of the methods it had evolved, was not given any opportunity of advising on the circumstances necessary for the continuance of those methods – indeed the chief architect of the work which was now to be the main function of RSS [Gill] was dismissed unseen. All questions of organisation, policy and personnel were decided by SIS although since SIS had never practised interception there was no one in SIS who could understand the questions they were deciding. *'Hinc illae lacrimae.'* 'Hence those tears'.[6]

Writing years later Trevor-Roper added the perspective that though Gill would not have been at ease among the 'self-important mandarins of SIS' he had been treated shabbily. He had, after all, 'thrown them a life belt which after they had run their own ship aground, had enabled them to be winched to safety, and afterwards, on dry land to congratulate themselves on what they would claim as their achievement.'

Notes
1. see Bibliography.
2. 'Sandy' Mansfield, 5th Lord Sandhurst 1920–2002, earlier a wine-merchant

and Special Constable in London, he won a DFC for his rôle as an intrepid RAF navigator and Squadron leader, impressing those who served with him with his courage as well as his ability to swallow a pint of beer while hanging upside down from the Mess bar. *Daily Telegraph* 6 July 2002.

3. Gill, Ernest Walter Brudenell, OBE, 1883–1959.

4. Strachey, Oliver, CBE, 1874–1960. In *Who's Who* and similar publications those who served in the secret world often took perverse pleasure in hiding their light under bushels such as 'Civil Assistant, War Office' or ' Special Duties,' meant to be understood only by the cognoscenti. Knox's entry was a masterpiece of its kind. His description of his career read, in its entirety: 'Has been engaged in work on East Indian Railway, on historical research and in the Foreign Office.'

5. *TRIPLEX*, p. 108.

6. The quotation from the Latin poet Terence, Publius Terentius Afer, 190–159BC, which reinforces the notion that Trevor-Roper was the author, would have struck many of its contemporary readers as an elegant and comprehensible closing line. Life has changed; several British Local Authorities have recently banned as 'elitist' the use in official documents of such intellectually challenging terms as 'e.g.', 'ad hoc', 'prima facie', and even 'vice versa'.

21

A Welcome in the Hillsides . . .

Back now to SNOW. When last seen, he was in Rotterdam with GW where he added fuel to Ritter's Cymric fantasy by delivering a Tar-scripted message that he had recruited fifteen men in South Wales, most of them Welsh and others in West Hartlepool and Middlesbrough, a plausible touch since his business associates at the Expanded Metals Company had a factory there. Scraps of Abwehr traffic[1] show Ritter reporting to Berlin without comment or qualification, vague but intriguing SNOW stories allegedly based on comments from well placed industry and Service sources, in reality created by Tar mainly with the help of the co-operative Wing Commander Boyle at the Air Ministry. A senior RAF intelligence officer had been relieved of his post. There was disquiet in senior RAF ranks and a loss of confidence in the 'top leadership'. Plans for a British landing in Belgium had been called off at the last minute. The scraps also show how the Abwehr system served RSS and GC& CS since Ritter's messages went not just to Berlin, but to stations in Kiel, Wilhelmshaven and Bremen, and from these no doubt repeated along an even more extensive network.

Ritter in turn asked SNOW what he could find out about Canadian factories which were said to be producing armaments for the UK. He also wanted to know whether he could recruit men to plant explosives on the ships on which this materiel would be carried to Britain. We can see the little Welshman nodding in glib agreement. Ritter told him samples of a new explosive would soon be sent to him in the UK concealed in batteries and, a nice touch, in loaves of Swedish bread. SNOW and GW thus came back to give Tar the 'valuable data' he had hoped for. He knew what the Germans were thinking of doing, and what they wanted to know.

And there was a bonus. Ritter had also given SNOW the name of another Abwehr agent CHARLIE, (identified by Guy Liddell as 'Eschborn'), who lived in Manchester and was a professional photographer who could prepare and develop microphotographs for him and told him he would be getting some money in the mail from another German source.

CHARLIE, British born son of a German family, had been recruited in 1938 by Ritter, claiming to be Dr HANSEN, threatened that if he did not help, the Abwehr would take reprisals against a brother who still lived in Germany. Before SNOW got in touch with him, Tar had been up to see him and persuaded him he was better off working as a double agent, a move CHARLIE accepted with relief. As to the money, when two £5 notes were picked up in SNOW's mail they were traced back, incongruously via the banking hall of Selfridges, the store in whose white tiled and chrome 'American Milk Bar', Tar and his brother had enjoyed ice creams all those years ago. The tellers had paid them out to a Mrs. Krafft, who found herself very quickly and without any publicity, exchanging her placid life as a Bournemouth Hausfrau for a cell in Holloway Prison. The Game was off to a good start.

And of key importance in a confidence trick, the potential 'mark' was equally convinced he had gained. Ritter could puff a cigar and rub his hands in satisfaction that he had a loyal and active agent in SNOW, a burgeoning network, supposedly secure communications channels via wireless and, through CHARLIE, microphotographs, and a direct line into a happily fictional snakepit of saboteurs in South Wales. SNOW did not let him down. In an analogy wartime audiences would have understood, he was playing the dummy 'Tim' with Tar in the rôle of his famous ventriloquist master Arthur Brough.[2]

He sent the Germans a steady stream of intelligence about troop sightings, bomb damage, RAF squadron strength, and anti-aircraft defences which must have given Ritter a degree of comfort that he was getting something for his money even though none of the information in itself was strategically vital or compromising. In April 1940, SNOW was also employed to suggest to the Germans that the impending, and in the event, abortive Allied attack on occupied Norway would be concentrated on Bergen rather than Trondheim. For Tar and his colleagues each exchange of messages, especially when the Abwehr HQ in Hamburg repeated them to Berlin and Abwehr outstations gave new insights in the German organisation and its codes. And there were other potentially valuable insights, such as when Ritter told SNOW that Germany 'had only 90 submarines left and found it very difficult to train the crews. They were also very expensive. They are therefore going to concentrate more on aerial warfare and are intending to attack shipping in the Irish Sea . . .'

This is where we came in. At a rendezvous in Antwerp in April 1940, Ritter told SNOW that their next meeting should be in the North Sea. He had heard that there was a good deal of smuggling through British east coast ports and suggested that it should be quite easy for SNOW to charter a trawler. Even in his wilder Walter Mitty moments SNOW might have been rather taken aback at what one MI5 officer described as 'this extraordinary project'. Ritter would come out from Germany by submarine or plane and SNOW could bring with him not only answers to the growing 'laundry list' of intelligence questions but also an agent SNOW had already unwisely suggested would benefit from training in Germany. This was Sam McCarthy, now to be known as 'BISCUIT' who after 'a prolonged career of petty larceny, dope smuggling and the con-fidence trick' . . . had 'reformed and since acted as a capable and honest informer [for MI5] in criminal matters'. He had nerve too, since he did not back off when Tar told him he was likely to be 'recruited' by SNOW to go into Germany to be trained by the Abwehr as a saboteur, though he was shrewd enough to ask how much he would be paid.

But how to get hold of a trawler? We know SNOW told Ritter a Welsh friend of his happened to own one, and that Ritter believed him. The truth was more complicated. Tar went to see the Fisheries Board in London and was put in touch with a family shipping firm in Grimsby who were willing to co-operate. Tar and a colleague went up there the next day and made meticulous arrangements with the owner and the skipper about how to get SNOW and BISCUIT on board, what the crew would be told – the pair were passed off as Government inspectors of some kind – how much the crew should be paid, and how MI5 were to be kept out of the limelight. BISCUIT and SNOW each knew the other to be under Tar's control – he came to Kings Cross to see them off on the 11.10am Grimsby train – which makes what happened on the journey and their arrival at 4.43pm even stranger. BISCUIT became convinced from SNOW'S comments and behaviour that he was actually working for the Germans and that when they met Ritter, SNOW would betray BISCUIT as a British 'plant'.

For his part SNOW 'for reasons which we cannot analyse', a slightly exasperated MI5 file note subsequently observed, convinced himself that BISCUIT would tell Ritter that SNOW himself was a double agent. BISCUIT's reaction was hardly surprising since according to a note scribbled that evening by BISCUIT, SNOW had started the conversation with the bitter comment that 'it would not be long before he got his own back'. He had gone out of his way to denigrate Tar and MI5: 'What a fat bundle Capt. R thought he would get out of this job. £500, that means £400 graft for him. They are all like that, mean lot of lousy grafting b's. My people pay well. They don't bleed them and use them for mugs.' He added to the impression that he was spying for the Germans by taking many photographs as the train rattled through eastern England and then produced his *pièce de résistance*, showing BISCUIT a compromising document, which could only have cemented in BISCUIT's mind that SNOW was not playing 'both ends against the middle' but was on the German side.

By the time they clambered stiffly out at Grimsby, BISCUIT could hardly wait to get to the hotel and telephone Tar to raise the alarm. Tar decided that the *Barbados* should sail, but not make the agreed rendezvous, and that SNOW should be carefully watched. He was, and when not long after they had reached the open sea an unidentified aircraft flew over and fired signal flares, BISCUIT, convinced SNOW had betrayed the plan, had him bundled down to the captain's tiny cabin and tied up. The *Barbados* hauled in its nets, doused its running lights and headed home.

There were three consequences. First, it was decided in London that SNOW should be arrested, though in the event this did not happen. Second and more dramatically, was Operation Lamp. Many in the intelligence community had bitter memories of the Venlo incident in 1939 when the Germans kidnapped two SIS officers on the Dutch border. Tar thought he too could play that game and turn the tables by capturing the elusive Ritter. After a series of hurried meetings with the Air Ministry, the Admiralty and the Vice-Admiral, Submarines he put the elements of the Operation together. The *Barbados* would be sent out again to a new rendezvous arranged with Ritter, this time manned by armed Naval ratings and equipped with depth charges and a Oerlikon gun. The submarine *Salmon* would patrol close by. SNOW would be on board the trawler watched by two officers. He was told by Tar that if there was any sign of his double-crossing at the rendezvous 'he would probably never come back to this country'. If on the other hand he helped in capturing Ritter, Tar might take him back as an agent. Tar's notes make it clear that though he was almost certain SNOW was betraying him and had even given his name to the Germans, he was still willing to give him the benefit of a small shard of doubt. He noted: 'His mind is a very odd affair and it does not work on very logical lines, and the arguments he put up for the things he said to BISCUIT were not exactly convincing but at the same time seemed to me to hold a certain amount of water.' But the Lamp never lit up. Ritter did not appear. There was a heavy fog and in subsequent messages, Ritter seemed to accept this as the reason they failed to make contact. It is an example of Tar's attention to detail that he took the trouble to arrange for the *Barbados* to be renamed and re-registered. If it was later captured by the Germans the innocent fishermen aboard might otherwise have had a hard time explaining their missions. His care notwithstanding, with the benefit of hindsight one team of post-war historians criticised the second foray as having 'piled folly on fiasco.'[3]

The third leaf of this convoluted triptych is the document which SNOW flashed at BISCUIT in the Grimsby train. Sometime earlier, to make SNOW's battery business cover look more authentic, Tar had recruited another of MI5's cast of extras, William Mair Rolph, to set up a company in London and give SNOW space in his basement office in Sackville Street, between Piccadilly and Vigo Street, (coincidentally from 1942 the new address of Tar's tailors Meyer and Mortimer, after they were bombed out of Conduit Street). Perhaps not one of Tar's best selections, Rolph was a cash-strapped restaurant manager, who had served with MI5 in the First World War and as a result was a member of 'The IP Club' created by Vernon Kell in 1919 as a social event for MI5 officers but which grew into a far more significant twice-yearly dinner, at which 'Prime Ministers, members of the Cabinet heads of the Army, Navy, Air, Force and Civil Service mingled with the ordinary club members . . .', as they left their cloaks and daggers at the door to wine, dine and gossip. When asked what the initials stood for, Kell is said to have responded 'Intelligent People' though it more probably stems from MI5's First World War designation as 'The Intelligence Police Service'. It was initially a 'men only' affair though wives were invited in later years.

It was the Guest List for the 1938 IP dinner – on 25 May, the last to be held and remembered by Constance Kell as a 'particularly glittering affair' – which SNOW had gleefully shown to BISCUIT, pointing out the names of Tar, Vernon Kell and "another son of a bitch, a high man in MI5. The Doctor will be glad . . . when our advance guard gets here, they will know who to get and where to get them." It is almost as if SNOW knew of the *Sonderfahndungsliste GB* the 'Arrest List' prepared under Himmler's direction of prominent British personalities to be seized when and if the Germans invaded.

Whether or not Tar knew, the irrepressible SNOW had in fact 'recruited' Rolph for his supposed network and even given him an 'Abwehr serial number.' Rolph was always pressed for money, and Tar's deal with him that MI5 would pay him £1 per day plus expenses was hardly generous, whereas SNOW had lent him sizeable amounts from time to time. SNOW claimed that when Rolph heard he was meeting Ritter, Rolph handed him the IP list and suggested he offer it to the Abwehr for £2,000. Brandishing the list, which had been found on SNOW after the trawler adventure, Tar and his colleague Richman Stopford tackled an 'agitated' Rolph in his basement office. Rummaging in his desk and safe, as well as his dustbin, they found several earlier IP guest lists, some MI5 related papers from the First World War, an amateur code he had devised to keep in touch with SNOW, and four pistols. After questioning him for several gruelling hours, in which in Tar's words he 'told lies continuously and repeatedly changed his story', Tar telephoned GW who was 'minding' SNOW and the latter was brought over for a confrontation with Rolph in which he repeated that Rolph had offered him the list.

Again, the black and white cinematic image is inescapable, the bare fly-specked light bulb hanging from the basement ceiling, the voices of Tar and Stopford barking questions at a sweating Rolph from the semi-darkness, probably doing a 'good cop, bad cop' routine, SNOW smirking in the background. Tar and Stopford hurried back along Piccadilly to their office to consult with their colleagues about what to do. Prosecuting Rolph was not an option since any even half-competent defence counsel would bring out MI5's 'Hidden Hand' and the SNOW aspects of the case.

Rolph resolved MI5's dilemma by putting his head in the greasy cooking stove in the back room of his basement, and turning on the gas. But if the sad facts – it is a bitter twist that what may well have been the first life lost in the Double Cross game of shadows should be British – reached the press, it might arouse German suspicions. The Abwehr knew of his supposed business connection with SNOW; in yet another sidebar adventure they had arranged for three Lascar seamen sent by 'Obed of Aden' to deliver radio valves to him at the Sackville Street address. Though the absence of comment from the file might suggest that fudging a death, like giving birth to a new identity, was all in a night's work, it must have caused considerable heart-searching and hand-wringing, and Tar's notes make oblique mention of an exchange with the Assistant Commissioner of Police in charge of Special Branch, Sir Norman Kendall. In the event the Westminster Coroner obliged with the verdict that the cause of death was an aortic aneurism. The formal notice in *The Times* Deaths column on 6 June 1940 recorded only that Rolph had died 'suddenly'.

By curious coincidence it was around this time that MI5 and SIS came close to getting their hands on Ritter, known to them at the time as 'Rantzau'. As Holland braced for the inevitable German invasion, its Government belatedly began to round up Nazi sympathisers and 'spies'. Liddell records on 9 May that among the latter was a 'de Rantzow' and that the Dutch had agreed to share any papers they uncovered. But the next day the Wehrmacht rolled in, and he was freed.

Like one of those painted plastic dolls with a weighted base that simply cannot be knocked over, none of this upset SNOW and the project. Far from it. On 4 June Guy Liddell noted in his diary, 'The general opinion now appears to be that SNOW is once more on the straight and narrow path. Personally I doubt it, though he has given us certain information [about Abwehr attempts to plant bombs on a cargo ship] which has proved to be reliable.' Tar shared these doubts; the microphone bugging of SNOW and LILY's home was stepped up and Tar warned LILY with menacing ambiguity that if SNOW stepped out of line again 'I would take steps to have him removed.' Not that the microphone buried in his living room wall troubled the feral SNOW; an earlier listener had noted that when he wanted to talk to LILY they moved into the kitchenette and thus out of range, or he simply turned up the volume of the radio-gramophone to drown out their conversation.

A week later Vernon Kell was axed. He died in 1942. His obituary in *The Times* on 7 April 1942 had its special poignancy. Signed only 'GM', it was undoubtedly written by Sir George Macdonagh, a brilliant military intelligence and staff officer. He praised Kell, a friend of 35 years, as a man whose 'tact, good sense, restraint and powers of deduction amounted almost to genius'. Macdonagh himself died in July 1942, just three months later. Like a Grimsby trawler heading into a North Sea squall, the Service embarked on the period of internal turmoil described earlier.

Whatever he really believed about the trawler fiasco, Ritter still wanted to meet BISCUIT, whom Tar brought into play like another pawn on the chessboard, sending him to Lisbon in July with papers which would, they hoped, convince the suspicious Portuguese police that he was a wine merchant.

Notes

1. Brammer, p. 172 et seq.
2. Brough's son Peter continued the family tradition in the 1950s with the manic-eyed dummy Archie Andrews.
3. Hinsley et al, Vol. iv p. 87.

22

Tea with BISCUIT

Portugal claimed – not too loudly as the tides of war ebbed and flowed – to be 'Britain's oldest ally', a relationship dating at least from the Treaty of Windsor in 1386 if not before, and some shop fronts along the black and white checkered pavements of Lisbon displayed Union flags discreetly in the corners of their Art Deco windows. There were the traditional ties of the wine trade through Oporto, and extensive British mining interests, while the older generation in the capital had vague memories that its rattling tramway system had been financed by capital raised in London. But their shrewd President Antonio Salazar[1] had decided to sit out this war as a neutral. Neutral as regards fighting, but not as regards money. Much as the Swedes had ore and ball bearings, the Turks chrome, and the Spanish manganese, Portugal had wolfram, the ore from which came the steel-hardening mineral tungsten desperately needed by both the German and the British war machines, much but not all of it the product of British owned mines. As historian Douglas Wheeler noted balancing their rival demands while maintaining his country's neutrality 'brought sleeplessness to Salazar and nightmares to Allied and Axis diplomats . . .' Though the facts remain elusive even today, it seems likely that through a complex set of banking deals the Germans paid for much of their share of the wolfram with gold they had plundered from the Central banks of the countries they conquered as well as that stolen, wrenched and blackmailed from their millions of Jewish victims.

For refugees from Occupied Europe, huddled at night in fleapit boarding houses, standing listlessly in ragged queues on the Tagus dockside to try to get berths on any ship going anywhere, Lisbon was a place of despair, hope dwindling along with whatever money they had left. Despair which grew sharper if they saw one or other of the Swedish liners *Drottingholm* and *Gripsholm*, for which Lisbon was a regular port of call as they criss-crossed the oceans, their berths reserved for the exchange of Allied and German diplomats and prisoners of war and unattainable for refugees. For nouveaux-riches '*wolframistas*', sleek Portuguese lawyers and bankers and exiles who had engineered the transfer of their fortunes away from the Nazis with the expensive help of discreet Swiss bankers, it was a comfortable moonlit 'no man's land' in which to wait out the war or a Pan Am Clipper flight via the Azores and Bermuda to the safety of New York.

It was a posting that intelligence officers from every side and touchline of the war, even the doctrinally ascetic Soviets, must have hankered after. No air raids, no food rationing, no superior officers demanding action and reports. For many it meant big houses with cool courtyards, and even cooler live-in 'secretaries', lunches by the sea, the gulls swooping over the Tagus, whiter and more perky than their shabby grey cousins mewling miserably over the Grimsby docks, long dinners of shellfish and steaks of a thickness and succulence which elsewhere were only a memory, washed down with *viñho verde*, the glamour of the Casino at Estoril, palm trees, bougainvillea, and above all, light. The blackout that clamped down gloomily on most of the belligerent European capitals at the end of each afternoon was unknown.

The intelligence players had a keen sense of what their opponents were up to: hotel concierges, restaurant head waiters, bank managers, Customs and other key Government officials were on several intelligence service payrolls, so information flowed freely if expensively. It also flowed to the Portuguese Secret Police, whose eyes were sharper than their appearance. The game, much of it focused on cornering as much as possible of the tungsten traffic for one side or the other, was more like ju-jitsu, trying to trip one's opponent, compromise him or deceive him rather than have him garroted by a gypsy in an Alfema back alley. A German author who spent time in Lisbon in those early war years[2] wrote that 'shoot-outs were simply unthinkable'.

It was a game played out in public as well as private. A probably apocryphal but not implausible story has it that when a group of British intelligence officers went in to a smart Lisbon restaurant one evening, a well-lubricated gaggle of Germans who knew who they were and who also knew that in the SIS codebook the cryptonym for Germany was '12 Land', ('Zwőlfland' in German), greeted them with a full throated chorus of their national Anthem, rendered as 'Zwőlfland, Zwőlfland Űber Alles.' We get a sense of the heady atmosphere in one of the lesser known quotes of the ubiquitous Kim Philby, recorded by a British SIS officer Kenneth Benton, who was driving him the 300 miles from Madrid to Lisbon 'one brilliant spring day'. 'All a man wants on a day like this,' Philby chuckled, as they ate and drank their way through the cork groves, 'is someone like Ginger Rogers and a fast car'.[3] As another of Tar's agents reported, between 7.00 and 9.00pm – as in Spain, dinner was a late affair – Abwehr officers were often to be seen meeting their contacts at the Douro Café or the York Bar. They were told not to visit the Arcadia and other 'public nightclubs' but went for 'amusement' to the relatively new Café Nina, 'financed by a wealthy Portuguese Jewess and managed by a Russian. I think he is an ex-army officer.' The intelligence game attracted its fair share of gifted amateurs too. One *femme fatale*, drawn not from a novelist's imagination but from the curling pages of the MI5 archives, can serve as an exotic proxy for the men and women, who slithered across the Lisbon landscape, conniving and surviving in any way they could. 'Maria' as she was known to the Abwehr is memorably portrayed in an MI5 note as 'aged thirty to thirty-five, well dressed, but not good looking, a heavy drinker and a drug addict who is very clever on the comparatively rare occasions when she is sober'.

She styled herself 'Marquesa', an honorific to which she was not entitled, not least because during the Spanish Civil War she was said to have murdered her noble husband to become the mistress of a senior Red officer. Before arriving in Lisbon she had been involved in several scandals involving 'men and money' in Biarritz and Cannes. She had been taken on by the Abwehr in Spain, and moved to Portugal when it became clear that she had been ostracised by what was left of Spanish high society. There she gambled, lost heavily and was often seen in the hearty company of free-spending officers of the American clandestine services in the Palace Hotel in Estoril. According to one intercepted German message she had disclosed to them early on in their relationship that she had in fact been working for the Americans for some time. They had instructed her to 'turn' a German agent, and believed she had done so successfully, not knowing she had revealed the plot to the Abwehr, who were then able to run the agent as a 'double' against the unwitting Americans.

None of these convolutions inhibited her from a liaison with one Bogomolets, who despite his Russian name (which translates as 'pilgrim' or 'a devout person') was a Rumanian with a British passport and was generally believed to be the head NKVD agent in Lisbon. Agents like the Marquesa came and went, greasy palms needed crossing with silver, gold or dollars, often loosely accounted for on grounds of 'secrecy'. There were deals to be done on the currency markets, bullion bought for the grossly overvalued Reichsmark the Germans printed in their occupied territories, escudos for precious dollars, flesh for visas. There were silk stockings, wines, perfumes and cigars to be bought and sent home. Many intelligence men were officially on their local Embassy staff. As they swept past the rickety taxis and donkeys laden with panniers of fruit and vegetables the cynical Portuguese muttered that the big black CD emblems on their Packards and Mercedes stood not for 'Corps Diplomatique' but *'Contrabandistas Distinguidos'*, ('Distinguished Smugglers').

BISCUIT spent some three weeks there in July 1940 mostly with Ritter's colleague Doebbler, a dashing international yachtsman with an Argentine passport. Ritter himself, who came from Germany for a short meeting, seemed to accept the story that the *Barbados* had made it out to the rendezvous point but had seen nothing in the fog. BISCUIT returned to London with a new wireless for SNOW, a fresh set of intelligence questions reduced to microphotographs which CHARLIE was to enlarge, and an alert that 'a South African' would soon be parachuted in to help SNOW; he would carry $3,000 in cash, and would be recognisable by his suntan (some might have thought that rather a give away in a locked down, rainy Britain). BISCUIT's pen portrait of Ritter, which we cited earlier, also noted snobbishly that he 'speaks with a broad New York accent, swears, is fond of telling filthy stories and is exceedingly common.'

Common or not, Ritter had a big job on his hands. In the summer of 1940 Hitler was pushing his Generals to prepare for Operation SEALION, his plan to knock Britain out of the war by a cross Channel invasion. This was grudgingly abandoned when the Royal Air Force trounced Goering's Luftwaffe in the battle of Britain, or better the battle over Britain, and the Germans failed to gain the mastery of the skies, which was an essential precondition to an invasion. As part of their planning the German High Command ordered the Abwehr undertake Operation LENA, otherwise HUMMER, the urgent recruiting of as many agents as possible to be parachuted into England to radio back military intelligence. On all the evidence Ritter's job, finding, training and equipping the hapless agents, was badly done on every count. Some were to be parachuted in by a special unit of Heinkel and Junkers 88 aircraft; others would land by sea on hopefully remote beaches. They were scantily trained since for the most part they were not intended to be long term undercover spies but rather as a first wave of "boots on the ground" who could send back information ahead of the planned invasion and then act as guides or scouts when the Germans swept ashore.

It was Ritter's knowledge of the invasion timing and his rôle in LENA which makes that trip out to the North Sea, with its many risks, seem so utterly foolhardy.

His more realistic colleagues talked of LENA (behind his back) as '*ein Himmelfahrtskommando*', or a suicide mission. They were right since apart from one unfortunate soul who committed suicide in a dank air raid shelter when his meagre funds ran out, the twenty-three agents in his multinational ragbag were all caught and those who were not adroitly recycled as double agents were executed.

What the Germans did not know was that through SNOW's radio and his feedback, Tar and his team were expecting them; their training and their movements were known, their cover identities, their landing sites, were all visible in the crystal ball in St. James's Street. Even the fake identity cards and ration books they carried had numbers and mis-spelled addresses made up by Tar's team and passed on through SNOW, instantly recognisable as false to an even half-alert policeman. That they were expected did not make Tar's task any easier. Some never appeared. Some refused to be 'turned'. No surprise, since in the real world a case officer's life is more a succession of frustrations and blind alleys punctuated by intermittent success, than vice versa.

For instance, we see him down in Wales with the Swansea MI5 Regional Liaison Officer hurriedly renting a house to shelter a group of saboteurs whom the Abwehr were supposedly sending over to help GW create mayhem. Nothing came of it (MI5 was unable to decide whether three Cubans who arrived on a trawler at Fishguard in November, 'overloaded with sabotage equipment' were the group they had been expecting). Another blind alley failed to lead to the 'the Infra-Red Man' who, according to an intercepted Abwehr message, was seeking to peddle the blueprint of a new British aircraft device. In the end he never appeared at the rendezvous – BISCUIT's Paddington flat – but the file notes show again the meticulous preparations Tar made, starting with the 'boffins' to see what sort of device it might be, and who might have had access to its plans, through to multiple versions of the script to be followed, installing microphones in the flat and a ciné camera across the road to film the delivery.

There were successes too. On 17 September 1940, two days after a heavy bombing raid on London's West End had caused heavy damage in Bond Street and around Tar's office, gutting Christopher Wren's 1670's St. James's Church 200 yards away on Piccadilly, a Swede came swinging down from the sky near Denton in Northants. We have long since given up expecting our actors to be James Bond clones or men of especially high or heroic principle. Goesta Caroli, who became Tar's agent SUMMER, was a rolling stone who had gathered debts rather than moss and had fallen into the German net largely because of financial misadventures, the last of them being when he 'failed disastrously with a silver fox farm . . . near Upsala'.

The highlights of his later story – his manic depressions, his attempts to escape – have been told elsewhere and need not detain us, other than as a reminder that though the individual cases have a sometimes impenetrable fascination, even at that early stage running Double Cross required Tar to thread his way along a spiders web of delicate connections. If one was damaged or compromised the entire structure might unravel. After SUMMER landed and found himself in some distress, Ritter radioed SNOW to go to his assistance, thus reinforcing Tar's feeling that they still regarded the ambivalent Welshman as their most important asset in Britain. SUMMER also gave Tar the names of two more agents who were on their way. After a spell at Camp 020, they too became Tar's property, key members of SNOW's notional network. But all the time the doubt nagged: what if SNOW was really betraying all this to the Germans?

Had the Infra-Red Man produced the blueprints, SNOW was to take them with him for his next, and climactic meeting with Ritter, which was again to be in Lisbon. He had also offered to bring two new 'sidekicks' (his term; he may have been thumbing through Latimer's hard-boiled novel), one of whom was to go on to Germany for training. In the end there were no blueprints and only one 'sidekick', Walter Dicketts, codenamed CELERY, a new recruit to Tar's band of strolling players. According to Liddell's laconic diary entry Dicketts was 'wanted by the police'. Masterman's later summary of the case comments that he 'served during the last war in a branch of air intelligence but since then had shown a less satisfactory record and had been involved after his return to civil life in a number of dubious financial dealings. He was therefore able to represent to the Germans that he had a grudge against this country inasmuch as his record made it impossible for him to regain his commission in the Air Force.' As a scholar, Masterman would well understand the Greek stylistic form *Litotes*, or 'measured understatement'; he was deploying it here to the full. Another Patrick Hamilton-style scenario is about to unfold.

Notes

1. Salazar, Antonio de Oliviera, 1889–1970, founder and leader of the authoritarian 'New State' régime which controlled every aspect of Portuguese life.
2. Seligo, p. 129.
3. Benton, p. 405.

23

The Odd Couple

Born in Putney in 1899 and schooled in Southend, Dicketts fudged his age and joined the Royal Naval Air Service at the outbreak of the First World War when he was just 15, and went on to work in Air Ministry Intelligence; given his youth he is unlikely to have risen to a senior position. After the First World War he was one of many ex-serviceman to find himself unable to cope with civilian life, but not all of them turned to crime.

His first recorded brush with the law was in 1921, when he was convicted of obtaining credit by false pretences. He and an accomplice had motored around the country staying at expensive hotels (without paying their bills) and in the process convincing their 'marks' into believing that they had an 'inside track' to the Army Canteen Board, from whose war surplus stores several million cigarettes could be bought at knockdown prices, offering the prospect of resale at a sizeable profit. Needless to say once the victims had paid cash in advance Dicketts and his partner, Percy Doland, moved on. There were no cigarettes. 'Wholesale dissipation', the judge harrumphed, as he sentenced Dicketts to nine months' hard labour. Two years later Dicketts, now an 'advertising agent' was in the dock again, charged with obtaining by fraud, a diamond wrist watch and a gold cigarette case from the jewellers Mappin & Webb. In 1929 Southend police were reported to be looking for him after he ran away with a 16-year-old girl, Alma Farqhar, and married her at a London Registry Office; the marriage was dissolved eighteen months later on the grounds of his adultery.[1]

He travelled far and fast, a roving Raffles. A 1929 Passport Office Bulletin warned British Consuls around the world that Dicketts, also using the names 'Morton' and 'Welfare' had been convicted of fraud in France, had spun yarns to get financial assistance from the British Consuls in Chattanooga, Tennessee, and Detroit, and had also left behind a group of aggrieved 'investors' after a visit to Barcelona. CELERY himself claimed in a later note to Tar that he knew France, Belgium, southern Italy and Bavaria well; Tar's eye may also have been caught by CELERY's claim that he had also travelled in Malaya and Java. Back in the UK he was again in trouble in 1930 and 1931 for obtaining money by false pretences. In 1933, by his account he was a 'Warden for the Unemployed' in Bristol, probably a reference to one of the "toughening-up" camps established by the Ministry of Labour to get hard-core and recalcitrant unemployed reacquainted with habits of discipline. Ex-Service officers and retired policemen were often put in charge.[2]

CELERY's first contact with SNOW was early in 1940, when he overheard him talking in a pub in Richmond – SNOW was then living high on the Hill, if not the hog, in Marlborough Road – about what he rapidly concluded was his work as a spy. They drifted into bibulous conversation about, of all things, their shared fondness for Mexican food, and SNOW soon told him he was a secret agent and could put work and money CELERY's way. And not just through spying. According to the MI5 listeners to the microphones in SNOW's flat, the two men also shared Gorse-like fantasies of producing ready-mixed mustard in tubes, and buying 'Mountain Glow' whisky and gin 'wholesale', a euphemism for the 'black market', relabelling it and selling it to restaurants with the help of the unfortunate Rolph; nothing came of them. Nor is there any sign that another SNOW project – a nightclub in Soho's Rupert Street, intended in part to serve as an outlet for the liquor – ever saw the light of day or night though he did get as far as choosing a name, the 'Rialto', perhaps a 'tip of the hat' to the Art Deco splendours of the nearby cinema of the same name.

SNOW and CELERY were period pieces, men of their times. Just as English murders of the 1930s and 1940s had a grisly, now outmoded, style of their own – privet-hedged suburban homes where miserable marriages were ended by gas or arsenic, bodies in suitcases deposited at Left Luggage Offices, throats slashed with razors, bodies dissolved in vats of acid. So too the English 'conmen' of the era had a patter which matched the times. An Army deserter posed as an officer, the son of a peer and, dressed in a clergyman's clothes obtained on credit in Salisbury, seduced the daughter of a Hampshire vicar. A smooth talking greengrocer posed as an SIS officer and an Army Major, a cashiered Colonel claimed to have access to profitable arms deals in China and Russia, another offered an entrée to a weapons contract with Abyssinia, and a Midlands couple masqueraded profitably for a while in a South Devon resort as the 'last of the Romanovs'.

Tar's watchers told him that CELERY and his wife were seeing a lot of SNOW and his wife. They portrayed CELERY as just under six feet tall, with 'black hair, well greased and brushed back, erect carriage . . . speaks in rather superior, loud tone of voice, while his wife was . . . about 29, wavy hair . . . pale face . . . smartly dressed . . . appearance of chorus girl.'

While they watched him, CELERY watched the Welshman, which may explain an eye-catching note by Tar in March 1940. He and Joan had driven to 'The Barn' pub, a short way down the Kingston Road from the Star and Garter Ex-Servicemen's Home which crowns Richmond Hill. They were due to meet SNOW and LILY; Tar was to pass over a 'loudspeaker' for SNOW's wireless set. Tar did not want to go in himself – he was in Seaforth officer's uniform, a rare sight even in wartime in suburban pubs – so Joan Robertson went in for ten minutes and then brought SNOW and LILY out to Tar's car. She told him that when they got up to go and meet Tar a man who had been sitting in the pub looking out at the car park had slipped out by the back door, leaving most of his beer undrunk . When Tar drove away he was sure he was being tailed though he could not make out the number of the car. Reporting the next morning to Guy Liddell he commented that 'SNOW's reaction to the whole affair was one of complete calm which made me wonder at the time if he was not double crossing me.' If the watcher was indeed CELERY it is quite plausible that SNOW would have encouraged him to observe his 'inside track' with British intelligence. (The episode is a good illustration of Joan's close involvement in Tar's strange dealings; she also entertained at least three of his double agents at home. Family memories are of a strong, gregarious personality, perhaps as shrewd a judge of character as Tar himself.)

The two men's tangled trail included visits, unexplained by SNOW to addresses in Norwood and Sheen, and a jaunt to Bournemouth and Devon with their wives, for which SNOW paid all the bills, even though the sharp-eyed CELERY noticed that he signed the hotel register as "T.A. Wilson." Drink flowed freely, and SNOW's tongue loosened. He bragged he had £1,000,000 at his disposal, and when they got back to Richmond he took CELERY up on his roof to show off his clandestine radio, claiming it had a world-wide reach, and told him the men in the flat next door were his 'henchmen'; they were actually Tar's MI5 watchers. When he poured generous shots of 'Mountain Glow' Scotch for CELERY (the brand name itself epitomises the entire sleazy adventure), he told him not to worry about the cost: they were 'having a drink on the Führer'. There were also defeatist diatribes which if anyone else had heard them, would have caused SNOW serious trouble. Britain was falsifying RAF casualty figures, Army morale was terrible, rich people were shifting their money abroad as fast as they could; Germany was bound to win the war.

When he thought he had heard and seen enough to prove that SNOW really was a German spy, CELERY decided to report him to his former colleagues at Air Ministry Intelligence. Though these were early days for Double Cross, the spider's web of official and personal relationships reacted effectively. The Ministry told Special Branch, the latter, who knew all about SNOW, alerted Tar. Quick checks by the Branch and Tar's team showed CELERY not only 'had form' but was currently wanted for bouncing a cheque in Wolverhampton. The police arranged to meet him at the buffet on Richmond Railway Station – another temple to the tea urn – where they promptly arrested him and took him to the local Police Station, down the hill from SNOW's home. Tar drove down to talk to him. He also joined the police search of CELERY's flat, which yielded nothing of interest. Tar quickly decided that CELERY was not, as he had at first feared, an Abwehr agent trying to penetrate the

SNOW operation. But what was his game? Based on CELERY'S record, he felt he had first marked SNOW down as a free-spending 'sucker' from whom he could charm money for his own get-rich-quick schemes. But when he realised there was something behind SNOW's bluster about spying, it had dawned on CELERY that by reporting him and offering to try to find out more, he might take the first step along the pebble-strewn uphill path back to respectability, even re-instatement in the RAF. Based on his intuition, Tar was prepared to take him on and as a first step fixed matters with the Chief Constable in Birmingham – to whom we remember, Tar was well known – so that the bouncing cheque charge would be smoothed over. The hearing went unreported and CELERY was fined £3.00, given his "form" no more than a mild slap on the wrist. We can assume that as CELERY was always short of money, the fine was chalked up as an MI5 expense.

It had suited Tar not to see CELERY defending himself in the dock, where he might have spoken out about SNOW, and CELERY was now in his debt. He was warned not to contact SNOW without permission from Special Branch. It is beyond any agent runner to script a case in any detail more than a few days ahead, sometimes a few hours or minutes at a time. Things change, 'stuff happens', hard facts melt in the daylight, black becomes white, or more often, grey. Flexibility, imagination and a cool head are essential. So it was here.

Over the summer, CELERY peppered the long-suffering Tar with volleys of letters and postcards, whose wheedling tone evokes the professional begging letter writer castigated by Charles Dickens in a diatribe of the same name.[3] But this may be unkind; the letters could equally well be the genuine calls for help of a drowning man trying to catch the attention of a passer by on the riverbank. Please help me with a job or a start in business (he even claimed acquaintance with Emperor Haile Sellassie of what was then Abyssinia). Could he work as Tar's chauffeur, could he "hot up" his car, or find an official position screening aliens? He was 'down to my last few shillings, he had no money for my wife and son, he had fourteen pawn tickets and nothing left to pawn, he could not work after a nasty fall in the blackout, he had to find cheaper lodgings, if Tar could help with a lump sum this would be the last letter he would write.' It was not but unlike the much-pestered Charles Dickens, who advised his readers 'to resolve at any sacrifice of feeling, to be deaf to such appeals'.

On one view, Tar was kindness itself, and on another pro-fessionalism personified, and kept CELERY going. He sent him a few pounds every fortnight or so, gently badgered the Air Ministry and even got himself into trouble with SIS by dropping a personal note to a friend there to see if they had a place for CELERY. The letter landed on the desk of Valentine Vivian who returned it directly to Liddell, with a pompous covering note complaining that Tar's approach outside established channels was a breach of protocol and that recommending to SIS a man with a criminal record was an initiative of 'doubtful propriety'. The twenty-first century SIS may well be more open-minded.

By October CELERY's persistence had paid off. Tar found the right way to use him, and sent him £35 to clear his debts. CELERY's gratitude was unfeigned. The task was a subtle Tar blend of objectives. CELERY thought he had been sent to various industrial towns to sniff around undercover and see what he could pick up about the security precautions at various ammunition and machine tool plants; this included looking for traces of IRA activity in Coventry and Communist infiltration of aircraft factories. Though only a few of his reports survive they show an ability to penetrate, to encourage loose talk, an eye for detail, and an almost photographic memory. Tar used CELERY's reports to point out weaknesses to his MI5 colleagues responsible for regional industrial security, an initiative they clearly viewed as meddling in things which were none of his business. But unknown to CELERY his material also fed Tar's insatiable professional appetite for information from which to prepare replies to questions asked by the Germans, or to offer up ostensibly new insights to reinforce the credibility of their notional agents.

CELERY was then put back in touch with SNOW, to pose as his 'sidekick' for the Lisbon trip, to whom would fall the dangerous mission of going into Germany for 'training'. According to Masterman, CELERY spoke fluent German (though CELERY's own notes and a postwar interrogation of an Abwehr officer contradict this) and was thought by MI5 to be able and observant, a combination that made the possibility of his actually going into wartime Germany attractive: '. . . we expected that he might bring back valuable information', Masterman noted.

As they got ready to leave, the two men circled each other warily, each jealous of his relationship with Tar, each mistrustful of the other's motives, sometimes arguing loudly, then making up, a truly 'Odd Couple' like rival leading men in a touring repertory company missing no opportunity to run to Tar, their producer and director, with disparaging tales about each other and the rest of the cast. SNOW talked too much, was drinking heavily, and spending lavishly on LILY, GW was 'an opinionated, mercenary man', CELERY was surely working for the Germans, CHARLIE likewise, BISCUIT was upsetting the MI5 minders – not least by condescendingly leaving a lavish tip for them on the mantelpiece as if he were a guest at a country house – and also behaving obnoxiously in public when he had too much to drink. BISCUIT himself even sneaked to Tar that one of the minders was seeing rather too much of a Richmond barmaid. For the most part, Tar took delivery of the delations with little more than a raised eyebrow and a wry smile. But even he could be infected by the prevailing paranoia, minuting that only one copy be made of a December 1941 note since 'CELERY is of the opinion that SNOW has people everywhere, even possibly in this department'.

Notes
1. *The Times*, 17 November 1921, 20 May 1929, 18 December 1930.
2. See, e.g. Gardiner, p. 165.
3. Dickens, Charles, *Household Words*, May 1850.

24

Thieves Fall Out

The passenger lists of flights operated in the Second World War by the erstwhile British Overseas Airways Corporation (BOAC), between the UK and neutral Lisbon would repay more detailed study and would probably make a good novel. All passengers inbound and outbound needed British Government (in other words MI5 or MI6) sanction. Since space was so limited – the need to carry a large fuel load left room for only eighteen passengers – priority out of Lisbon was given to agents and escapers scrambling to London from Occupied Europe, and in both directions to SIS, SOE and MI5 officers, Whitehall trade and propaganda officials and ambiguous 'businessmen'. The DC3 aircraft, manned by émigré crews from the Dutch airline KLM flew low – at a bumpy 1,000 to 3,000 feet, and only in daylight. Until the fall of France in 1940 some left from the Art Deco terminal at Shoreham on the Sussex coast – Britain's first commercial airport, opened in 1911. When it closed, the flights ran between Whitchurch, outside Bristol, and Lisbon's Portela field, where arriving and departing passengers came under the sharp-eyed scrutiny of the Portuguese Political Police and a scrum of watchers in crumpled linen suits sent by half a dozen competing belligerent and neutral spy agencies to see who was coming and going. It was a scene described by the local BOAC manager as 'like [the movie] Casablanca, but twentyfold'.[1]

SNOW flew to Lisbon on 15 February 1941, telling the British Passport Control officials he was going to buy sardines. The bright lights he could see as the plane came in over the Portuguese capital must have been a startling contrast to London where the 'blackout' at the time started at 6.45 in the evening and ran till 7.42 the next morning. Lisbon's Abwehr Station was a major operation, on paper at least. Debriefing and briefing agents like SNOW and CELERY was part of a much larger task, in which wheeling, dealing and bribing for tungsten loomed large. But recruiting and running agents also kept many of its officers at full stretch. Refugees and escaped French, Polish or Czech prisoners of war, trying to get to England to join their armies in exile, found themselves buttonholed by inquisitive and appraising Germans or their Portuguese agents. The docks were trawled for seamen who might talk carelessly about convoy procedures or even better, those who might be persuaded into sailing to England as intelligence or sabotage agents. The Germans were closely watched by the Portuguese Political Police, who also suborned their locally engaged staff, and their radio traffic was being decrypted in Britain and read by Tar and his team sometimes even before it had reached the last Abwehr outstation on the circulation list. And the man on whom the Abwehr relied as their main 'talent spotter' in the dockside bars and bordellos was actually an SIS asset.

Just before the Lisbon trip CELERY told Tar that SNOW was 'both mad and double-crossing us', which makes it mildly surprising or a tribute to Tar's powers of persuasion and reassurance, that he went ahead with it, taking a cargo boat from Newport. It had to dog-leg across the Bay of Biscay to avoid German U Boats, delaying his arrival and leaving SNOW to face Ritter on his own. SNOW's later account of what happened was judged by MI5 as 'in the highest degree confused and gave every impression of being untruthful.'

SNOW claimed that Ritter confronted him with the accusation that he was working under British control, arguing that there was no way otherwise he could have got one of the coveted seats on the Lisbon flight. He had admitted it, but stammered that this had been going on only for the past two and a half months, after someone had betrayed him. Never one to tell a story simply, he claimed that he had told Ritter he had included 'bluff checks' in his recent messages to tip off the Hamburg operators that he was working under British control but they were 'so lousy they failed to spot them'. Ritter had reacted by suggesting that SNOW go back to England as if nothing had happened, and pretend to carry on as before, only now using special code words in his message to indicate what was true and what was British deception material. A few days later, CELERY arrived, and in telling his side of the story later, he was adamant that though he saw SNOW before he met Ritter on his own, SNOW did not tell him that Ritter now knew he, and by extension CELERY were under British control. If this was true it was a staggering act of deceit. All the more since he was about to be sent into Germany. If SNOW had given the game away, the chances of his coming back were slim.

SNOW'S version was that he did warn CELERY but that the latter, saying he was 'one hundred percent for the Doctor', still decided to go ahead with the plan to travel to Hamburg for 'training', with an Abwehr officer as escort. According to Masterman's subsequent summary of the case, that while he was there CELERY was subjected to 'the closest interrogation on his past and present activities'. Ritter's 1972 memoirs tell us that this involved him completing many questionnaires and answering shoals of questions from visiting experts from Berlin about the RAF, and his technical knowledge, but was not 'interrogation' with its chilling twenty-first century connotations.

Ritter remembered that CELERY was allowed to walk about the city on his own, though trailed by the Gestapo, who reported he had made no suspicious contacts. His benign treatment, hardly matching a situation in which he was suspected to be working under British control, is confirmed by the post-war questioning of his Abwehr escorting officer. He told the British they travelled from Hamburg to Berlin in the comfort of an express train and CELERY was put up in a suite at the Hotel Adlon, the capital's finest hotel then and arguably still today. (In his own comments on the Abwehr in Spain and Portugal, Benton[2] observes that it was 'a gentlemanly organisation. They believed in treating their spies well, accommodated them in good hotels and sent them on by sleeper or first class reserved seats.') Ritter adds some stitches of embroidery, telling us that when it was time for CELERY to go back to Lisbon, the Abwehr chief, Admiral Canaris asked why Ritter wasn't simply going to hold him as a prisoner of war. 'Because I gave him my word,

Admiral', Ritter told him. 'Very well', Canaris said quietly, 'in that case there's nothing more to be said.'

CELERY rejoined SNOW in Lisbon three weeks later 'without mishap', and without training but his agile mind loaded with detailed observations, on everything he had seen and heard; descriptions of the many Abwehr officers he had met, comments on the Luftwaffe, on warship construction in the Hamburg yards, even German thinking about an invasion of Britain. He also claimed that many of the Abwehr officers and German diplomats he had met were under so much pressure that they were taking drugs – veronal to sleep and cocaine to keep them alert. He brought back samples which at Tar's request Victor Rothschild, the brilliant scientist who was yet another of MI5's topflight wartime recruits,[3] sent to the Medical Research Council asking for comments. Regrettably their reply is not on the file.

The notes of CELERY'S debriefing, mainly by Tar, fill many pages of the files and were immediately sent by dispatch rider to SIS and the Service Ministries. Tar's bet-hedging covering memorandum points out that CELERY had been 'undoubtedly impressed by what he had seen, which may have coloured his judgements,' and the possibility that much of what he had learned 'was being planted on him', could not be ruled out. Nevertheless, 'we believe [the] source to be speaking the truth and have so far no proof that he is trying to double cross us. He has got a very good memory indeed and the facts mentioned may therefore be accurate as far as he knows them.' What he remembered about Ritter's comments on the supremely delicate subject of 'peace feelers' was not of direct relevance to him but must have rung bells elsewhere in Whitehall. It leads us to another of those tantalising 'floaters', half-glimpsed plots drifting in the margins.

Notes

1. Most flights went unchallenged by the Luftwaffe. The shooting down of a DC3 carrying among others the celebrated actor Leslie Howard in April 1943, on which conspiracy buffs still feast, seems to have been a German operational mistake.
2. Benton, p. 381.
3. Rothschild, Nathaniel Mayer Victor, 3rd Baron, GBE, GM, PhD, ScD, FRS, 1910–90.

25

Peace For Our Time

CELERY claimed Ritter had told him that 'most right-thinking Germans' wanted peace with England. It was for England to make the first move, and if CELERY were to come back to him with some sort of official support he could introduce him to Goering.

Ritter's message implies that he believed that if not a British agent, CELERY was someone with valuable access in London. His comments may have been part of a complex series of shadow plays, whose high point was to come a few months later when Hitler's deputy Rudolf Hess parachuted into Scotland from a Messerschmitt 110, he had commandeered and flown solo across the North Sea. It was the first page in a bewildering chapter of history, seized on at the time by backbench MPs in the House of Commons, to put a nervously evasive Government on the defensive, and which created a new and still flourishing niche for writers on the Second World War history and intelligence.

Hess told the puzzled policemen who took him into custody that he was seeking to contact the Duke of Hamilton, an RAF Wing Commander, whom he believed could give him an entrée into the British political 'establishment' to explore the possibilities of a peace deal.[1]

The approach to the Duke had originated with Hess's friend and advisor Albrecht Haushofer, who had met Hamilton in Germany and was convinced he knew 'all the important people in London and had access to Churchill and the King'. In September 1940, Hess approved a letter from Haushofer to the Duke, suggesting they meet in Lisbon to explore this acutely sensitive theme. The letter was intercepted by the British Censor. Rightly so, since it reeked of the clandestine: signed only 'A' it was sent from an address in Portugal known to be a German wolfram-buying 'front' via an elderly lady in Cambridge, 'a typical grandmother' in the words of the MI5 officer who interviewed her.

Fifty years later when he was asked by the Duke's son for his recollections, Tar's memory, preserved in his papers in the form of a draft evidently typed with two fingers, was clear. Hess was not lured to Britain as part of an SIS plot, as some claimed, and still claim. And the initial thought that the approach should be followed up in a bid to use Haushofer as a conduit for disinformation or deception was not followed through because Tar was 'not prepared to open up a link with a man about whom very little was known, on the off chance of creating a channel through which false information could be fed. No-one knew where the other end came out. Besides if we had taken up the offer, how were we to know what effect the affair might have on other double agent cases and we were not prepared to risk it.'

Though Hess goes unmentioned in the index of the new authorised history the MI5 files give us a fuller story of the rôle of Tar and his colleagues, John Marriott and Jack Curry among them, even though they leave several questions unanswered and are certainly not the complete picture of the workings of Whitehall, notably SIS.

The first question is why Haushofer's letter, dated 23 September 1940, and speedily intercepted by the Censor, was not forwarded on to the Duke, and why it did not reach MI5 until 15 November, even though the Foreign Office had a copy. It was fortunate that copies existed since in another puzzle, the original letter went missing. No-one quite knew why, but the most plausible explanation on offer was that it must have been 'mislaid' when the bomb-damaged MI5 Registry files were moved to Blenheim. And it was not until much later, April 1941, that Tar interviewed the Duke at the Air Ministry. In the course of a long conversation he sounded him out on the idea of going to Lisbon, and noted: 'Hamilton at the beginning of the war [was] and still is a member of the community which sincerely believes that Great Britain will be willing to make peace with Germany providing the present régime in Germany were superseded by some reasonable form of government. This view, however, is tempered by the fact that he now considers that the only thing that this country can do is to fight this war to the finish, no matter what disaster and destruction befalls both countries. He is a slow-witted man but at the same time gets there in the end; and I feel that if he is properly schooled before leaving for Lisbon, he could do a very useful job of work.' The Duke was in principle willing to go, though with several sensible caveats. But there were still doubts. How could the long delay in replying be explained away? And surely Cabinet approval would be needed for such a political initiative.

On the night of 10/11 May, Hess put an end to the dithering when he plummeted down into the Scottish gorse. It made the Haushofer ploy redundant, though to MI5's chagrin the bemused and, many claim, demented, Hess was handed over to SIS for interrogation. MI5 also found itself having to explain to an angry Lord Swinton at the Security Executive, why he had not been kept informed.

In fact the Double Cross channels seem to have been used several times in the orchestration of 'peace misinformation' though on a matter so politically supercharged, MI5 were probably not kept fully 'in the loop,' as modern jargon has it, on all the twists and turns. SIS seem to have had more of a rôle to play. For instance in January 1941, while senior Civil Servants, spies and politicians were still circling warily around the Haushofer letter like dogs sniffing a lump of poisoned meat, Victor Cavendish Bentinck at the Foreign Office authorised, via SIS, a message from Tar's agent TRICYCLE, Dusko Popov telling the Germans that three named members of the House of Lords (each of whom would be known in Berlin as being identified in various ways with the push for appeasement or with extreme Right Wing movements) 'were prepared to accept peace terms'.

On 15 June TRICYCLE's notional sub agent BALLOON, (who had been pitched to the Germans as a disgraced Army officer turned reckless racing driver) was authorised to send a message reporting that in some British eyes Hess's mission 'was a peace move dictated by fear of Russia'. On 28 June TRICYCLE himself was cleared to pass on to the Abwehr the confusing notion that Hess 'might play an important rôle, that there was no peace party in England and the appeasers had lost all influence'.

One day perhaps more of the story will emerge. Meantime we can pick up again the adventures of our Second World War versions of Don Quixote and Sancho Panza.

Note

1. Douglas-Hamilton, Douglas, 14th Duke of Hamilton, 1903–73, boxer, aviator and politician and the first man to pilot an aircraft over Everest.

1. Tar in genial retirement

2. At four months

3. Dressed *de rigueur* in plus fours, even at 13, taking a smooth
swing at Ballater

4. At Charterhouse, in centre of first
standing row

No. 1 COMPANY, CHAMPION COMPANY—SPRING TERM, 1928.

5. Tar in the Champion Company at
Sandhurst, Spring 1928

6. Newly commissioned as a subaltern in
the Seaforth Highlanders

7. Best Man at John Kell's
wedding

8. Tar's wedding in April 1936

9. At the outbreak of the Second World War – "a dashing military type"

10. Tar in 1942. The strain of running Double Cross for MI5 is beginning to show

11. Babs the dog that almost scuppered D-Day

12. Arthur George Owens, the double agent SNOW – an appropriately blurred image of this complex spy

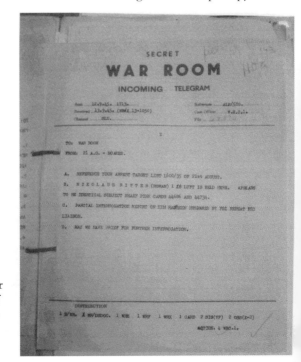

13. A 'secret' cable to Tar's War Room reporting the capture of senior Abwehr officer Niklaus Ritter

14. Tar in cheerful mood wearing his renowned 'passion pants' in Germany
in the first months of peace

15. Joan Robertson in 1952

16. Holloway Farm where Tar and Joan lived for ten years from 1949

17. Agents and case officers in October 1981. Tar is standing third from left. Eddie Chapman, agent ZIGZAG, is standing third from right with Christopher Harman on his right. Double Cross agent BRUTUS is seated in the centre holding a book. JEFF and MUTT are on his right

18. Tar and a colleague outside the former MI5 office in St James's Street

26

Fresh CELERY

CELERY told Tar that Ritter had described SNOW as lazy, drinking to excess, living on his nerves and spending too much money 'but we don't mind, we have plenty of it here'. Despite all that he still trusted him and implied that though his intelligence contribution was not great, the Abwehr had other plans for him, probably after a German invasion. When CELERY tried to probe, Ritter told him: 'Don't ask too many questions, but SNOW is a very clever chemist. In fact in some ways he is brilliant.' Whether this was just a diversionary throwaway or had some substance in the plan to poison Britain's reservoirs, earlier mooted with GW, we will never know.

For Tar however the more urgent concern was less what CELERY had seen, or been told, but what had happened in Lisbon, whether SNOW had betrayed the case, and by extensions others of his agents and several of the MI5 team might be 'blown'.

When they got back to England the pair were separated, searched and questioned, SNOW sticking firmly to his story. Tar actually knew the essence of the tale already. While in Lisbon SNOW's primary British contact had been the local SIS Station Head, Ralph Jarvis to whom he seems to have given useful insights into the local Abwehr setup; an SIS note sent during the fateful trip records, in a far cry from that 1936 frostiness that 'he has been a useful ally out here and in some ways I am sorry he is going . . .' But it was soon overtaken by an SIS letter to Tar even before SNOW left Lisbon, reporting the 'disquieting news' of the encounter between Ritter and SNOW but adding the puzzling postscript that despite his confession to Ritter, SNOW had been sent back to England with £10,000, new instructions and several detonators cleverly hidden in

Parker fountain pens. But if SNOW had, as he might have put it himself, 'spilled the beans', why was he being allowed to carry on and showered with largesse?

Meetings between Liddell, Tar, Dick White, Masterman and John Marriott, who had been helping Tar on the case, and incessant interrogation of the two protagonists, never really got to the bottom of it all. As Masterman sighs in his book[1] 'the riddle of the Sphinx and the doctrine of the Trinity are straightforward and simple affairs compared to this . . . enquiry.'

All the more so when to try to complete the jigsaw, we drop in the pieces supplied by Ritter. We begin with a leap in time and geography to 1946 and to what more settled years had been the therapeutic mud baths of the spa town of Bad Nenndorf, now in the British Zone of Germany. The spa complex now had the resonant title of 'No.74 Combined Detailed Interrogation Centre Western European Area'. It is where Ritter was held in one of the makeshift cells converted out of the rows of tiled treatment rooms, though the sunken baths had been roughly filled in with cement to make a level floor. He was questioned first by the FBI, seeking to find out more about his US activities and then by John Gwyer, one of the solicitors who had been drawn into MI5. Ritter had had nothing to 'sell' and nothing to play for. He was not a war criminal and though there was some ambiguity over his Nazi Party membership, he hoped soon to be free to rebuild his life. Gwyer found him 'relatively explicit'. Ritter said that even before the last Lisbon rendezvous he had 'very little confidence in SNOW as his faith had been shaken first by the North Sea episode and secondly by the ease with which he had been able to arrange passages to Lisbon for himself and CELERY from England'. He had formed the impression, reinforced by comments from SNOW, that the British had sent CELERY onto the playing field to penetrate SNOW's network. If so the game was essentially over. But there was the 'bare possibility' that CELERY could be deployed to stave off disaster, in line with Ritter's desire to 'leave something behind him' when he was posted to Libya.[2] He therefore decided to allow CELERY to go to Hamburg. He told Gywer that while there CELERY had admitted to being a penetration agent but had offered his services to the Germans. 'These were accepted not so much from any confidence in CELERY but more in the hope the case might after all be rescued from disaster . . .'

So SNOW and CELERY had been allowed to go home. (To the relief among others of CELERY's wife Kay who had been justifiably worried at the thought of his going to Germany and whom Tar had to soothe over tea and cakes at the Grosvenor House Hotel.) As to the £10,000 in cash, Ritter claimed stoutly, and Gwyer seems to have accepted, that this must have come from another Abwehr branch since he was always careful not to give his agents too much money at any one time. Perhaps the most telling disclosure from Gwyer's questioning is that he understood Ritter had 'not found it prudent' to tell his Abwehr colleagues about his suspicions of the two men. Had he done so the Double Cross system might have been holed below the waterline.

Leaping again, this time to 1972 and the leafy Hamburg suburb where Ritter wrote his memoirs, we find some colour, and many more confusing and self-serving 'quasi-facts'. He and SNOW had met at the Estoril villa of an Abwehr agent called 'Don Carlos', with cocktails served by the Don's German-speaking secretary Juanita. JOHNNY, as he called him, was ill at ease and in answer to a direct question from Ritter, admitted that he had offered to work for the British; it was the only way he could get permission to leave for Lisbon. In the process he had given an unnamed intelligence 'Captain' (probably Tar) a shorthand, sanitised version of his Abwehr relationship. But his real loyalty lay, as it always had with Ritter and the Germans. If he went back to England the British would give him material to feed to the Germans but he alone could tell Ritter what was true and what was false. So Ritter had allowed him to return, concluding that 'Our little JOHNNY played his unremitting and fascinating game out right to the end. Over the years he had kept up his connections with the British secret service and had occasionally sold them information but all the time he was working loyally for us. The British are right to claim that JOHNNY worked for their intelligence service. But what the British did not know was that he did so only with my agreement and encouragement.'

'Today I have no doubt that JOHNNY was a master spy. The information he brought us was of the greatest possible value for Germany.'

John Masterman was right. But Tar was not a man to waste time unravelling the riddle of the Sphinx and he cut through the doubts and prevarication with the crisp judgement that the case was indeed 'blown'. SNOW was arrested in March 1941 and locked up in Stafford Prison. An MI5 operator who had studied his transmitting style radioed the Abwehr to say that because of illness it was 'Impossible to carry on. Will call you 1130 to see if any further instructions. If not I am going to pack up here and hide all gear. Regards.'

Replying for Ritter, who was by then in Libya, Hamburg tapped back 'Agree. Standing by even days. Best wishes. Regards.' We will look later at whether Ritter was disingenuous, deluded or even deceitful, but it is interesting to note that his professional antennae did twitch. When these messages were copied to him in Libya he commented for the benefit of Hamburg and, unknown to him, also Bletchley Park and Tar, that if there was any further contact with SNOW, he was to be closely questioned about his supposed illness, 'there is something fishy about it'.

Though SNOW was a detainee rather than a criminal prisoner, the distinction must have seemed a fine one as the cell doors clanged behind him. A short while later SNOW's son by his first marriage, (known in the files as 'SNOW JR', as if he were a younger brother in a public school register), a 21-year-old engineer, told MI5 he had information which would enable him to 'enter and leave enemy territory' and offered to do so for MI5. Tar decided that he did not, and that it was 'reasonably clear' he was just making a bid to secure his father's release. His view was confirmed when the young man then admitted that in 1939 he had mapped the RAF aerodromes at Biggin Hill and Kenley for his father, and had sent the plans to an address in Hamburg which his father had actually told him was a German intelligence mail drop. Not surprisingly, despite the rather brave gesture of filial support, MI5 told the Home Office he represented 'a grave potential danger' and should be detained. Tar went down to Surrey to orchestrate the arrest and search his flat, and JUNIOR – described by Liddell in his diary as 'a frightful little worm' – found himself at the Peveril Internment Camp on the Isle of Man a forlorn figure, trying to keep afloat amidst the ideological and linguistic confusion of a pot pourri of hapless foreign scientists, waiters and musicians, as well as a heavy mob of British fascists.

Tar's damage assessment after SNOW's arrest noted the other double agents who could be exposed as a result, and the MI5 personnel whose names, his among them, might have become known to the Germans. Ritter does not mention Tar by name in his memoirs but refers more than once to 'my English opponent' as if he knew it was an individual rather than an organisation. In the event agent TATE, who might logically have been the first to be suspected by the Germans, continued triumphantly until the last days of the war, and GW was able to carry on with his Spanish connection.

And what of SNOW, our anti-hero? In August 1941 Tar recorded that he had attempted to escape from Stafford, and ordered that a telephone tap be put back on Lily's phone in case he tried to contact her directly or through a 'bent' warder. In a later letter to Tar, SNOW observes, without self pity, and pointing out that he did not complain at the time, that he was badly treated in Stafford, spending seven months in solitary confinement and at one point being denied a visit to the prison barber until 'my hair grew shoulder length'. It is possible that both measures stemmed from the escape attempt, but at this distance in time they might seem harsh for a man who had never been convicted and had been locked up on no more than an unchallenged MI5 denunciation.

Never one to lose the opportunity to make his point he told Tar that 'As you are aware, I have done a considerable lot for this country and your dept. although not perhaps seeing eye to eye in our methods of arriving at a given point.' He was 'consumed with rage' at having to waste his time in jail when he could be doing useful work, and asked Tar to find a way for him to help. He could not. In the meantime though, on 26 September 1942, Tar did have something special to celebrate, the birth of his and Joan's daughter, Belinda. Underscoring the sense of MI5 as a 'family firm', Guy

Liddell was her godfather, and a good one; two silver gift spoons still remain in the family as testimony.

But in 1943 to the surprise of MI5 the Home Office transferred him to Dartmoor Prison. Even though he was not there as a rock-picking criminal but held in the Hospital Wing, designated as Camp 001, along with other political and security detainees. Compared to the sunny streets of Lisbon, Dartmoor was a rainy, granite tomb. But the adrenalin rush of playing the double game soon overrode any depression. In notes to Tar and at discreet sessions with visiting MI5 officers making the long trek from St James's Street, he was keen to pass on tidbits, for instance that a Roman Catholic priest who ministered to the detainees was acting as a courier. When the V1 flying bomb attacks began in London another letter brought 'Buster' Milmo down to Dartmoor to be told the news had reminded SNOW of a long-forgotten conversation he had once had in Germany with a scientist introduced by Ritter, who had told him the Nazis had a flesh-eating acid compound which would make a terrible weapon if only they had some way to deliver it. Perhaps they would use the new rockets? Echoing the many others who had come away baffled from encounters with the Welshman, Milmo reported wearily to Tar that 'This story may be five percent true. I doubt if it is more and have no idea where the five percent lies.'

More valuably, SNOW wormed his way into the confidence of a German whom MI5 suspected of being a latent agent but against whom they had no evidence, and wheedled enough out of him to enable MI5 to get him to confess. SNOW justified this by telling Tar in a letter in July 1943 that 'as I have taken a solemn vow to assist England, yourself and the Service for which I worked from 1936 to 1941, I am in duty bound to report this and all other matters . . .'

We know that Tar himself had the knack of winning and holding his agents' trust even when, as with SNOW, he had had to take drastic action. That SNOW was not bitter, might be inferred by the cheery tailpiece of a letter from Dartmoor of 4 December 1943 'wishing you and Mrs. Robertson and your daughter all the very best for Xmas and the New Year.' It was not quite his last farewell.

When faced with someone who had been in and out of German hands, and might have been 'turned', MI5's policy was to believe they were guilty unless they could prove their innocence; a high threshold for most, and one applied to CELERY by some of Tar's colleagues. Tar, though, stood by his man.

He went so far as to send a note to his Director, David Petrie, to say he had told CELERY at the outset that if things worked out he would make every effort to see he was considered for an RAF commission, to 'redeem himself in the eyes of the community.' Whatever his past faults CELERY was loyal, and had done 'a brave deed' by going into Germany. Tar must have known it was a lost cause but it was characteristic of his loyalty to those who had helped him that he even suggested it.

But even if he could not get the coveted commission, after some hand-wringing in St James's Street (the ever cautious John Marriott suggested that if he were not given another job, CELERY could become 'a disappointed and dangerous man, capable of doing harm') and in SIS' Broadway Buildings, CELERY was given one more mission. His Abwehr escorting officer on the trip to Germany had been Peter Sessler, a tall 25-year-old who had once played soccer for the German Youth Team. A note by Tar describes Sessler as 'good looking . . . with a four inch scar across his left cheek . . .' While they were travelling he had made several comments suggesting he had strong anti-Nazi leanings. These may have been no more than standard *agent provocateur* tactics to test CELERY, but was it worth trying to see if he could be turned around? After much debate – it was clearly a policy matter of such importance that it was referred to and initially rejected by the W Board – MI5 decided to send CELERY back to Lisbon to see what could be done. It is interesting that the plan was developed by CELERY himself, again with all the best trade craft trappings. He had given himself the alias Walter Drexner, Sessler would be smuggled out with phoney seaman's papers as George Sinclair and would be paid $3,000. He would not be detained, and the British would do their best to get him via Ottawa to Milwaukee, where his father had been living for some years. CELERY was warned he was not to use 'force or drugs'.

He came back empty-handed. Sessler, who had seen and would go on to see more frontline service, resisted the siren call, saying $3,000 was not enough 'to change everything'. It is of passing interest that he did not report CELERY's pitch to his Abwehr colleagues.

While these cases and many others consumed Tar and his team by day and on many nights, the organisation of which they were a critical part had grown out of all recognition. It is tempting to segué seamlessly from SNOW and CELERY into the very different but equally compelling TREASURE history. But we can pause for a few pages to get the "inside" view of how MI5's part in the carapace of a nation at war, and especially its counter – intelligence strategies, had evolved since those early days of the flat in Norbiton, trysts in pubs and railway buffets, and surreptitious visits to left-luggage offices.

Notes
1. J. C. Masterman, *Double-cross System in the War of 1939 to 1945*, p. 92.
2. He was sent to command a unit, known as 'Sonderkommando Ritter', with orders to set up agent networks in Egypt and French North Africa.

27

Stock Taking

We have come a long way from Richmond station. It is 1943 and we are looking at MI5's Country HQ at Blenheim Palace. Its pillared reception rooms, some with ceilings painted by Sir John Thornhill, are now partitioned with plywood and lined with filing cabinets, and barbed wire and sentry posts girdle the magnificent grounds, whose stately elms were planted to replicate the positions of the Duke's troops at the battle of Blenheim in 1704. It is a bitterly cold January day, and we meet Tar, this time not as the ace agent runner, but as a lecturer, a master of his own subject. He and the other speakers had come to the comparative tranquillity of the Oxfordshire countryside from a London under daily siege from the sky. As they sat in their St James's Street offices (which Philby thought compared well in their tidiness and air of efficiency to the 'dingy halls' and 'rabbit hutches' of SIS), they were all too aware of the bombs and incendiaries which fell in nearby Bond Street, St James's Square and Piccadilly. And coming to work after a fitful night of sirens, searchlights and bombs, crunching through broken glass across nightmare urban landscapes, gaping spaces and gutted houses shored up by wooden scaffolding where a week earlier there had been Georgian or Victorian façades.

One exception was the pragmatic and ascetic Masterman who decided that being close to the office and, as far as possible underground, was the best combination for a place to spend the night. After being bombed out of two flats, he found himself a mattress and space (even though he was not a member) in what in peacetime had been the semi-basement barber's shop of the Reform Club where the bath water was as cold as the marble floor but which had the advantage of being just a few hundred yards from the office.

As a twenty-four hour counterpoint, everyone in the office, top to bottom, had worries about a fiancé, husband, brother or sister in harm's way in a desert, a jungle or at sea.[1]

Even if wives and families had moved out to the comparative safety of the countryside, travel was a stop and start struggle; admonitory placards at railway stations asked 'Is your journey REALLY necessary?' and buses made unscheduled diversions as roads were blocked by rubble, unexploded bombs or leaking gas mains. Dust and the smell of unlaundered clothes, sweat, soot and punctured drains clogged the nostrils. Everything – food, clothing, cigarettes, eggs, soap – was rationed or in short supply; shops made defiant displays out of empty cartons of tinned foods that existed only in memory and cardboard cut outs of bunches of Fyffes' bananas, the closest most would come to the real fruit until long after the war ended.

It was probably easier to get divorced than to go through the paperwork of changing one's officially designated butcher. Wives counted their ration coupons, sewed and mended, turned cuffs and collars, and did their best to make family meals out of powdered eggs and offal, washed down with the four ounces of tea allowed each week. As the writer Leslie Blanche recorded 'lemons were becoming as rare as caviar, and sugar as precious as cocaine'. For those with money, there were exceptions, as there always are in times of war and shortage. The Black Market thrived and West End hotels and restaurants, officially limited to charging no more than five shillings a head for a meal, provided a full gourmet menu by adding swingeing 'cover' and service charges .

The year 1942 was when the pendulum swung. In February, Singapore had fallen to the Japanese, the 'largest capitulation' in British history, in Winston Churchill's words and a month later as Tar and his parents may have noted, the Japanese occupied his birthplace of Medan, as part of their drive across the Far East. But November saw the Eighth Army's victory at el Alamein, portrayed by a now more upbeat Churchill as 'not the end, nor is it even the beginning of the end but it is perhaps the end of the beginning'. As 1943 opened the starving, freezing German armies besieged in Stalingrad were close to surrender, and though Nazi U Boats were still ravaging Atlantic convoys, in just a few months the insights into their movements fed to the Admiralty by the code-breakers at Bletchley Park would force Grand Admiral Doenitz to pull his raiders out of danger. Bomb-heavy RAF and US aircraft droned through the skies above Europe and North Africa to wreak increasing havoc.

On the home front the publication just before Christmas of Sir William Beveridge's recommendations for social insurance and a National Health Service held out the promise of better things to come when the war ended. For those who wanted their pleasure now, London's West End had thirty theatres competing for audiences, alongside ten cinemas, one of the latter offering the chance to swap the real war for Hollywood's version, watching Errol Flynn and Ronald Reagan playing downed aircrew escaping from the Nazis in a now forgotten drama, *Desperate Journey*.

The secret world too was expecting its first taste of US culture, preparing for the arrival that summer of the first outriders from the US Office of Strategic Services, or OSS, from which would later emerge today's Central Intelligence Agency. Among them were the Yale academic Norman Holmes Pearson, who contributed the introduction to Masterman's revealing book, (and also co-edited with W. H. Auden an important collection of British poetry), and the enigmatic, intellectual, and deeply cunning James Jesus Angleton.[2] Neither seem to match the condescending picture painted by the acerbic journalist Malcolm Muggeridge, a wartime SIS recruit then working in Section V under Philby. Muggeridge, who makes a later appearance in the TREASURE saga, wrote:

'Ah, those first OSS arrivals in London! How well I remember them arriving like *jeunes filles en fleur* straight from a finishing school, all fresh and innocent, to start work in our frowsty old intelligence brothel. All too soon they were ravished and corrupted, becoming indistinguishable from seasoned pros who had been in the game for a quarter of a century or more.'[3]

Though the initial US unit was designated 'X-2', probably as a whimsical reflection of Tar's team, and was privy to all Double Cross and Most Secret Source materials, its principal link was with SIS, with which it shared offices in Philby's Section V Ryder Street HQ.

Thus if there was any 'ravishing' done it was by Philby rather than by Tar and his team. 'Seduction' may in fact be a better word since despite the paranoia, which was a part of his DNA, Angleton was totally taken in by Philby.

But the London visitors to Blenheim had left all this behind them – for a short while at least.

Their audience was a contingent of new MI5 recruits, shuffling in their seats, pulling at cigarettes or sucking pipes, gas masks in canvas cases tucked under their chairs. Destined for security and counter-intelligence posts in the Middle East or with the Allied armies in Europe whenever the much-anticipated Second Front was launched, they were about to sit through a five-day 'Lecture Course on Counter Espionage and Counter Sabotage Methods', some of the notes for which have survived in the archives.

Those intelligence neophytes at Blenheim were much like Jesuit seminarians filing into a chilly chapel to hear their Father Provincial, played by Guy Liddell explain the inner mysteries of their mission. He laid heavy emphasis on secrecy, in particular the 'extremely serious' consequences of any outsider getting even a hint that MI5's Most Secret Sources even existed, let alone what they revealed. They could take only brief notes, and the Course papers would be collected up when it closed. He was followed by a phalanx of his senior officers, including Tar, and a cross-section of the new blood MI5 had brought in to meet the challenges of the War. Victor Rothschild was a brilliant and brave scientist as well as the jazz-loving third baron. Helenus Milmo, nicknamed "Buster"[4] was a distinguished barrister, though in the years ahead his bruising cross-examination style would singularly fail to make a chink in the armour of the ever-artful Kim Philby when the latter came under suspicion; they probably knew each other too well. Herbert Hart, who also spoke,[5] had been a barrister at the Chancery Bar and after the war, went on to have a career of much distinction as an academic and jurist. Maxwell Knight, of the M Organisation, though not one of the newer breed,[6] was not just a skilled agent runner and orchestrator of penetration operations; he would later be known as a naturalist as well as an author and broadcaster.

Nor was another of the speakers a scholastic 'slouch.' Anthony Blunt, last seen in Wormwood Scrubs, was no doubt keeping a furtive eye out for candidate catamites, and memorising names, faces and facts for the delectation of his NKVD masters; we know from Moscow's Second World War files that he gave the Russians many MI5 names, described how Double Cross worked and highlighted Tar's rôle. To stretch the religious simile to breaking point, he was the Judas in their midst, even though years later some of the Registry girls remembered his charm and the impromptu walking tours he gave them to spotlight the history and glories of the Blenheim Palace.

Blunt aside, the Blenheim line-up bore out the post-war comment by Dick White, who joined MI5 in the 1930s after a spell as a South London schoolteacher and went on to head both MI5 and SIS, that 'in the national interest . . . we probably appropriated too much talent . . . perhaps we were too greedy'.[7]

It also brings up a perspective all too easy to ignore, the team's relative youth. Writers and their readers tend to fix on an image of an individual at a certain age – Tar in genial retirement, Philby in early middle age lying through his teeth to a gaggle of journalists, an avuncular Liddell on the front cover of his Diaries, a 1960's portrait photograph of Victor Rothschild, the essence of urbane gravitas. But when the Second World War began Tar as we have noted, was just 30, as was the 'Byronically handsome' Victor Rothschild, give or take a few months. Tomas Harris, who ran GARBO, was 31 and Dick White 33. Blunt was 32. Guy Liddell was 47, and Masterman 46. Even the urbane doyen of the intelligence world, Stewart Menzies of SIS, was just 49. Only David Petrie at 60 qualifies as an 'elder statesman'. Indeed several of those involved were by any standard striplings – Philby was 27, Trevor-Roper, the enfant terrible or as the Abwehr might have said, *das schreckliches Kind*, was just 25 and Hugh Astor joined in his early 20s.

Age matters. Historian Dominic Lieven believes that the youth and energy of some of its military leaders played a part in Russia's victory over Napoleon. Aleksandr Chernyshev and Johann von Diebitsch were 28 when they were both promoted to the rank of

Lieutenant General. Count von Nesselrode was the same age when the Tsar sent him to Paris in 1808 as his master spy, a rôle in which he was extremely successful.

We cannot put an age to Felix Cowgill of SIS. Last seen when we looked at the RSS, he was another veteran of the Indian Police, dismissed by Philby in a characteristically snide note as a man whose 'intellectual endowment was slender. As an intelligence officer he was inhibited by lack of imagination, inattention to detail and sheer ignorance of the world we were fighting in.'[8] Cowgill who in this context might be said to represent a rival religious order, perhaps the secretive Opus Dei, was also billed to speak, but at the last minute his place was taken by a Broadway colleague, a Major, whose name has been redacted but from other indications was probably Frank Foley.[9]

If we borrow the Test match analogy quoted earlier after Guy Liddell opened the bowling, Dick White came on from the Pavilion End to deliver his 'Introduction to Organisation and Method for Counter Espionage Work', (quite advanced management jargon for its time). Though Dick White was billed as "Mr", Tar who then took the podium, was by now Major Robertson. He ran a full day's session, the morning given over to 'The Running of Double Agents as a Source of Counter Espionage Intelligence', followed in the afternoon by 'Strategic Deception as a By-product to the Running of Double Agents'. Sadly, his speaking notes have not been preserved in the Archives but White's comments show how the system evolved and credit Tar with that one key step across the grimy landing in Wormwood Scrubs. Other speakers lifted the lid on interrogation of spies and travellers from abroad at the London Reception Centre, the rambling Victorian Gothic pile on Wandsworth Common, once the Royal Victoria Patriotic Schools. It is not clear from the notes whether much if anything was said on another integral part of the system, Camp 020 on Ham Common. Once Latchmere House, a hospital for 'neurasthenic' officers after the First World War, it was now another set of forbidding high-fenced buildings, to which captured spies, or anyone who had failed to pass muster at Wandsworth, were sent to be cracked through a mix of unpleasantly harsh (but never physical) interrogation, the judicious use of tidbits from Abwehr intercepts to foster the impression of British omniscience, threats of execution, planted microphones, and ingratiating 'stool pigeons'. Its numerical designation was most likely a play on Double Cross.

There were lectures on the running of 'straight' agents for counter-espionage, the detention and prevention of sabotage, port and travel control, and 'foreign intelligence services', no doubt a summary of the close ties with émigré government services in London such as the Poles and Czechs. Anthony Blunt described what MI5 was up to in 'The Study of Diplomatic Communications as a Source of Counter Espionage Intelligence', a nice euphemism for the rifling and deft resealing of supposedly sacrosanct diplomatic bags, tapping phones and placing domestic staff in Embassies to rummage through waste paper baskets. No doubt the Russians took care, on his advice, not to fall into the same traps.

But as those who listened to Tar and his colleagues that chilly morning were soon to hear, the success of Double Cross was attributable not just to skill and cunning but in great measure to those Most Secret Sources, whose importance was underlined by the fact that the topic was tackled by no less than three separate speakers. Herbert Hart spoke on 'Intercept intelligence and its uses', Major Morton Evans laid out the intricacies of the 'Interception and discrimination of Axis secret communications and its bearing on detection of illicit wireless telegraphy' while Malcolm Frost, one of Swinton's 'impositions' brought over from the BBC, took as his theme the more succinct 'Investigation into illicit wireless telegraphy'.[10]

White's remarks, the transcript of which fills eleven single-spaced small-type pages, show us what MI5 thought it had accomplished and how.[11]

First MI5 was defending a country at war, a war in which the only enemy was Germany. Apart from a sideswipe at 'Jap agents pouring into India', White makes no mention of any threat from other belligerents, or the dangerously ambivalent rôle of supposed neutrals such as Spain and Portugal, the exposure in Gibraltar or the strategic vulnerability of Ireland. Nor does he speak to subversive or espionage threats from the British Communists or underground Soviet networks, despite MI5's visceral suspicions about 'the Red Menace'.

Some of the background sketched by White we know already, notably the 'comparative bankruptcy', the 'absolute darkness' of knowledge about the Abwehr; in 1936 MI5 had just one officer dealing with 'the German aspect' and even in 1938 just two, for whom it was not even a fulltime job. They had been held back by the diversion into Fifth Column scares and the internment of aliens in the first year of war, and the resulting strain on the Registry. The arrival in London of the exiled Czech government, its intelligence service and its extensive files on the Abwehr had been a boon but the real entry point had been the Most Secret Sources, and the impetus this had given to the build up of Tar's war machine.

White stressed that MI5 was just one part, though an important one, in the larger British and Imperial intelligence and security machine. SIS and GC&CS at Bletchley Park were perhaps its most important partners. He shed some light on the shape of SIS at the time, highlighting MI5's reliance on its counter-intelligence work overseas; Section V had started the war with four officers; it now had 100. But MI5 also worked closely with the Metropolitan and regional Police forces, the Post Office mail openers with their steam kettles and bamboo tweezers, the phone tappers, and the world-wide censorship network, the immigration and Customs services, the Special Operations Executive, the Service ministries, and the Home Office. It also had to liaise with British service attachés overseas, with the service intelligence branches such as MI14 which studied the German army and MI9 which worked clandestinely in harness with SIS to return POW from enemy occupied territory, and with foreign services including the FBI and the newly formed Office of Strategic Services.

The list went on – ministries such as the Foreign Office and the Ministry of Economic Warfare, the BBC Monitoring Service – and his audience might have wondered whether there was any time left for field work. If they did, White would have confirmed their fears with the admonition that modern counter-espionage 'does not depend on high grade sleuthing but on steady, systematic clerical work'.

While the essence of our story is Tar as an autodidact of espionage, he was also the consummate Whitehall operator, an instinctive 'manager', to use a rather dull word about a man who wasn't a 'networker' in modern business jargon. As the case files show, he also had valuable access elsewhere in Whitehall and across the country, well beyond the network sketched by Dick White: the Ministries which issued 'genuine' identity cards, ration books and petrol coupons for real and notional agents, the Ministry of Information, the Fisheries Board, the Port of London Waterguard, the Department of Motor Vehicle Licences, the Registrar-General, Chief Constables and co-operative Detective Inspectors, Prison Governors, even the Westminster Coroner. His charm – a colleague said it 'could melt an iceberg' – and unruffled diplomacy were in some ways as essential to his success as his agent handling skills.

White sketched in more nuanced colours the same picture as Petrie of the prewar MI5 working mainly through letter and telephone interception and surveillance, accumulating 'enormous numbers of personal files [but] extremely few subject files which gave the objects and methods of the German secret service'.

White told his listeners that since the start of the war, 73 German agents had been caught or identified in the UK and another 49 in British possessions or British-controlled territory, the latter in many cases with the help of the letter-steamers and luggage-rummagers of the Censorship and MI5's overseas Security Officers. (White spared his listeners the other side of the coin. As the history of Camp 020 shows[12] like guddling trout, when some fish are captured for the pot, others released, Double Cross had its harsh side. Agents had to die, if only to lull the Germans into believing that British security was hard at work, and that the agents who survived were working diligently in the Nazi cause through skill, the support of existing agents and good luck rather than British deception. In all some nineteen Abwehr agents sent to the UK in the Second World War were executed, some because they were captured in a blaze of publicity that made turning them implausible, some who were obdurate even under pressure, a few who went to their deaths because politicians felt the public needed a victim. Though MI5 had a voice in their fate the ultimate decisions were a matter for the Home Office, and the Law Officers.)

Gradually peeling away the veils, White revealed that MI5 also controlled 'a considerable and at least partially successful number of double agents', operations made possible by possession of those Most Secret Sources, describing them as 'surely as potent a counter-espionage weapon as has ever fallen to the lot of any security service'. MI5 was now well placed 'to orient ourselves with some fair sense of certainty' in figuring out what its German adversaries were up to.

Everything they had learned had convinced MI5 that the Germans had made almost no effort to build up intelligence networks in Britain before the war. First and foremost, because they believed that their propaganda and British appeasement sentiments would keep Britain out of any war, and that even if they did not 'the state of our disarmament [sic] would make it impossible to fight'. Berlin also mistakenly believed that Germans working in Britain who were members of the Nazi Party's 'Foreign Organisation' could be relied on for at least basic industrial and commercial intelligence. In any event from 1933 to 1937 Germany was dealing with its own 'internal problems,' a succinct summary of Hitler's rise to dictatorial power, and after that it had to focus its intelligence efforts against his next victims – Austria, Czechoslovakia, Poland, France and Belgium. White added, perhaps a touch cynically, that even after September 1939 the Germans were 'probably justified' in believing that as long as France was in the war, the Abwehr in France could collect intelligence about Britain through its sources there.

But most importantly, White told his audience how the Most Secret Sources had been revealed. 'It . . . was really derived from intelligence . . . we got out of the case of SNOW.'

Tar's subsequent deft handling of SNOW and his cadre of fictional subagents had deluded the Abwehr into believing they already had a network on which they could rely. Those who take national pride in the extraordinary success of Double Cross, might be slightly taken aback by White's comment that the French too deserved credit: 'They suggested collaboration with SIS in this matter. The French collected a large number of double agents and some became 'double double' agents. The French made several ventures in this work and it produced important results. We ourselves appreciated its importance after the outbreak of war and it was then we went into it in a big way.'

There is a touch of shorthand in White's remarks. Pierre Paillole's memoir of his years as a senior French counter-intelligence officer before and during the Second World War gives an impressive and detailed account of successful French efforts through double agents and code breaking to penetrate and understand the work and personalities of the Abwehr stations which ringed France's frontiers. They had even come close to replicating an Enigma coding machine. According to Paillole all the intelligence the French collected was shared with SIS via 'Biffy' Dunderdale and 'Uncle Tom' Greene in Paris and at London briefings with Menzies and Cowgill. It was at one of those encounters that Cowgill told Paillole 'You are our teachers'.[13]

It seems surprising given the amount of detail the French passed to SIS, that MI5's own knowledge of the Abwehr in the run up to the war was so sketchy. It is possible that Cowgill was even then applying his own rigid 'need to know' criteria.[14]

We are telling Tar's story and it is natural to portray the Double Cross plots, like any other extraordinary endeavour, in singular terms. And men as sharp and judgemental as Trevor-Roper and Masterman, had no doubt that it was Tar's achievement. But we need to remember that as the SNOW case developed and the agents and scripts multiplied, a disciplined and co-ordinated overlay was essential. The first level was the team work and diligence of Tar and his colleagues, led with discreet professionalism and sound judgement by Guy Liddell, and their ability to work swiftly, seamlessly and in deepest secrecy. But double agents' scripts had to tally, and it was beyond the remit of MI5 to decide what intelligence, real, confected or 'tweaked' could be given to the Germans, whether it was military or related to bomb damage or civilian morale. In the early SNOW days RAF Wing Commander Archie Boyle, a man of shrewd judgement, readily gave Tar the clearances he needed on air matters, in the process rather 'chancing his arm' but more was needed.

Though Whitehall's committee traditions are often scorned as a prescription for indecision and point-scoring, bureaucratic infrastructure which guided and supported Tar's Double Cross operations proved highly productive. Nominally at the apex of the pyramid sat the W Board, a small group of senior officials, (initially the Directors of Intelligence of the three fighting services, the Chief of SIS and the Head of MI5's B Division responsible for counter-espionage), but it soon found it could safely leave most of the detailed work to the Twenty (from the Roman numerals XX which were the shorthand for Double Cross) Committee whose members covered the whole spectrum of Service, Intelligence and civilian authority. From its formation in 1941 it met no less than 226 times before the war ended, and proved a harmonious, constructive and effective 'clearing house' for all double agent issues. Masterman records that MI5's recommendations were invariably followed, an outcome no doubt facilitated by the fact that he was the Committee's Chairman. The secretary was John Marriott, a solicitor with thick-lensed glasses and a deep suspicion of all things foreign and Tar was the MI5 representative. It was nevertheless a system of checks, balances and support, what would today be termed a 'model of corporate governance' in marked contrast to the undisciplined Abwehr.

We should not leave this review without a further comment on the Blunt/Burgess/Philby nexus. Blunt had actually persuaded Liddell to use Guy Burgess as an agent to help run two London cases for MI5, and to arrange for his call-up to military service to be deferred. When flushed with that success, he suggested Burgess be taken on as an officer, Liddell was inclined to do so but the sage and suspicious Jack Curry vetoed the idea, partly on the grounds of Burgess' promiscuous homosexuality, and partly because he was not convinced Burgess had as he claimed, wholly disavowed his undergraduate Communism. Liddell did not agree but did not press the point and after Burgess defected had the grace to tell Curry his judgement had saved the Service from what 'might have been a catastrophe'.[15]

Liddell's ambivalence was in stark contrast to the brisk reaction of Colin Gubbins, when he became the prime mover of SOE in 1940.[16] When he first clapped eyes on Burgess in the corridors of its Baker Street HQ, he had him fired immediately, as 'a manifest security risk'.[17] As with Philby, immersion in the files leaves the impression that Blunt's value to the Soviets has been somewhat underplayed. A 1941 memorandum describes his rôle as being 'to correlate all investigations and enquiries concerned with the activities and communications of Foreign Diplomats and Consular officials in this country'. Other Sections dealing with the countries concerned were to keep Blunt informed of 'any developments' and he was also to act as MI5's liaison with the Foreign Office and 'other Government Departments' on policy questions relating to foreign diplomats. The Soviet intelligence archives unveiled by the assiduous Nigel West show that part of the task involved spreading disinformation among foreign diplomats and correspondents in London.[18]

The note concludes enigmatically that Blunt 'will also carry out certain special liaison and investigation work' for Guy Liddell. Philby and Blunt will often have run into each other in the corridors of St James's Street, encounters freighted, like a clandestine love affair, with the furtive frisson of a secret shared. Each had known since the early days of the war that the other was working for Moscow. As Blunt wrote in the twilight of a highly convoluted life,[19] he had been in charge of a unit of the Field Security Police near Boulogne when he ran into Philby, then a *Times* correspondent attached to the British Expeditionary Force HQ at Arras. The two had known each other casually as undergraduates, introduced by their mutual friend, Burgess, whose seductive advocacy of the Communist cause had won over the impressionable Blunt. Though an intellectually persuasive advocate, Burgess was also an incorrigible and indefatigable gossip and had told Blunt that Philby was also working for the Russians. When Philby and Blunt met again in France, Blunt told him he was too, which apparently Philby had not known. Blunt does not tell us how Philby responded. Though he must have been at the least disconcerted both by yet more evidence of Burgess' indiscretion and Blunt's own breach of basic security, he no doubt displayed his usual sangfroid.[20]

Notes

1. At least Tar's parents were relatively safe. They had moved in 1939 from their home on the Chelsea Embankment to Newtonmore in the Cairngorms, 30 miles or so from the site of the family tragedy all those years earlier at Dulnain. John Argyll died there in 1943. Mim moved back to London where she lived until her death in 1962, surrounded by her watercolours, her fine porcelain, her extended family and surely sustained by her pride in Tar and his brother. The Healing family mill, whose huge French burr stones had begun to grind in 1865, closed a year later.
2. See Mangold.
3. See Holzman, p. 37.
4. Milmo, Sir Helenus Patrick Joseph, 1908–88, Queen's Bench Division Judge, 1964–82.
5. Hart, Professor Herbert Lionel Adolphus, QC, 1907–92.
6. Knight, Charles Henry Maxwell, OBE, 1900–68.
7. Masterman, *On The Chariot Wheel*, p. 219.
8. See Philby, p. 55.
9. Foley, Francis Edward, 1884–1958. Joined SIS after the First World War. If what is claimed about Kell's recruiting prejudices is correct, as a Roman Catholic who as a young student had contemplated entering the priesthood, Foley would have been summarily disqualified as a candidate for MI5.
10. How military ranks fitted with the hierarchy of MI5 would make an interesting study in practical democracy, since in 1941 Guy Liddell is identified in the Organisation Chart as a Captain, his Assistant Director, Dick White has no military rank, while Tar, who as the head of Section B1a reports to White, is already a Major. The 1943 Chart shows Liddell still in charge and still a Captain, White is his Deputy Director and still without rank, while Tar has advanced to Lieutenant Colonel. But White would soon leapfrog him. A report on his visit to Cairo that summer indicates that White had meanwhile been vaulted out of civilian life straight into the rank of Brigadier, probably to give him appropriate "clout" in dealing with the status conscious local Army brasshats .
11. National Archives.
12. Hoare, p. 368.
13. Paillole, p. 126.
14. Long before the phrase 'honourable correspondents' became a term of art in Anglo-Saxon spy literature for the unofficial, trusted assets of an intelligence service, the French were applying it to a mixed bag of unofficial agents,

among them the celebrated African-American singer and dancer Joséphine Baker.

15. Andrew, *Defence of the Realm*, pp. 271–2.
16. Gubbins, Major-General Sir Colin McVean, KCMG, DSO, MC, 1896–1976.
17. Information from Professor M. R. D. Foot.
18. *TRIPLEX*, p. 277.
19. Blunt, *Memoirs*.
20. Burgess' persona – the promiscuous and predatory homosexuality, about which he gossiped according to Blunt with considerable exaggeration, his garlic chewing, the dirty fingernails and general slovenliness – would have made him appear even to most cynical eyes a wildly improbable candidate for a Soviet secret agent, in a sense the best type of cover. On the other hand Blunt noted in his afterthoughts that 'I have known few people with whom I have more enjoyed looking at pictures or buildings.'

28

All the World's a Stage . . .

This then was the machinery which supported Tar as the show's producer, much as beneath and behind the stage of a major theatre, out of sight of the audience, there are trapdoors, pulleys, trapeze cables, concealed drop curtains, 'flies', smoke machines, spotlights and loudspeakers, all the paraphernalia needed to stage a memorable production. And we have mentioned but probably not yet given enough credit to the rôle of SIS, whose stations in Lisbon, Madrid and other neutral outposts were often the first to snare and screen prospective Double Cross agents, and who were responsible for 'babysitting' them on their dangerous encounters with the Abwehr. We have met the show's impresario.

As for Tar's 'cast' we remind ourselves again that in telling the story we are following the footsteps and the keyboard tracks of many others. Though they are classic cases of spy craft and counter-espionage, rehashing in detail the headline-grabbing cases which have attracted most attention, serves little purpose save to emphasise Tar's breadth of responsibility, his ingenuity and his ability to handle characters just as complex as SNOW. There was ZIGZAG, in real life the swaggering safebreaker Eddie Chapman, TRICYCLE, the daring Yugoslav playboy Dusko Popov, said to have been given his code-name because of his predilection for what was once euphemistically called 'troilism' but is now blazoned in the headlines of red-top newspapers as 'three in a bed sex', or the Catalan Juan Pujol, code-named GARBO and perhaps the biggest star of them all in terms of his contribution to D-Day. GARBO would not have achieved what he did without his case officer the coruscating art dealer, artist and collector Tomas Harris, who turned out to be the perfect foil for GARBO's extraordinary imagination.[1] There was even the dead tramp who posthumously played the leading rôle in Operation MINCEMEAT.

But to pick up on the shared passion for cricket of many of those in the story, not least Tar's mother, going back over the story of these stars is rather like describing the Australian 1948 Test team, nicknamed 'the Invincibles', in terms of Bradman, Lindwall and Keith Miller, and ignoring the lesser lights such as Ron Saggers, Doug Ring and Sam Loxton, now forgotten but without whom there would have been no team and no unbroken run of victories.

In 1943, the year we visited Blenheim, Tar's staff prepared a stack of memoranda on active and latent agents. Since these do not take the stories through to the end of the war, they do not always tell us how they ended, though much of that information is available elsewhere in the archives or in the extensive literature. But if we take a cross section, we can see what Tar's team looked like, so to speak, lower down the batting order.

They highlight the extraordinary variety of the agents' backgrounds and the ways in which they were recruited by the Germans and the British. Those who swung out of the night sky on a parachute, or splashed haplessly ashore from a rubber dinghy have tended to attract more attention than the majority, who arrived as refugees, or escaping Allied prisoners of war, or simply as part of the human detritus of war, and were sifted first at the RVPS and if there were doubts about them, at Camp 020.

Following them alphabetically is not only equitable but has the advantage of allowing us to open with the glamorous BRONX, divorcée daughter of a Peruvian diplomat who had been accredited to Pétain's Vichy government but was now in Madrid. She was, Section B1a noted with a hint of a middle-class sniff 'a typical member of the cosmopolitan "smart set"' who had lived in Paris and the South of France. Less typically, after reaching England when the war started she had been recruited by SIS and sent back to France, where she 'accomplished a successful mission' for three fraught months in 1942. Quite what this was the note does not reveal but it certainly put her in contact with the Abwehr, who as she told MI5 after her return, had asked her to supply industrial intelligence by letter to a cover address, first in the Unoccupied Zone of France, and later Lisbon. She was to be paid £100 a month via Switzerland, dressed up as alimony from her husband. Christopher Harmer dubbed her 'BRONX' after a then popular cocktail, essentially a Bond-style martini also shaken not stirred, but with orange juice and red vermouth added.[2]

Under his guidance she began by sending off 'low grade industrial information and political chatter' scribbled in invisible ink between the lines of conventional letters. She was then used with success to confuse the Germans with 'chaff', (some purportedly picked up from a drunken officer in the 400 Club and passed on in an improbable code involving payments to 'dentists' and 'doctors'), about rumoured Allied landings on the Atlantic coast of France, and in southern Norway. Her partying circuit was at the highest level – many noble Lords came a'leaping – though one wet-lipped comment on her file suggested she might be a lesbian – and she ran up large gambling debts. She kept writing to D-Day and beyond, diverting one SS tank division from Normandy to the Atlantic coast, and her seventeenth and final letter on 3 May 1945 was an elegant Tar/Harmer 'dangle' to try to smoke out Nazi post-war plans. She told her Abwehr controller 'Events succeed each other so quickly that everyone here thinks of the war being over but no one knows who is really in command in Germany. It seems to me useless to send you military information but I think I could from time to time send you political observations which would be of use to you in the reconstruction of Germany once this terrible period is over.'

If BRONX was 'glamorous', BRUTUS, Roman Garby Czerniawski of the Polish Air Force, in his 30s when the war started, would qualify for 'brave', 'dashing' or any other of the adjectives that rightly characterise the bold Polish spirit. After his country fell, he escaped to the Polish Forces HQ in exile in Paris, spent a short time in jail when the Germans marched in, escaped again into the Unoccupied Zone but soon returned to Paris undercover to build and run the Interallié network, an asset of SIS rather than the Special Operations Executive. He did this for a year, sending London what the file calls 'extremely detailed and valuable' reports, until the network was penetrated and rounded up by the Abwehr through a double agent ploy of their own, using a Frenchwoman, Mathilde le Carré, nicknamed 'the Cat'. BRUTUS spent several months in jail. Between March and June 1942 he was in delicate negotiations with the Abwehr, who were pressing him to go to England as their agent, to report on aircraft production military movements and 'the possibilities of German-Polish collaboration'. This he eventually agreed to do. The W Board note suggests that this was because the Germans held several of his relatives as hostages. An authoritative later history tells us that in fact he agreed to work with the Germans to save the lives of members of his network.[3] The Germans gave him a radio and a confected cover story of escape and evasion, which he tried out once on MI5 before telling the truth and agreeing to work for Tar. Delicately handled by Hugh Astor, adventurous and distinguished scion of the family which had once owned *The Times*,[4] he became one of the most prolific suppliers of a mass of credible disinformation, right up to and past D-Day, ostensibly based on his position in the Polish HQ in London. The most reliable source on FORTITUDE[5] tells us that judging by the Germans' intercepted messages, BRUTUS's reputation with the Germans as a trustworthy agent stood as high as those of the far better publicised GARBO and TRICYCLE.

'Trouble' might have been a better name for another young Polish airman who joined Tar's team as CARELESS. Or even, at the end 'Sadness.' Like BRUTUS he got to Paris after Poland fell and left again, but in his case because he was in trouble with the police. He reached Spain where he was snared by a wallet-waving Abwehr agent, and trained in a spy's black arts with the aim of using them in London to join the RAF and send reports on deliveries of US aircraft. His contacts aroused the suspicions of his compatriots in exile and after a voyage to Glasgow replete with accusations and admissions reminiscent of that earlier 'Ship of Fools' trip on the *Barbados*, he found himself working for Tar, but sending his reports not from some suburban safe house but from a cell in Brixton Prison where he spent five months while his story was checked. He told the Germans his health had led the RAF to turn him down but that he had joined Balloon Command. He was eventually released and sent to join the Pioneer Corps, that rag, tag and bobtail collection of German and Austrian refugees, misfits and the unfit, a move he deeply resented. He wanted to rejoin the Poles but the latter still distrusted him and told Tar if they ever got their hands on CARELESS they would throw him in jail. Though MI5 had persuaded themselves otherwise, the Poles were convinced that he had betrayed Polish escape lines to the Germans.

Meantime CARELESS had begun to be a source of much fretting in St James's Street: he went absent without leave, bounced cheques, and 'got drunk at inconvenient moments'. Though the Most Secret Sources showed the Germans were satisfied with what CARELESS was supplying, his instability – at one point he even attempted suicide – suggested to B1a that the case should be closed. A file note fulminated that CARELESS was, 'a wastrel and a blackguard of high order who has proved himself time and time again not only to be utterly irresponsible but totally untrustworthy'. They stayed their hands for a while because of a worry that shutting him down might compromise GARBO, a far more significant asset. But when he continued to misbehave, he was thrown into an internment camp. In retaliation he went on 'writer's strike'. The case had to come to an end, happily without risk to GARBO. But it was not an end for CARELESS or his compatriots. For the latter revenge was a dish best eaten cold, washed down with a bottle of vodka. They would not give up on the charge that he was a traitor. After the war he faced deportation, technically a matter for the Home Office. Though MI5 expressed mild concern that if he was sent back he might well be shot, they did not prevail and 'home' he went, to what, we do not know.

We need hover only briefly over DRAGONFLY, born in England to long-resident German parents, a small-scale business man some of whose dealings were recorded as 'somewhat shady'. His case was not spectacular, but is of interest because the original 'pitch' that he work for the Abwehr came from his sister in Germany, and because he eventually found himself working under the remote control of TREASURE's handler Emile Kliemann. He turned himself into the

British in London and agreed to work for Tar. Like so many others he took the mystery man's flight to Lisbon to meet the Germans, returning with 'a considerable amount' of cash, a cover address for letters and one of Kliemann's favourite toys, 'a wireless set disguised as a portable gramophone'. Like the banks and bordellos, the radio shops in Lisbon must have done brisk business supplying the Abwehr.

Though they were unrelated cases FATHER and FIDO both represented yet another Abwehr obsession, to get their hands on a British fighter aircraft. FATHER, Henri Arents, was a Belgian pilot originally recruited by the Abwehr for a mission to the US to collect intelligence on aircraft production. Turned down for a visa he told the Germans he would go to the UK and volunteer for the RAF. He revealed his story to SIS in Lisbon and offered to become a double agent. The London screeners thought him 'trustworthy' and he was taken on with 'real' cover as a serving RAF officer. By 1943 he had become a test pilot at the Vickers factory which produced the Battle of Britain-winning Spitfire fighter. The opportunity was irresistible. So much so that the W Board system found it more and more difficult to concoct plausible responses to German questions without revealing too many secrets. The Germans swallowed unhesitatingly the story that FATHER had been posted abroad. Again truth and fiction were deftly merged. He was in fact sent to the Far East. The Germans attracted by the new potential this offered, made considerable efforts to send him a wireless via Istanbul and Bombay. He used it to send high grade 'chaff' until August 1944, when 'real personal difficulties' dictated that he be sent home. But even then the merry-go-round continued. Before he left, FATHER notionally recruited a subagent, an Indian attached to Strategic Air HQ in Calcutta to whom he notionally handed his set.[6]

FIDO, a young French air force pilot, had been suborned by the Abwehr in Paris, again with the aim of getting him into the RAF as a fighter pilot in the UK or even North Africa, to 'shoot down as many German planes as possible in order to establish confidence', (the Abwehr evidently applied the Nelson touch in facing what in the business sphere would rightly be called a serious 'conflict of

interest') and eventually fly back to Nazi territory with 'the latest
type of plane he could find'. In the meantime he was to send back
by letter whatever data he could collect on aviation, troop movements and technical developments.

Once in London, he opened up fully to the Wandsworth interrogators who passed him on to the taciturn men in St James's Street
as 'a quiet and thoughtful type of Frenchman with a rather earnest
outlook on life'. The plan was to send him on a training course for
six to nine months to see how he, and the German handling of him,
developed, but the file note suggests the case went nowhere, perhaps
because of some lingering questions over his reliability.

As SNOW taught us, Wales was another Abwehr obsession. One
of those used to pander to it was GWLADYS, an odd soubriquet for
a young Welshman with a flair for languages, who chose to join the
Merchant Navy from Oxford instead of the armed forces. He spent
two years as a seaman including a harrowing encounter with a
torpedo, before he applied to train as a radio operator. Tar's
antennae were by then well tuned – a roving Welshman who spoke
Norwegian, French and Spanish, with 'some knowledge' of
German, Portuguese, Italian and Swedish was a valuable asset. He
became a 'mole' inside the Welsh Nationalist party. On a voyage to
Dublin he flaunted his Nationalist fervour to such good effect that
he came into contact with the Pan Celtic Union whose cranky
ambition was to build a Welsh, Irish and Scottish nationalist
coalition to fight 'English domination and British imperialism'. The
Union was keen to enlist the support of nationalist Bretons and the
next scene in the plot, arranged via SIS, was to 'dangle' GWLADYS
in front of the Abwehr, who were known also to be keen to
encourage the Bretons, and get them to ship copies of the Pan-
Union manifesto to Brittany in the diplomatic bag. Welzien of the
Lisbon Abwehr took the bait on GWLADYS's next voyage, and also
asked him a few questions about the ship he was on, and its sailing
route, but the case seems to have faded away either, as the file implies
because the Abwehr in Lisbon were in some internal disarray at the
time, or more likely because they sensibly decided not to spend any
time chasing such a will o' the wisp project.

We can wonder whether Philby ever heard about JOSEF, also a seaman, but who in contrast to GWLADYS was not only a Russian and a Communist but a former Soviet secret policeman.

Thirty years old, 'undoubtedly clever and astute', JOSEF first came to MI5's attention after sabotage incidents on a Dutch ship 'which were never satisfactorily explained' and when he sailed into the UK in March 1941 he found himself held for seventeen months at the London Reception Centre. His 'get out of jail free' card was an improbable friendship he struck up with a fellow internee, a Mr. Matsumoto, who was paying the price for serving as the Honorary Press Attaché at the Japanese Embassy. No doubt remembering his Moscow training about the value of stool pigeons, JOSEF reported their conversations to the officer in charge of the Centre and soon found himself enlisted as an agent on the first of several voyages under seaman cover to Lisbon. There he called at Matsumoto's introduction on the Japanese Legation and met at various times the Assistant Military, Naval and Press attachés and two 'sabotage experts' whom he believed were Hungarians. He gave them some information on Clyde shipbuilding and outlined a plan for sabotage in Glasgow docks. His new friends told him to go back to Britain, and stay there. He was instructed to focus on getting intelligence back to them by courier on ship and landing barge building, and convoy movements and elaborate his sabotage plans. Though he sent several messages to them, for whatever reason, perhaps Japanese timidity and inexperience at the game, the 'dangle' did not work and the case petered out in 1944.

MUTT and JEFF merit inclusion in this selective and idiosyncratic cast list for two reasons. First, unlike most of the others they were sent over by the Germans primarily as saboteurs. Thus the games Tar and Christopher Harmer had to play were far more complex. Second, along with TATE they had the distinction of being the only double agents whom we know Tar invited to spend time at his home, an illustration of his relationship techniques. Joan Robertson was loyal and stoic and knew how the game was played, but it is doubtful Tar shared with her that JEFF was described on the MI5 file as 'an undesirable character'. Even with 'minders' from the

Field Security Police any wartime household might justifiably have felt alarmed at entertaining German agents who may have been persuaded to work for the British but of whose real loyalties there was no definitive or secure test.

John Moe, alias MUTT, was 30, the son of a Norwegian-British marriage. Born in London, he moved to Norway with his parents when he was just two years of age. Even seen against the background of our litany of implausible and exotic case histories, his chosen career as a ladies' hairdresser seems an unusual jumping off point for a sabotage mission. But when the Norwegian economy collapsed after the German occupation in April 1940, just getting enough to eat became the priority. There was not much demand for permanent waving and highlights. Casting around for a job he was introduced by a mutual friend to JEFF, Tor Glad, who found him a place in the German Censorship Office in Oslo where he was already working; JEFF had been on the Abwehr payroll as an informer since the war started.[7] We can now "fast forward" to April 1941.

MUTT and JEFF, now trained by the Abwehr in codes, radio work and in the use of explosives, splash ashore on a chilly Aberdeenshire beach. A German seaplane, reminding us of Ritter, had dropped them offshore and they crested the grey swells in a rubber dinghy. They lost no time in turning themselves in and a conveyor belt involving the police, the MI5 Regional Security Officer, a long train ride to London and a Black Maria brought them to Camp 020 on Ham Common and a new beginning as two more valuable assets for Tar, operating out of an anonymous semi-detached house in Hendon. Though sabotage was their main mission, the Abwehr had also instructed them to report on RAF aerodromes, troop movements and on civilian morale, a brief wide enough to allow Tar and Christopher Harmer to use them to begin their new careers by feeding back deception information about a supposed British plan to invade Norway. That was easier than sabotage, which required action that would be visible, attract press coverage that would get back to the Germans, but which was neither damaging nor seriously alarming. Action which called for exquisitely careful co-ordination with the local police, emergency services and journalists. Their 'bombing' of a power station in Bury St. Edmunds, a food depot in Wealdstone and a clutch of empty Army huts so impressed their controllers that the Abwehr not only replenished their cash via the mail but arranged for the Luftwaffe to make four parachute drops of wireless equipment, cash and sabotage gear in the remote Highlands. That the sabotage gear turned out to have originated with SOE, probably captured by the Germans in one of their own successful deception operations in Occupied Europe, did not detract from MI5's satisfaction at this haul.

As we have seen, many Double Cross cases faded or were allowed to fade discreetly from sight either because of waning German interest in the product or more often because of an agent's actual or perceived instability. Here JEFF faded first, bored, drinking too much, and prone to indiscretion. He knew too much to be allowed to roam free, and found himself, to his angry disappointment, interned on the Isle of Man. His wireless remained with MUTT who operated it adroitly in JEFF's 'handwriting' without raising German suspicions. MUTT's war ended satisfactorily. JEFF's might have finished badly. He was deported to Norway to face charges from his earlier alleged collaboration with the Germans but that 'Hidden Hand' got to work and the charges were dropped.

It would be simple to run through the entire alphabet but these summaries are sufficient to show the human difficulties with which Tar and his team had to grapple daily if not hourly over and above scripting, clearing and synchronising the streams of information to be put across to the other side.

As the agents told their stories, Tar and his colleagues had a formidable task. First came the key character assessments. Who could be trusted? What were their motives? Where did their loyalties lie? If they passed the close questioning, the records checks and in the final analysis the inquisitors' indefinable litmus test – red or blue, good or bad – and were accepted as double agent material they then had to be assigned to a case officer, found somewhere to live, to write their secret letters, and tap out their messages with an MI5 operator at their elbow. They needed identity cards, ration books, petrol coupons, money, housekeepers, 'minders' and real jobs or plausible cover stories. A discreet eye had to be kept on their love lives, how much they drank, what they gossiped about in pubs, any signs of depression or second thoughts. One estimate[8] is that it took a team of nine or ten headed by the case officer to 'service' each agent. The 1943 memoranda profiled more than 30 agents. By no means were all run simultaneously, some were dormant, some faded quickly, some needed far more care and feeding than others, and some support teams looked after more than one agent. But the figures do give a broad sense of the overall logistical challenge Tar faced, a challenge made even more daunting by the need to keep each case in its own watertight security compartment.

Once the agents were 'bedded down' the team were faced with the 'Rubik's Cube' challenge of finding, creating, clearing and co-ordinating the responses to the Abwehr's instructions and queries, making sure not only that each piece of the deception jigsaw did not have some latent operational or strategic risk, but fitted the ones around it. Whatever was reported by the agents and the growing number of their completely fictional sub-agents were events and scenes which they themselves had witnessed – which meant taking them as far afield as Scotland, the major port cities, the industrial Midlands and the West Country – or could plausibly claim to have seen for themselves in their notional jobs or had maybe heard from some loose-lipped but well placed contact.

These were not just troop sightings, bomb damage reports or even faked sabotage attempts. There were sophisticated rumours supposed to emanate from senior Civil Servants, a bold and successful plan to delude the Japanese, via the agents, and waves of spurious radio traffic, that the aircraft carrier *Indefatigable* had been commissioned a year before her actual launch. The D-Day deception apart, which stands in a class of its own, one of the more significant feints in terms of its tactical impact was the false information put across via TATE about the laying of new minefields which, reinforced by the happy accident of a U Boat sinking in the area, convinced the Germans to order their submarines to stay clear of a 3,600 square mile swathe of sea south west of Fastnet Rock, thus clearing it for Naval and convoy traffic.

Writing long after the war Tar cited this as one of B1a's most successful deceptions. The other – FORTITUDE apart – was the deft and politically sensitive web of delusions that were spun to mislead the Germans – successfully about the mean point of impact of their V1 and V2 rockets, which must have saved thousands of lives.

The stream of flimsy decrypts provided by the Most Secret Sources had to be read and re-read with care and suspicion, cross-checked and collated, to see how the stories were being received, and how the Abwehr was assessing its agents and their material, and what plans were being concocted for new arrivals. Hardly less complex was devising schemes to enable the Abwehr to send money into Britain for their supposed agents without knowing they were doing so under British control. The inventiveness of St James's Street (one of whose imported talents was the City banker Sir Edward Baring, related by marriage to Liddell) was matched by the gullibility of the Germans. Onto the deception stage were wheeled fictional Spanish traders who needed pesetas in Spain and as neutral citizens were happy to pay out sterling to an agent in London in exchange, and a London theatrical producer nervous about the outcome of the war, delighted and relieved to pay sterling to an intermediary against dollar credits in Lisbon.

On top of all this, Tar and his colleagues needed 'people skills' of a high order to deal with those in Whitehall who fretted, rightly, about giving the Germans any information of strategic or defence importance and with their opposite numbers in SIS, still guarding their right to control agents and intelligence one inch outside the Three Mile Limit; SIS ran double agents of its own for counter-espionage purposes,[9] but told MI5 as little as possible about them. At a more human level Tar and his team had to cope with their agents' tantrums, worries, the occasionally difficult relationships some of them had with their national governments in exile in London and their domestic travails.

The files are full of personal dramas in which Tar and others mixed the rôle of 'Agony Aunt' and 'Ace of Spies'. GARBO's wife Carmen Aracelli, was a temperamental Spaniard, who had been his active partner from the start of his espionage career when she helped him in his first approach to the British. She had joined him in London in 1942 but in June 1943 complained to MI5 that she felt neglected, and wanted to return to Spain. If MI5 wouldn't give her an exit visa she would go to the Spanish Embassy and tell them everything. Though Liddell thought she deserved to be locked up, he concluded with regret that there were no grounds for doing so.[10]

The active minds at St. James's Street produced several flights of fancy. One was to warn the Spanish Embassy that a woman answering her description intended to assassinate the Ambassador, so that she would be 'flung out' if she made any approach. This was abandoned, on the grounds that it would mean the police getting involved 'which would be a bore'. Despite the flimsy legal basis Tar was sent to warn her that even threatening to go to the Embassy might have dire consequences for her under the draconian Defence Regulations. A hysterical call then brought GARBO'S radio operator to her flat, where he found her in a room 'full of gas' though he concluded it was 'a bit of play acting for his benefit'. Tomas Harris's wife Hilda, was sent in to calm her down. The next morning it was Tar's turn again. He persuaded Aracelli to sign a statement that it was all her fault and that she would behave. But more was needed. The final page in the plot called for her to be taken down to Camp 020 at Ham in a Black Maria where she found her husband, who had allegedly been locked up.

The story – in the scripting of which GARBO himself had an active hand – was that because of her behaviour MI5 had decided to shut the case down and asked him to send one final message, at which he 'blew up', refused and threatened to give the whole show away. Hence his arrest. Shocked, Carmen said it was her fault, and after another heavyweight warning the next morning at MI5's 'front office' in Northumberland Avenue she promised she would make no more trouble and the couple were reconciled. According to the same Liddell diary entry GARBO told MI5 it was 'one of the most distasteful things that he had had to do in his life'.

Day and night, seven days a week, Tar could not afford to drop or muddle any of the tangled threads or to lower his guard, either with his agents or with the Germans. It was not just an office job. As well as MUTT and JEFF, TATE too spent time at Tar's home. To judge from scraps of correspondence TATE was there for some time, a spell he remembered with nostalgia much after the war, though he seems to have forgotten the evening when the Robertsons' cook – who did not know who this guttural guest really was, waved her carving knife menacingly to demonstrate how, if she came across a German parachutist she would cut his throat. TATE himself had no idea that behind the geniality, the welcome to the family home, lay a grimmer reality. As long as a German invasion remained a threat MI5 had to worry about their double agents falling into enemy hands. The careful contingency plans called for them to be moved to three hotels in North Wales. Those who were not trusted were to travel in handcuffs, under armed escort. And as Tar told 'Tin Eye' Stephens at Camp 020, 'If there is any risk of the more dangerous cases falling into enemy hands, they will be liquidated forcibly.' David Petrie was more specific telling TATE's designated escort, 'As it is of vital importance that TATE should not fall into the hands of the enemy, you must be prepared to take any step necessary to prevent this happening.'[11]

But, surprisingly, given the workload he had to juggle, double agents were not Tar's sole focus. In the style of a chess grandmaster hopping from table to table playing simultaneous games, he found his professional and diplomatic skills much in demand in MI5's sticky relationships with another of the secret world's silos.

Notes

1. Harris, Tomas, 1908–64. Given our sense of MI5 as 'a family firm' it is not surprising to find that his considerable achievements in the field of art as a dealer, collector, scholar and artist should have been captured for the *Oxford Dictionary of National Biography*, Article 33731, by his friend, MI5 colleague and fellow connoisseur Anthony Blunt who also wrote the catalogue for a 1975 exhibition of Harris' work at the Courtauld Institute. Both were close friends of Guy Burgess.
2. In 1934 it was ranked third among 'The World's 10 Most Famous Cocktails'.
3. See Foot, M.R.D. and Dear, C. B.
4. Astor, the Hon Hugh Waldorf, 1920–99.
5. Hesketh, p. 186.
6. Howard, p. 208.

7. He later stoutly denied he had ever actually given them any information.
8. Holzman, p. 46.
9. See e.g. Jefferys.
10. Liddell, 22 June 1943.
11. Andrew, *Defence of the Realm*, p. 258.

29

Setting Europe Ablaze

Baker Street – named after William Baker its eighteenth century developer – is best known as the fictional home of Sherlock Holmes. Tar became familiar with it in the Second World War when several buildings there were taken over by the all too real Special Operations Executive (SOE) whose mission was 'to set Europe ablaze' through sabotage and subversion. Rather like Lord Swinton, it was a cuckoo plopped into the Whitehall intelligence nest by Winston Churchill in 1940. SOE and the brave agents, among them young women, girls even, of great spirit, who were sent on dangerous and often fatal missions in Occupied Europe, made an invaluable contribution to winning the war. But it also made enemies for Whitehall, which reinforced its tendency to be secretive, defensive, even prickly.

It was well aware that its older rival SIS, some of whose functions it had usurped, regarded SOE as an unprofessional and insecure upstart whose noisy ways might upset its delicate intelligence networks overseas, as well as a competitor for scarce resources, not least aircraft. It knew too that in its principal rôle as defender of the security of the Realm, MI5 had doubts about whether SOE checked its recruits carefully enough, whether its methods in the field, especially its communications, were secure, and whether SOE agents returning to the UK from their missions might include men and women who had been 'turned' by the Germans.

Even though it would not take long to show that some of the doubts were tragically justified, SOE tended to bristle when in its view, MI5 tried to do its job and meddled in a quasi-military mission which SOE was fulfilling with energy and against the odds. The last thing it needed was the heavy-handed interference of quasi-policemen or for that matter, the hauteur of SIS. An SOE internal note complained that an SIS proposal about signals traffic had 'an under-tone of condescending patronage bordering on the impertinent'.[1]

Communications between MI5 and SOE were thus initially stilted, with heavy emphasis by SOE on the formalities of who was authorised to talk to whom, and how SOE should be referred to in secret and semi-secret correspondence, bureaucratic mumbo-jumbo of a sort which again suggests SOE were anxious to use the shield of secrecy to ward off outside interest, especially from another practitioner of the black arts.

With his now well-honed skills in handling awkward people, and his technical knowledge, Tar made a valuable contribution to the edgy relationship. In an early attempt to cross the moat, he had circulated a note within B Division in November 1941 suggesting that if he had access to SOE signals traffic, and could get a sense of the form and content of messages sent back by SOE agents 'under field conditions' it would help him and his colleagues as they drafted material for their double agents to put across to the Germans. He would also like to know when one of their agents 'went bad' or was captured with his wireless; there could be 'real value in luring the Germans into deceptive traffic by pretending London did not know the set had fallen into German hands'. The first suggestion went nowhere; the second took a while to come to fruition, not least because SOE was institutionally disinclined even in the face of solid evidence, to admit that any of its people had been 'blown', or in intelligence jargon, 'brulé'.

But Tar persisted and a month later we find him at a private dinner with SOE's head of security Lt. Commander John Senter,[2] who had himself spent some time at MI5, and Colonel Munn, who ran the SOE Training Schools at Beaulieu (and would later do the same job for SIS and its rather smaller and bleaker establishment at Fort Monckton, near Gosport). In one of his rather rare positive comments, Philby remembered Munn as 'a young colonel of the sensible type as opposed to the no-nonsense military type, the mystical military and the plain silly military'.

Tar gave them a brief and no doubt carefully honed summary of what went on in St James's Street and wrung out of Senter the concession that a small group of MI5 officers – Tar would be the first – could attend the SOE training course, though he 'most forcibly impressed' on Tar that this was a personal favour and was not to be made widely known within MI5.

Tar went to Beaulieu for ten chilly days in February. His record of what he was told in that cluster of 'Stockbroker Tudor' mansions dotted around Lord Montagu's estate on the Solent reads like an espionage writer's notebook, except that the training was in deadly earnest, an attempt in an all too short spell to force-feed agents with the skills, disciplines and tricks which might – if he or she also had luck on their side – keep them from death at the hands of the Germans. Caution, secrecy, the 'need to know', blending in, alley-cat alertness and distrust, displaying leadership, were leitmotivs, along with the more pragmatic subjects like memory training, resisting interrogation, and coding. But unpleasant reality was not shirked. SOE officers in the field dealing with a local agent who might have 'gone bad' faced 'an awkward problem . . . the semi-honest man is the most difficult to deal with . . . It is a mistake to bump the man off. What are you going to do with the body?'

And in an echo of language we have heard from Tar, their advice was to warn anyone about whom there were doubts 'that if he goes bad you cannot be responsible for the consequences. Try to avoid telling him this directly, rather, insinuate it . . . Tell him the [SOE] security organisation is very strong.'

In the field, network organisers should not carry a gun, if they were stopped and searched it would mean instant incrimination. For some reason a piece of lead pipe was thought less of a give-away, while in Norway a knife was unexceptional, since they were carried by men of all classes.

But if their luck ran out and they faced an 'extreme emergency' the agents could fall back on the 'L' or lethal pill, which was claimed to act instantaneously though it is hard to know how this could be proved.

Tar did not take part in one of the standard 96 hour practical exercises, in which SOE trainees were sent 'blind' to an urban or industrial area, told to find somewhere to stay (in itself not easy in wartime) and given a local factory or communications hub as an observation target, or a more mundane field assignment such as roaming a provincial art gallery to pick up or conceal clandestine correspondence behind one of the more remote exhibits. What they did not know was the local police and even the gallery attendants had been tipped off about 'suspicious characters' and that they were likely to end up in a cell trying to defend their cover story and avoid the ignominy of calling home to the Training School. But Tar, always a lateral thinker, did warn SOE that the Germans knew the names and locations of many of the factories important for the British war effort. If a trainee was sent to find out about the security, staffing or production levels of one of these plants, and later fell into German hands, he might be forced into giving them damaging information.

Tar told John Senter, perhaps with a touch of deliberate flattery, the course had taught him more about counter-espionage than all his years at MI5, though he also offered some professional comments on the course material. His notes would be a handy primer for agent runners anywhere.

Any mission stood or fell on the cover story. 'From a certain amount of experience of interrogating people, not that I am an authority on the subject, it is practically impossible by ordinary, straightforward interrogation to break down a person who has a watertight and genuine story', Tar wrote. Perhaps with GARBO's case officer Tomas Harris in mind, he gave as an example that 'if you say you are an art dealer you must (a) be an expert in art and (b) make some pretension of dealing in art treasures.' But sometimes there was a case for a story so improbable that it had to be true. He cited the example (maybe he had been late home once too often) of the man who turns up an hour late for dinner and makes an 'ordinary, humdrum' excuse which in normal circumstances would not be believed. 'But if he produces a story with a wealth of detail, which is quite out of the ordinary, he will probably get away with it.' He recommended that SOE agents should be professionally interrogated on their cover stories before they went into the field. He even advised on questioning technique. 'It is a hundred to one that if you [as interrogator] affect to be ignorant of a certain point, and possibly make a thoroughly misleading statement on purpose, you will nearly always be taken up by a person who is anxious to display his greater knowledge, thus obtaining the desired answer.'

Clothing was important. Sounding a touch like the fictional Baker Street detective, Tar recalled a case 'where a man's story broke down because the state of his boots did not conform to the story he tried to put across'.

So too were papers. The Abwehr had 'fallen down badly' by sending agents into the UK with identity cards which did not stand up to scrutiny. They had made the 'unforgivable mistake' of writing the address in a Continental script, and the cards had been folded by machine rather than by hand. (He did not mention that through SNOW he had helped confuse the issue by giving the Abwehr examples of entirely bogus and thus easily recognised, card numbers.) Ideally identity papers for agents sent to Europe should be obtained on the ground, rather than forged at SOE's 'documents factory' at the former Briggens Hotel near Harlow.

How should agents travel in territories where there were strict police controls? Obviously they stood a better chance of slipping through at morning and evening rush hours. In describing Tar's work we have used several similes from the film world and it is interesting to see that, in advising how an agent should best describe to his handler someone he or she had met, 'a useful method which has served us in very good stead is to compare a person with a film star, such as Clark Gable, or a smaller version of Charles Laughton. We had a case not so long ago when one of our people in Spain described a German agent as being like a man in a certain Austin Reed advertisement.' (Such comparisons date and fade fast; today's would presumably be with George Clooney or a pectorally perfect model for Calvin Klein underwear.)

There was also surveillance. A man and woman together 'never arouse the same suspicion as a lone man or even two men loitering' but it was also vital to ensure the watchers themselves were not under observation, though this could get complicated. He recalled MI5's trailing of a suspected Russian agent in London some years earlier, in which the street line-up swiftly evolved into: 'suspect, our watcher, his [NKVD] watcher, our watcher'. Unfortunately he does not relate how the impasse ended. Better to avoid encounters which could be observed, for which cinemas were ideal. Buses, trains and trams were also useful rendezvous sites, while cars were good for private conversation and also made shadowing easier to spot.

The best way for a wireless operator to stay out of German hands was to run the set from a city building, not out in the country where direction finders could quickly home in, to keep messages short and to try to send them in a style which made them seem like regular military or commercial signals, If an agent was on the run, Tar counselled primly, 'the asylum offered by houses of ill-repute and kindred establishments should not be overlooked'. They had a tradition of asking no questions and were susceptible to 'commodity bribes' such as soap. (Here his English background may have led him astray. Someone more familiar with the facts of French life would have been aware that 'maisons de tolérance' from the exotic Le Chabanais in Paris, a favoured haunt of King Edward VII, to the prison-like Palais Oriental in Reims, were regulated by the local vice squads. Their proprietors and their gangster backers thus lived in uneasy but mutually profitable collaboration with the police, a murky mix of black market racketeering and back handers in which the police made good use of the owners and their girls as informers. In the words of one social historian, for the police the brothel regime 'existed only with them, through them, and around them'.)

Tar also told SOE of a technique they might like to consider, which was for agents in the field to send the German authorities a stream of anonymous letters denouncing real or fictitious suspects. It was a time consuming exercise but would take the Germans' 'eye off the ball'. MI5 had itself tried it on a very small scale but the results 'if any, were a little disappointing'. (One target of these false missives was the German Ambassador in Dublin.)

Reporting back to his MI5 colleagues Tar noted he had been much impressed by SOE's teaching on how to sabotage factories – rather than blow up the plant itself, look for the small vulnerable point which, if damaged would bring production to a halt. He evidently enjoyed retelling the story of one SOE harassment initiative which fed powdered glass into the artificial fibre used to make German uniforms. 'The result was amazing, as it not only had the effect of making the wearers scratch themselves but when they did so it tore their skin to ribbons.'

Tar was one of the few MI5 officers trusted by SOE. When after another Whitehall turf war SOE had finally wrested control from SIS of its radio communications, it was Tar to whom they turned for help. Which radio frequencies in Europe were not being used by commercial or Government transmitters? What did MI5 know about German wireless sets and the instructions given to their operators? Could he tell them about German wireless detection methods? Tar helped as best he could,[3] though when he came back from Beaulieu he had advised (presciently but in vain, given SOE's later travails), that radio traffic between the field and London was 'extremely dangerous' and should be kept to an absolute minimum. He saw no reason why its agents needed to be in 'continuous communication' with the UK.

He did not tell SOE that he was playing exactly the same game and knew phoney traffic when he saw it. He could not. To give even a hint to an organisation which did not 'need to know', to use the official jargon, and was in any case suspected of being less than tight-lipped, risked revealing the acutely sensitive secrets of the Double Cross agenda. But as an example when the Germans rolled up an SOE network around Toulouse, and began to play its radio back to London, it was Tar's experience and decisive judgement which cut through much Baker Street vacillation with the crisp view that the set was in German control, and traffic should be shut down. When SOE worried about the nervousness (perfectly understandable to most people) of some of their agents at the prospect of being parachuted into hostile territory by night, they turned to Tar to ask for access to some of the German agents held at Camp 020 at Ham, hoping to quiz them about their own reactions.

He also gave them information on the Germans' invisible inks (one made up as an eye lotion and which at a pinch could be used for that purpose), and their sabotage devices (thought by SOE to be inferior to the British equivalent). Tar was one of the main advocates for the creation of a series of 'panels' at which MI5 and SOE could discuss their mutual problems and challenges. (He represented his Service on two of these, one dealing with 'Security of the Training of SOE personnel and the interchange of personnel and intelligence', and the second which looked at 'the Security of SOE Communications'.

In the first capacity he pushed for visits by SOE officers to MI5 though Petrie initially wrote crabbily that he did not care for the idea of 'strangers' visiting Camp 020 and Guy Liddell fretted about how much could be said about the Most Secret Sources, (to which SOE did not have access) and the first draft of the programme for the five-day tour of MI5 (it did include Camp 020) by Lt. Colonel S. H. C. Woolrych, Chief Instructor at SOE's Beaulieu schools is written out in Tar's own hand.

Much as Tar had recorded how impressed he had been by what he saw at Beaulieu, in thanking him for his tour, Woolrych was at pains to praise B1a for its 'most patient, painstaking and scientific approach'. He told Tar he had come away with a 'general impression of quiet efficiency, of a smooth running machine which sifts, scrutinises and compares every shred of evidence going through its hands collected by its various agencies and of the careful building up of a picture from innumerable shreds of evidence . . .' coupled with 'a refreshing absence of the stunts and gadgets so dear to the hearts of those who are anxious to produce impressions rather than results'. Faced with the diligence of MI5 the life of a German spy in Britain was, he concluded, an 'extremely hazardous occupation'.

Many more glimpses of Tar are to be found in Christopher Moran's fascinating study of SOE's Security Section and need only be summarised here to underscore the breadth of his involvement. At times he was almost an umpire, called on when SOE felt MI5 had overstepped the mark in its attempts to ferret out insecurity. More often we see him, backed by Christopher Harmer, giving dispassionate and probably often unwelcome advice on SOE wireless sets and agents that might have been 'blown'. His main interest was always to see whether the sets might be used for deception but, surveying potentially 'blown' operations across a spectrum from France, the Low Countries to Norway he usually decided they could not, often because the situation on the ground was so confused. Even if it was not, luring the Germans into using a captured agent for a protracted 'game' ran counter to SOE's primary objective of extricating their man or woman out of a potentially lethal situation as fast as possible.

This did not stop him giving trenchant advice that London should 'mark time' when doubts, soon proved correct, were raised about the security of the SOE circuits around Toulouse, or the penetration of SOE's Belgian networks; unknown to London by the end of 1942 all their eight wireless sets were in German hands. In citing these examples, it is easy to lose sight of the fact that as the records show, each one involved much careful thought, detailed analysis, a flow of memoranda, internal debate at St James's Street, and then often difficult exchanges with SOE and the other agencies. Playing sets back was fraught with problems. As one file note pointed out B1a wanted to use a set known to be in German hands to ask about the production of certain factories in France. But their questions '. . . might have led to the enemy thinking that these factories would be bombed and transferring flak (anti-aircraft batteries) from other parts of the country. If in fact the factory was on the Air Ministry (target) programme it followed that our aircraft might meet with a hot reception.'

SOE has often been criticised. But whether its contribution to European Resistance is measured in terms of freeing up Divisions which the Allies were able to deploy elsewhere, or the months by which it foreshortened the Second World War, it was considerable. At the time some Country Section heads in SOE may have felt MI5 were more of a hindrance than a help, but this is clearly not the case.

Unloved to the last, SOE was summarily dissolved at the end of 1945. The Labour government was anxious not to be seen sustaining an organisation devoted to sabotage and subversion which, in several countries in Europe, had backed the wrong political 'horse'. And the Foreign Office had long felt that there was room for only one organisation to operate covertly overseas and that was SIS over which it had policy control.

SOE's demise was so sudden that when its chief, Sir Colin Gubbins[4] wrote to David Petrie on 18 January 1946, thanking MI5 for its co-operation, he added rather poignantly 'Please do not trouble to reply, as I am now leaving and my staff has broken up.'

Notes
1. Mackenzie, p. 385.
2. Senter, Lt. Commander (later Sir) John W., QC, RNVR, 1905–66.
3. The frequency list came from the BBC Monitoring Service, then at Wood Norton Hall near Evesham, in the heart of Grice-Hutchinson country, but he did not tell SOE the source. It is an illustration of SOE's isolation from the world that they did not have their own relationship there. The Hall is now a rather comfortable hotel.
4. Gubbins, Major-General Sir Colin McVean, KCMG, DSO, MC, 1896–1976.

30

Pigeon Pie

Yet another perspective on Tar's capacity for what in modern jargon would be called 'thinking outside the box', is a story which might have served as the plot-line for an episode in *Blackadder* or *Dad's Army* and one nicely told by Emily Jane Wilson.[1]

The wartime MI5 had assets which its twenty-first century counterparts would probably have to eschew for fear of falling foul of 'health and safety' regulations or seeing Thames House picketed by animal rights activists.

When intercepted German traffic in December 1942 revealed that ZIGZAG was to parachute down in the Cambrian Hills, Guy Liddell commented that 'we are getting out the bloodhounds which we purchased at considerable expense at the beginning of the war, and never used.'

Odder in modern eyes, was the fixation with pigeons. Given the centuries over which their homing instincts had been used to make them discreet and reliable message carriers, it is perhaps not surprising that MI5, defending the Realm, should have created a Falconry Unit based in the Scilly Isles – perhaps one of the nicer postings in the midst of a world war – to bring down German birds flapping high on their way to and from agents in the UK. They downed just three, all of them turning out to belong to aggrieved British fanciers. (Some time earlier the *New York Times* had reported without a hint of irony that a carrier pigeon caught with plans of a Yugoslav fort ringed to one leg had been 'sentenced to death' in Belgrade. Whether the sentence was carried out and if so, how, is not known.)

But along with Flight Lieutenant Walker, who ran MI5's 'Lights and Pigeons' section, Tar saw another exciting dimension, the chance to turn the German pigeon service inside out, much as he was doing with the Abwehr agents. Pigeons were used not just by the Army and RAF for routine message-carrying but also by SOE to send the Resistance in Europe intelligence questions to which London badly needed answers. Some of those birds would inevitably fall into German hands and the initial idea was send them out with phoney questionnaires, to give the Germans a misleading idea of where British tactical interests lay and the potential targets on which they wanted information. The technique was first used, to no discernible effect as part of the deception measures for Operation Starkey in July 1943.

But Tar's questing mind went further. As chicks, all professionally run European pigeons had – and still have – a unique national identification ring clamped on one leg, said to be impossible to alter without tell-tale soldering and even then, impossible to fit to another grown bird. It was perhaps the challenge of this that drove Tar on; nobody in B Division had yet encountered a document that could not be forged, a lock that would resist picking, and what was creating phoney pigeon rings compared to whistling up a trawler or procuring a dead body. Britain's ring-making master craftsman was duly enlisted. His skills opened the door of the pigeon loft for supposedly German birds to be sent out from England, and dropped by parachute in wicker baskets which would open when they touched ground, close enough to Germany to encourage them to make a Nazi loft one of their first stops on the long flight home.

The allure of the scheme was twofold. At a minimum, the rather far-fetched reasoning went, the Germans, thinking them to be *echt Deutsch*, by virtue of the false rings, might be tempted to use them to send messages to agents in England. When they reached the Channel coast their instincts would lead them to their own home lofts and put the messages they were carrying into MI5's hands. Even better, if the German handlers checked carefully and realised they had some birds with apparently identical rings, the confusion would lead them to stop sending pigeons out until they had double checked each ring and culled the suspects from their lofts in an avian replay of the Massacre of St. Bartholomew's Eve. Under the plan, some 350 hapless birds were dropped by parachute over Holland and Belgium, again with no recorded result.

But Tar had more important themes on his mind than conjuring tricks with *Columba livia domestica*. As they became more confident that they did indeed control all the German agents in the UK and many elsewhere, Section B1a had begun to argue as early as 1942 that the edifice of illusion they had created could be used far more powerfully as a weapon for deception rather than penetration and control, that they could shift from defence to offence, from the back foot to the front, to use the cricketing terms with which they had grown up.

John Marriott noted[2] that the double agents must be getting the reputation 'of men who seldom or never say anything untrue, but who equally, as must be apparent to the Germans, never say anything which is new.' Had the time not come to 'aim at supplying the Germans with so much inaccurate information that the intelligence reports furnished by the Abwehr to the German High Command based on that information would themselves be misleading and wrong?' One member of the Committee complained that 'our agent goes on a tour and produces a sort of bowdlerised Baedeker. He sees nothing exciting, he sees so few troops of so few units that one would think there were no troops in England; he sees few aerodromes though every 'recce' by the Germans must have shown the country stiff with them, no factory was making armaments anywhere . . .'

These memoranda may have been part of a concerted campaign since 'Policy Papers' written at the time show the deception guidelines laid down by the main Whitehall constituents – the fighting services and the Home Defence Executive – were beginning to shift. The RAF in particular was already looking for a major change in emphasis. For the past year the theme they had sought to put across to the Germans via Double Cross was 'belittlement', gulling them into believing that the RAF had fewer, and poorer aircraft than the Luftwaffe. It was also presented as badly trained, which had led to many accidents which in turn had weakened morale. The aim had been 'to hide expansion and create surprise when the increased strength became operative'. The time had now come to put across a message of 'strength'.

To take another contrarian example, the Home Forces' policy was to exaggerate Britain's defences. Thus anything which supported the idea that Britain was impregnable could be put across, but reports which suggested the opposite, which spoke of low spirits in the armed forces, were to be avoided. Some matters were simply never to be mentioned in Double Cross traffic, e.g. the War Office dictum that the Germans were not to be told anything about 'our gas offensive weapons . . . nor any rumours that we intend to use gas'. In the words of the 1940's hit song by Johnny Mercer, 'Acc-ent-uate the positive, E-liminate the negative . . .'

On 15 July 1942 we find Tar himself made the same case.[3] First, as to control, 'It is reasonably certain that the only network of agents possessed by the Germans in this country is that which is now under the control of the Security Service.' Why was he so sure? The Post Office monitoring known Abwehr cover addresses had revealed no uncontrolled agents. There was no evidence of payments being made through the carefully watched banking channels in Lisbon and Madrid. In fact one controlled agent had £18,000 available in England for disbursements but had not been instructed to make any. Finally RSS had not picked up any signals which might be from uncontrolled transmitters. It was simply inconceivable that another network was operating. 'It follows from this that if we, being in control of the network, chose to say one thing, and a single agent who is not controlled, to say another, it is we who stand a better chance.' Nor could the whole thing be an elaborate Abwehr hoax involving decoys and some deeply-buried parallel network. Through the Most Secret Sources, MI5 had watched the Germans arranging to send agents over, to pay them and passing on their reports from one station to another; 'in two or three cases we have been able to observe the action (which has been rapid and extensive) taken by the Germans on the basis of these agents' reports'.

Thus 'the combined General Staff in this country have in MI5 double agents a powerful means of exercising influence over the OKW German High Command'.

His suggestion was that 'to fill the German files with what the British would like to see there', an Inter-Service section should be created for the task. He was pushing on an open door, or even perhaps, mixing a metaphor, knowing it was open and wanting to make sure MI5 had a seat at the table inside since others were thinking the same way.

The notion of a clear and co-ordinated deception strategy had caught the attention of the Prime Minister and the Joint Planning Staff. Colonel J H "Johnny" Bevan, an Old Etonian stockbroker whose easy charm was on a par with Tar's,[4] took command of the London Controlling Section, whose deliberately anodyne name belied its considerable task of preparing 'deception plans on a world wide basis with the object of causing the enemy to waste his resources' and pursue 'any matter calculated to mystify or mislead the enemy wherever military advantage may be so gained'. He joined the Double Cross Committee, but declined to take its Chair, a decision which left MI5 in what Masterman told Liddell was its proper rôle. 'I am convinced that the Security Service alone is in a position to run double agents but at the same time the running of them depends upon retaining the goodwill and full support of all the Services,' which would be provided via Bevan. The dots were soon to be joined up, and 'close and continuous informal liaison' began between Bevan's small staff at Storey's Gate and Tar and his team in St. James's. Bevan also had the important job of co-ordinating with the Allied deception machine for the Mediterranean and Middle East, known as A Force and run from Cairo by the redoubtable Dudley Clarke.[5]

It may have been Clarke's penchant for the clandestine which led to his arrest and three weeks' detention in Madrid in 1942 for an unofficial rendezvous with, in one version, a potential German agent, in another the SIS Head of Station. As Clarke was dressed, rather fetchingly, it should be said, in a floral print frock, elbow length gloves, a turban style hat, high heels and a brassiere, the photographs taken by Franco's police and gleefully passed to London raised many eyebrows, Churchill's among them. Clarke gave the Spanish police confused explanations for being dressed as he was, none of which as the British Embassy told Whitehall 'square with the fact that the garments and shoes fitted him'. Clarke was too valuable a player and emerged from the episode with little more than a mild reproof for not clearing his trip with his superiors.

Partly because space does not permit, and partly because A Force was essentially a strategic military arm, not a counter-intelligence operation, we will not dwell on it here.[6]

The ruse which, rightly, has attracted more attention than most was the brilliantly successful 1943 deception known officially as "Operation MINCEMEAT" and in the public mind as the saga of The Man Who Never Was. The refrigerated body of a Welsh tramp, dressed with difficulty in an officer's uniform of the Royal Marines, was slipped into Spanish coastal waters from a Royal Navy submarine. It was hoped when the body floated ashore the artfully-forged, supposedly Top Secret papers he was carrying would swiftly reach the Germans and persuade them that the Allies were targeting Greece and Sardinia, rather than the real goal of Sicily, for their major thrust in the Mediterranean. The story has been told, filmed and recently retold in detail. There may not have been the plethora of parents suggested by the old saw that 'success has a thousand fathers, failure is an orphan'. But there were several in the wartime intelligence world, including Ian Fleming, himself an officer in Naval Intelligence and Dennis Wheatley, the prolific author of bodice-ripping, Black Magic novels, who subsequently claimed credit for the idea.

But as Ben MacIntyre and Denis Smyth have separately demonstrated,[7] even though Tar was 'present at the birth' chairing the Whitehall meeting at which the idea was first laid out to Bevan, there are two men above all who can properly claim to have created the deception. One is Ewen Montagu, who oversaw the meticulous execution.[8] The other is the imaginative, larger than life RAF officer Charles Cholmondeley, remembered by Tar[9] as 'a most extraordinary and delightful man who worked in my section largely as an ideas man and it was he who really triggered off the whole concept of MINCEMEAT. He was really quite unique.'[10]

Tar's tale is studded with unlikely combinations – SNOW and

CELERY are just one example, the Montagu – Cholmondeley duo is another. The former was the irascible, restless barrister scion of a wealthy Jewish family, whose brother Ivor was as ardent a Communist as he was table tennis player; unknown to Ewen he was under close MI5 surveillance. Behind the very English Cholmondeley's gawky frame, his horn-rimmed glasses and a handlebar moustache generally associated with Battle of Britain pilots, lurked the frustration of being classified unfit to fly, the imagination of a novelist and a catholic range of interests from restoring antique cars to the mating habits of insects. It would be interesting to know what Montagu, a man with an eye for the ladies, thought when his rôle in the film of *The Man Who Never Was* was taken by the droll American Clifton Webb, well known in Hollywood as a 'confirmed bachelor.'

Planting false information on the enemy directly rather than via double agents was not a new ploy. In the First World War desert campaign the Turks, then fighting on the side of the Kaiser's Germany, were hoodwinked into misreading the British plan for the third battle of Gaza. Central to a sweeping, intricately orchestrated strategic and operational scheme, including bogus wireless traffic, was the 'loss' in a contrived encounter with a Turkish patrol, of a haversack stuffed with carefully prepared British staff papers purporting to describe their battle strategy.[11]

Using a dead body was a macabre evolution. It was first suggested by Cholmondeley, who proposed parachuting a corpse into France with a radio strapped to the body, to fool the Germans into thinking he was a British secret agent who had been killed in a faulty landing and tempting them to 'play' the set back to London as the start of a deception game. 'Does anyone know where we can get a corpse?' Montagu remembers him asking. An echo of the 'where can we get a trawler' question in the SNOW imbroglio. But we can surely detect Tar's hand in the suggestion that the team approach the Westminster Coroner, Bentley Purchase, who had been helpful in fudging the Rolph death. One of Tar's secretaries was involved in playing the part of the dead man's supposed fiancée, and Tar was also named in Top Secret cables to Spain as the person to whom any documents recovered from the sodden cadaver were to be sent. He also pitched in with sage advice – 'make no comment' – when a US radio station got hold of the gist of the story towards the end of the war.

In his Foreword to Montagu's 1977 book, Hugh Trevor-Roper wrote that its author 'more than any other man was personally responsible' for the operation, and characterises the book as 'enjoyable and accurate'. But he may have forgotten this encomium when he wrote in February 1993 to Tar,[12] telling him a complicated story about a misfired attempt to write an obituary for Dick White and adding that he intended to write something nonetheless. 'It will incidentally touch on the nimble kleptomania of J C Masterman and Ewen Montagu . . .' implying perhaps that the latter was not entitled to as much credit as he claimed. Bevan thought both Cholmondeley and Montagu equally deserving of recognition. His commendation of the latter's 'tireless energy' perhaps understated Montagu's mastery of the bureaucratic jungle and his tenacity, as approval for every piece of the jigsaw had to be sought not just up and down Whitehall, but ultimately from Churchill and General Eisenhower. (How Trevor-Roper would have characterised Blunt's betrayal of the MINCEMEAT plan to his Soviet handlers we do not know. An accurate summary, no doubt based on more timely reports, appeared in a comprehensive NKVD appreciation of British deception schemes in May 1944.)[13]

Given Tar's own agile mind and his collegiate approach to running the double agents, it is fair to allot him a share of the credit for this ghoulish masterpiece of stage management, an apt adjective since Masterman recalls that at one point he actually saw 'the large tin container which housed the body' in the St James's Street office. To borrow another sporting analogy, if a striker and a supporting midfielder weave through the opposing team and score 'a goal in a million' some of the crowd's roars of applause must be for the team manager and his tactics.

MINCEMEAT was elegant, bold, orchestrated with exquisite care, and fooled not just the Abwehr in Spain but their chief evaluator in Germany. But one German historian[14] believes it 'made no lasting and no decisive impression on Hitler and his planners', whose subsequent dispositions were far more influenced by concerns over the stability of their Italian allies and their strategic position in the Balkans. (Hitler had actually speculated that the corpse might have been a British 'plant'.)

Unlike MINCEMEAT, the D-Day deception plan FORTITUDE, was not conceived in a flash of imagination. It took time and intense and complex large-scale planning. Decisions had to be agreed and co-ordinated by American and British Generals, Admirals, and Air Marshals and their staff officers. Tar and his team nevertheless had a pivotal rôle to play. The agents who had been so carefully managed and manipulated by Tar and his team to win the hearts and minds of their German controllers were now to enjoy what in another Second World War context might have been called 'their finest hour'.

The objectives were to exaggerate the size of the assembling invasion force, to fool the Germans about the invasion date and even more critically, mislead them about where the main thrust of the invasion would be. The deception continued even after the landings, manoeuvring the Germans into holding back key forces in the belief that Normandy was a feint and that the real blow would fall across the short Channel crossing to the Pas de Calais. Deception and its rôle in the war strategy has been meticulously studied by Sir Michael Howard as a contribution to the official *History of British Intelligence in the Second World War* to which those in search of more detail can valuably turn. Likewise Operation FORTITUDE has been described with elegance and in 500 pages of detail by one of the central participants, Roger Hesketh, the Old Etonian barrister whose private passion for architecture gave him the eye for detail so essential in such an audacious and staggeringly complex endeavour. His book, written between 1945 and 1948, was long held in the Whitehall oubliette by the guardians of the Official Secrets Act and not published commercially until 1999. Hesketh was Bevan's Officer in Charge of Special Means, the euphemism for the back channels along which calibrated, co-ordinated deception information was to reach the enemy, and thus worked closely with Tar whose key double agents were among the most 'Special' of the 'Means'. In a meeting at which one might have wished to be 'a fly on the wall', we see a glimpse of Hesketh and Tar together at a planning session early in 1944 chaired by the Director of Military Intelligence, Major-General H. N. M. Davidson, and also attended by Guy Liddell, Bevan of LCS, and, for SIS Sir Stewart Menzies and Felix Cowgill.

The 'grand design' of deception was difficult enough to lay out, agree with all the many constituencies involved, and co-ordinate. It was a masterpiece of staff work. But once the main lines were set, Tar and his colleagues had to manage the equally challenging intricacies of execution. Information had to be collected, collated, checked to make sure it matched policy and strategy, and distilled into plausible nuggets that would carry weight with the Germans individually or cumulatively, matched against what other agents had sent or were about to send, and then cleared by the relevant Service Department (including the Foreign Office if it had a political dimension), before it could be coded and tapped into the ether, or laboriously penned in secret ink for letter traffic via neutral capitals.

Even that was not simple. Though the working estimate was two weeks, there was no guarantee when a letter would reach the Germans, so the timing had to be calibrated to try to ensure information did not get to them too soon or too late. The elegant symmetry of Double Cross – embodied in those matching Roman numerals whose *double entendre* was understood only by a handful of 'insiders', meant that the Most Secret Sources often served as a check that the data had reached them and more vitally, how they reacted to it. A file note shows that feeding the machine and its constant demands for more, was far from easy. Most stories were developed by 'the case officers' imagination' based on the policy directives, or by the more creative agents such as GARBO and TRICYCLE. But none of them could be everywhere and see everything. So everything was grist to the mill. The British and North American press was scoured, even the Canadian Hansard, as were the summaries of the BCC's foreign language monitoring service (of which John Marriott's brother was conveniently

Director), there were reports from Regional Security Officers and Chief Constables, even sightings and rumours passed on by the secretaries, including some of those at SIS Section V. It is little wonder that Tar told Frank Foley of SIS, who were running double agents of their own, that MI5 was too stretched to supply them with material though Tar would take responsibility for clearing whatever SIS concocted.

The Double Cross contribution to FORTITUDE was invaluable. But it was part of a far larger machine. Fictitious Army divisions had to be created in false locations, fitted in to phony but plausible Orders of Battle, matched by spurious but carefully orchestrated troop and convoy movements. Wireless filled the airwaves day and night with equally carefully contrived signals traffic supporting the deceptions, and intended to be monitored by the Wehrmacht's ever alert operational-level intercept service. Dummy landing craft were built and deceptively deployed in Dover and the Norfolk Broads, mocked up fighter planes and tanks that were no more than wood and canvas artefacts were carefully positioned to catch the eye of roving Luftwaffe reconnaissance. One of those involved in building the fictitious Orders of Battle was Anthony Blunt who later recalled 'I nearly always got it wrong and had to do it all over again.' That still left him time to pass over to the Russians a copy of the entire FORTITUDE operational plan and details of the rôle of Double Cross within it.

The effort was immense though, as Trevor-Roper commented, '. . . it was sad in a way that Luftwaffe's powers were already much reduced and that the Germans had not developed wireless interception with the same ingenuity and thoroughness that the British had, and so they were unable to get the full benefit of the visual deception and bogus wireless traffic that was laid on for them.'

A sense of how it all came together, like an hourglass with sand, mixed grains of truth and falsehood, flowing from the planners in the upper bowl through LCS and Tar and his colleagues at the narrow connecting tube, to stream steadily down to the ravenous Germans in the sphere below, is best found in the 130 pages of Appendices to Hesketh's book. One for example, sets out in neat columns the real facts, the version of the facts to be put across by Double Cross, and the date on which this was to be done. Some of the moves were subtle; on 6 April all Service leave was to be stopped but the Germans were to be told it was continuing though frequently interrupted by large scale exercises. Tar and his case officers had first of all to manoeuvre, or notionally manouevre their agents and imaginary sub-agents in to positions or situations where they could plausibly claim to have seen the formations on whose movements they were reporting, or picked up the high level chitchat they were purporting to pass on. The planners' detailed guidance then had to be distilled into believable messages and sent as the timetable dictated. All of this from a city still under the threat of Hitler's V weapons.

The contribution of Double Cross is underscored in Hesketh's thirteenth Appendix, where he sets out on the left the messages put out from London, from February to December 1944, mainly by GARBO and the Polish officer BRUTUS, though TATE and FREAK also 'scored', as did the troublesome TREASURE (whom we shall shortly meet), and in the right hand column their evaluation in the German High Command's daily intelligence summary, neatly picked up from their intercepted signals traffic. Almost every message is accepted without question as coming from Abwehr sources variously described as 'credible', 'particularly trustworthy', 'prudent', 'good' or 'proven'. GARBO and his fictional network of agents and subagents were so much in demand that he was provided with an office in Jermyn Street, handily placed between Tar's operational hub in St James's Street and the Allied HQ in St James's Square, fitted with a scrambler telephone for even faster communications. As one of the official Histories recounts,[15] the communications were all the faster since they involved 'a handful of men who knew each other intimately and cut corners'. They included, of course, for MI5 Tar, John Masterman, John Marriott, Tomas Harris, Hugh Astor, Christopher Harmer and other case officers, and for London Controlling Section Colonel Beavan, Hesketh and Sir Ronald Wingate. In the rueful words of the History they 'conducted business with a speed and informality which, unfortunately, has left practically no traces for the historian'.

The pièce de resistance is to be found in Hesketh's frontispiece, the German teleprinter copy of a GARBO report of 9 January 1944, indicating that the invasion would 'probably take place in the Pas de Calais area' and that troop concentrations in the South West were a diversion. It was initialled by General Alfred Jodl, the High Command's Chief of Operations Staff, and judging from a pencilled hieroglyph at the top of the copy, seen by Hitler himself.

Notes

1. Wilson, pp. 168 and 199–200.
2. Howard, p. 12.
3. Howard, p. 20.
4. Bevan, John Henry, 1894–1978.
5. Clarke, Colonel later Brigadier Dudley Wrangel, CB, CBE, 1899–1974, another Charterhouse Old Boy.
6. But see for instance, Holt and Tar's views on p. 294.
7. See Macintyre and also Smyth.
8. Montagu, the Hon E. 1901–85, lawyer, the Second World War Royal Navy officer, serving in the Admiralty's NID 17M intelligence section. Member of the Double Cross Committee.
9. Mure papers.
10. One wonders what the plodding Abwehr analysts would have made of the fact that his name is actually pronounced as "Chumley"; another cunning Anglo-Saxon subterfuge?
11. Wavell, Field Marshal Archibald Percival, 1st Viscount, GCB, GCSI, GCIE, CMG, PC, 1883–1950, Commander British Forces Middle East in the Second World War, Viceroy of India.
12. Personal papers.
13. *TRIPLEX*, p. 276.
14. See Müller, K-J.
15. Hinsley et al, Vol 5, p. 110.

31

TREASURE Trove

Borrowing from the theatre again, if GARBO was one of Tar's stars, TREASURE, Nataliya 'Lily' Sergueiew, was part of the supporting cast and briefly a prima donna. She may not have had many memorable lines, and like other ladies of the chorus over the ages, her temperamental tantrums gave Tar as producer a disproportionate amount of trouble. But her story is worth telling in some detail as an unusual perspective on the 1930s.

Artist, author, journalist, and intrepid traveller, and not a fan of Tar's she was another of the many double agents whose real loyalties he and his colleagues had to measure day and night. As well as a full MI5 file which could fairly have had the subtitle 'The Dog That Threatened D-Day' or in a Chekhovian allusion closer to her Russian roots, 'The Lady With The Little Dog', she is, unusually, survived by two books she wrote describing her remarkable prewar journeys and a third on her wartime experiences. Worries about what the latter contained led Tar to go unusual lengths to try to suppress it, not least perhaps because he knew she felt he and his 'gang' had treated her badly. She also features, unfavourably, in the autobiography of her cousin, a distinguished Cambridge academic, and in a better light in the recollections of Kenneth Benton, whom we last met on a sunny drive with his SIS colleague Kim Philby and who was her first contact in the British secret underworld.

One of the fascinations of exploring Tar's history is that the 'backstories' are often even more intriguing than the deception operations themselves. So it is with Lily, as we shall call her until she becomes double agent TREASURE.

Born in St. Petersburg in 1912, she and her sister fled with their parents after the October Revolution turned their comfortable world upside down. Like so many other White Russians their perilous journey across Europe's fluid and suspicious frontiers ended in Paris. They must have smuggled valuable heirlooms with them since in their early years they lived comfortably, with a maid, a cook an English Governess for the girls and income enough to send Lily to the Convent de l'Assumption from which she emerged speaking English as fluently as French and her native Russian, though a drive-by of their apartment building in the 17th Arrondissement suggests the area is now much less 'bourgeois' and far more mixed than it was in her childhood.

In the nineteenth and early twentieth century, Paris had been a refuge for many political exiles escaping the long arm of the Tsarist secret police. Now, ironically, it was home to some 40,000 of those once loyal to the Tsar, a world with its own churches, choirs, charities, newspapers, bookstores, grocers, ballet, theatres, dance halls, veterans' associations and political groups, bickering bitterly about how a new non-Bolshevik Russia could be created, and what its constitutional and political shape should be. The 3,000 Russian taxi drivers even had two Unions of their own.

Most of the White Russians had been declared stateless by the Bolsheviks. Unless and until, like Lily's parents, they could become naturalised, the refugee 'passports' issued by the League of Nations were their only proof of identity. Despite the congeniality and sense of community it was a mini-world riven by mistrust and uncertainty. Paris was an obvious target for a Bolshevik régime paranoid about White Russian and foreign plots to undermine it. So Moscow's secret police had a sizeable presence of skilled personnel, complemented by cunning, murderous undercover agents sent out from Moscow.

Early adepts of the double agent game, they had penetrated many of those White Russian groups, as Lily and her family were soon to discover.

European politics of the 1930s created yet more layers of uncertainty, not unlike a set of Russian Matryoshka dolls. France itself was in constant political upheaval. Governments rose and fell; Left battled Right in the press, the National Assembly and in the streets, using bombs and bullets when polemics were not enough.

There was uncertainty too beyond the frontiers, Germany had struck at France in 1870 and again in 1914, and embedded in Nazi policy was the conviction that the Armistice had been neither a surrender nor a defeat; the nation and its army had been 'stabbed in the back' by Republicans and Communists. If Germany under Hitler armed itself for another war, what would that mean for the émigré communities in France?

Many of these murky currents infused the already turbulent streams of émigré politics. Would some sort of sub-rosa cooperation with the Nazis actually advance the cause by undermining the Bolsheviks. These were streams in which Moscow's skilled intelligence officers fished adroitly and mercilessly. They killed rather than 'guddled'. Lily's mother Mariya was a Miller, a surname which sounds stoutly British but which is actually the Russian version of Müller. Mariya's brother and Lily's uncle, Evgenyi-Lüdwig Karlovich Miller, a distinguished soldier and later a General; his Germanic second name reflects the family's Baltic roots. In exile he seems to have modified the surname further to the Frenchified 'de Miller' but the generally accepted Russian spelling is plain 'Miller'. Her father Sergei, remembered by the family as 'a lovely, civilised man' had been a promising young diplomat under the Tsar. A family quarrel, later healed, turned their romance into an elopement.

General Miller's kidnap and murder and Maryia's secretarial job on the fringes of an early Second World War French Resistance network are sub-plots that must wait their chronological turn.

Where Lily's family (she was christened Natalya, but as a child she tossed her curls and insisted on it being shortened to 'Lily' and it stuck) spent the first two years after the Revolution she does not tell us. Most likely Berlin, which had a flourishing émigré colony, or Prague, where there were Miller relatives, but by 1920 they were in Paris.

In twenty-first century Paris svelte 'new' Russian women in sable, with a designer hand bag on one arm and a podgy Armani-clad 'sugar-daddy' on the other are a boon to the boutiques and five star hotels. But if one looks around, it is still possible to find remnants of the thriving Russian community that Lily and her parents knew; the Alexander Nevsky Cathedral, the Petrograd Restaurant across the road, and a few steps away, the Daru Restaurant, opened in 1918.

The 1920's émigrés were a broad cross-section. The Grand Dukes and dispossessed industrial magnates like the oligarchs of today, gravitated to palaces and ornate villas on the French Riviera, so reminiscent of the Crimea. But the less well off worked long and hard in factories like the Renault plant.

Mariya Sergueiew was a strict mother. She insisted on reading any book that came to their home before the girls were allowed to look at it and ensured that the governess escorted them to the convent door and collected them when it was time to return home. The girls were not allowed to go to a cinema unless Mariya went with them.

Much against her parents' wishes, Lily went on to study art for four years at the prestigious Academie Julian in the rue du Berri. They thought it a venue for 'all sorts of debauchery' and urged her not to talk to other students at lunchtime, and insisted that the governess escorted her home at the end of each day.

One of Lily's aunts was Mother Superior of a Russian Orthodox convent in Portugal; her sister Marousya married a French Count and moved to Algiers, while another cousin was the redoubtable Elizabeth Hill, on her way to becoming Professor of Russian at Cambridge. Her father also an émigré from St Petersburg, had been a comfortably-off member of the British merchant community there and her mother was also a Miller. Elizabeth was to become the prime mover behind Britain's Cold War programme in which young National Service conscripts underwent intensive learning of Russian at the Joint Services School for Linguists.[3] Known to her awed students there and at the university (though not to her imperious face) as 'Lisa', to Lily she was 'Cousin Bessie' and she too has her part – played with great reluctance – in Lily's story.

In 1931, the worldwide aftershocks of the Wall Street Crash – so recently and scarily replayed that we all know how it must have felt – reached Paris and the Millers were suddenly hard up. The family lost their maid and their cook, and Lily's father Sergei, had to scrabble for a living selling second hand cars. Lily's mother began, discreetly, to sell some of her jewels and began working as a secretary. Lily, who claimed later and demonstrated in some of her travel writing, that art was her passion, had to give up the Academie and, as she put it, swap her artist's smock for an apron and her paintbrush for a broom, and learn to clean, to cook, do the shopping, the laundry and other chores. Lily also lost her over-attentive English governess, the only bright spot for her in those difficult times.

Back in Paris she put her book together, organised an exhibition of pictures she had painted along the way, and then set off with a French girlfriend on a bicycle tour through Germany, Czechoslovakia, Austria and Yugoslavia, where their saddle-sore arrival in Belgrade coincided with the pomp and circumstance of the funeral of King Alexander[1], assassinated by a marksman for the Bulgarian 'Black Hand' as he arrived in Marseilles on a State Visit to France.

The XX archives record without comment or any sign of follow-up that while there Lily interviewed Hermann Goering, who represented Germany at the funeral. The interview itself, published in the Right-wing Paris newspaper *Le Petit Journal* did not reveal anything which might have disconcerted the chancelleries of Europe.

Her story is an amalgam of Patrick Leigh Fermor's *Wanderjähre* and the plot of a 1930's Eric Ambler novel. Seeing the opportunity to make a book out of the adventure – travellers' tales were very much in vogue – she set out in 1933 with little more than a rucksack, a tent and stout hobnailed boots, to walk from Paris to Warsaw, a distance of some 1,000 miles, with only the occasional lapse into hitch-hiking or train rides. Because the original publisher went bankrupt the book she wrote didn't appear until 1946, by which time she had had further adventures enough to fill another two books. By then also the cities and villages she remembered, the art galleries which had given her so much pleasure along the way, had been reduced to dust and ashes. But her comments reveal her sharp eye, as do her drawings.

The story deserves more space than is available here, but two aspects bring us back to double agents. First, the enigmatic Richard Dassel, whom Lily met in Berlin. Ostensibly a well-connected journalist, he had been born in one of the Baltic states, like the Millers, and like them he had grown up one hundred percent Russian. In the First World War he served as a Captain in a crack Tsarist cavalry regiment, and was badly wounded in Rumania. After the Armistice and the resulting redrawing of boundaries and shifting of populations, he had acquired German citizenship. Though Lily didn't realise it until much later, he was in fact a 'talent spotter' for German intelligence and much of their relationship can be seen through the prism of a covert 'grooming' exercise.

She might have been more suspicious had she known that in 1929, Dassel had been implicated in a plot to foist on a US correspondent in Berlin, documents purporting to show that two US Senators were on Moscow's payroll. The documents were forged.

Dassel gave the eager young writer several high-level introductions in Berlin, which she exploited with characteristic vigour but with limited success, though she did at least get a handshake, an exchange of pleasantries and an autographed photograph from Franz von Papen, the aristocratic schemer who did much to engineer Hitler's accession to ultimate power.

Lily's bid to visit a concentration camp – foul enough places already but not the 'killing fields' they would soon become – was refused but by way of compensation, she was allowed to spend three days in a work camp for unemployed house maids and shop girls whose days were spent sawing logs, picking potatoes and playing open air games. Their evenings were given over to sewing to the accompaniment of readings of inspirational Nazi 'literature'.

She then bullied her way to a much sought after press pass for the Berlin session of the trial of the alleged Reichstag arsonists. The trial had aroused an international furore, skilfully stoked by Communist propagandists around the world, and the Gestapo became suspicious of Lily's Russian origins, her nomadic ramblings across the Reich and her obstinate pursuit of a press pass. No sooner had she entered the smoke-stained Reichstag building, to which the trial had briefly moved from Leipzig, than she was smoothly shunted aside, searched, and driven off to the main Berlin jail in Alexanderplatz.

After three days staring at the walls, marching to the communal showers and making a nuisance of herself, she was bundled into a glossy red-upholstered Packard and taken to Gestapo HQ in Prinz-Albrecht-Strasse. There she was grilled politely but in minute detail, about the purpose of her trip, why she wanted to attend the trial and her family background. After a full day of this, the Gestapo drove her off to the house where she was staying, where her belongings and letters were carefully examined. She was then released, with urbane courtesy coupled with clear warnings about what not to write when she got home and continued her long march to Warsaw.

Her description of the experience and her jail house sketches present it as a funny little sideshow, in which she was the star but it must have been extremely stressful even for a young woman who was relatively nerveless.

The relevance of all this is that in other security areas, not least its almost paranoid suspicions of SOE agents returning from Occupied France, MI5 were wary in the extreme about anyone who had been in German hands. What had they said? Had they been 'turned'? Yet when Lily told her story to her British interrogators, it was simply noted without comment. Likewise her relationship with Dassel. (He was married with two children, and there is no hint of any romatic attachment.)

In 1936 she went to Czechoslovakia for him. He had been commissioned to write about 'local opinion' there but had other things to do in Berlin. He would put his name to the article but would pay Lily his fee. At the time the country was already seen as the possible flashpoint for another European war, looking fearfully over its shoulders at Hitler's secessionist ambitions for the German-speaking population of the Sudetenland. What Lily wrote for him cannot now be traced.

In February 1937, Dassel asked her to go to Spain to report on the Civil War. She was unable to obtain a visa and he was not enthusiastic about her suggestion that she should stay in Paris and interview French volunteers returning from the conflict. From an historical perspective we may regret she didn't go, as she might well have met Kim Philby, then setting out on his long road as a Soviet agent. As we have noted, he was under cover as a correspondent for the London *Times*, accredited to General Franco's forces, who would be the eventual victors thanks to the brutal generosity of Hitler and Mussolini.

Shortly afterwards, Dassel shed his Clark Kent suit and revealed his real rôle as a German intelligence officer. Would she work as one of his agents, not against her beloved France, but against Bolshevism, which had usurped her parents' equally beloved Russia? Given her émigrée background and especially the family links to General Miller and his rabidly anti-Communist Russian Armed Forces Union, it was a nicely judged pitch, but as she told the British later, she turned him down flat, and he did not pursue the idea. But as we shall see, she later turned the approach around and to Tar's eventual advantage.

That is the version she later gave the British interrogators. They seem not to have questioned it, nor did they explore the labyrinthine plotting, deceit and betrayal which just three nonths later culminated in General Miller's high-noon kidnap on a Paris street by Soviet secret police thugs. They drugged him, stuffed him into a packing chest, and shipped him off to Russia in a Soviet cargo boat, coincidentally named after Lenin's sister. In Moscow he was jailed, interrogated, shot in the back of the head just before midnight, and his corpse thrown into the Lubyanka's basement furnace.

It is too distant from our main theme to occupy us at length here. In any event various versions of the story of the general and his treacherous deputy Nikolai Skoblin have been told, retold and even filmed by among others Vladimir Nabokov, Marina Grey and Mary-Kay Wilmers. For us, it serves as a reminder of the deep and dangerous currents in which the Russian emigré community in Paris tried to stay afloat, but often drowned. As we shall see, some of it bears the fingerprints of the shadowy Dassel. It may have been the climate of fear and rumour it created which prompted Lily to embark on yet another hair-raising solo adventure, shortly before the kidnapping was dramatically explored in a Paris court room in a blaze of press publicity and a fusilade of ever wilder allegations and rumours. Skoblin had vanished, leaving his wife, the folk singer

Nadezhda Plevitskaya to face rather than perform the music. Instead of the bouquets and shouts of 'encore' to which she had grown accustomed in her glittering career, she was sentenced to twenty years' hard labour for her stoutly denied complicity in what was in effect an unproven crime without corpse, blood or smoking gun. Soon after the Germans occupied France she died in Rennes prison and was buried in an unmarked grave, having allegedly confessed to a priest and a French policeman on her death bed, that she had actually helped Skoblin build his alibi but did not know what he planned. Even that may not be the whole truth but it is outside our scope.[2]

Later in the war when Lily had become Tar's TREASURE, her gullible Abwehr controller, Emile Kliemann shared a strange memory with her. Just a few days after Paris fell, he told her he had been asked to help an important emissary from Berlin seize all the files in the French archives relating to the kidnapping and the trial. The emissary was none other than Dassel. He may also have been one of the two German officers, one calling himself Grimm, who visited poor Plevitskaya in jail at the same time.

The files were taken back to Berlin. When the German capital fell to the Russians in 1945, the files were shipped to Moscow, where along with French military, diplomatic and intelligence archives, they mouldered until some were repatriated to Paris in the brief period of 'Glasnost' in the 1990s.

The unstable Europe of 1938 was an extraordinary time and place for Lily to choose for her next solo adventure, a bicycle ride from Paris to Saigon. Twelve months and some 3,000 hair raising miles later, she had reached Aleppo in Syria. Her gruelling ride made a fascinating and well illustrated book. It will be covered in detail in a forthcoming biography.

The outbreak of war in September 1939 found her in Beirut where she worked as a Red Cross nurse. In December 1940, to her parents' relief – her father broke out his last bottle of champagne – she arrived back in Paris where she found nothing had changed.

Her parents' narrow street, its shops, its corner bar, looked just the same, as did the Grands Boulevards, the Luxembourg Gardens and the chilly quais along the Seine. But at a human level it was a city whose heart had been cut out like an Aztec sacrifice. Swastika flags fluttered, staff cars roared importantly down the centre of deserted cobbled roadways and Parisians had to step off the pavement to allow strutting soldiers to pass.

This seems to have been the turning point for Lily, the moment at which in a dangerous ju-jitsu move, she turned Dassel's pitch around. She wrote to him in Berlin, hinting that she was now willing to work for him. He hurried to Paris where, framed by the red plush upholstery and gilded mirrors of Maxim's restaurant, which had been quickly taken up as a plush Nazi watering hole, she made her own pitch.

She declared with masterly sincerity that her adopted country had fallen into defeat and occupation because Britain had simply left France in the lurch. So it was her duty, her conviction, that to help France she should accept his earlier proposal to work for the Germans against the British. Dassel accepted this without hesitation. Equally, when she eventually reached London and became TREASURE, Tar and his inquisitors took at face value her equally sincere assertion that the only way France would really be free was with British help, and that her duty was to work for the British against the Nazis. To pull this off, she had offered Dassel her services in the hope this would bring her into contact with the British.

Dassel started her off on what was to prove a far more harrowing, dangerous and often more frustrating adventure than anything she had done before the war. By the end of January she was in Berlin where she again convinced another team of German officers of her loyalty and bona fides. But they seem to have been uncertain about where best to use her. Syria? North Africa? Australia where she had a cousin serving with the Air Force? The debate went backwards and forwards and she was not sent into action finally until June 1943.

Some of the waiting time was spent in detailed tradecraft training – learning how to operate a radio, how to use pyramidon and quinine as secret inks – but most of it was just waiting, punctuated by expensive black market lunches.

Eventually, Lily convinced her controller Kliemann, an air

intelligence specialist based in Paris, that she could be of more help in Britain, where she had friends and a well-placed relative, namely her unwitting cousin, Lisa Hill, in Cambridge.

Dr Hill was then also working on Soviet and Yugoslav affairs for the Ministry of Information, a position which may have piqued the Abwehr's interest. Lily later told the British that Kliemann, a dapper, somewhat portly Austrian in his mid-forties with a pencil moustache, slicked back hair, a dueling scar, a German wife and a French mistress, who combined spying with being a skilled amateur violinist and collecting antique porcelain, was "an old fool" and easy to manipulate. Though from her account he was also badly organised, turning up hours, sometimes days, late for meetings, inept and as gullible as Ritter, Tar warned her not to underestimate him.

To judge from the archives Lily's reading of Kliemann was close to the mark. When he fell into British hands after the war, his first postwar interrogators judged that he had been 'as idle as possible and took no interest in what his colleagues were doing as long as he could with our help hold on to his job in Paris and to Yvonne (his mistress Yvonne Delidaise)'. He was not a career intelligence man, having joined the Abwehr at the outbreak of war, and then moving between jobs in mail censorship and travel pass control before finding himself working as an agent runner.

Under Kliemann's bumbling 'control', Lily set off on wild goose chases to Vichy, Marseilles and Lyon, usually accompanied by her dog, to get transit papers and exit visas which would allow her to enter Portugal or Spain and travel from there to England. It is a curious reflection on the limitations of German power in a country half of which they occupied, with the other half run by their Vichy puppets, that this was far from easy, with one bureaucratic hurdle after another, despite Kliemann's background in the travel pass office; his inattention and dilatoriness played their part. It all took so long that she teased Kliemann that she was losing sight of her mission; she felt as though she was reading a novel in serialised instalments, forgetting half way through what the plot was all about.

Lily wrote to Dr Hill several times in this period telling her in 'very veiled terms' that she was working for the Germans but wanted to get in touch with the British. Her cousin did not reply. Given her own hard-won position in the British academic world and her relationships with the British Government and the intelligence services at various levels, those of her students who remember Lisa Hill fondly (the present author among them) can well imagine that she would not have wanted anything to do with an approach from a maverick cousin last heard of cycling to Saigon and who now hinted at German intelligence ties. Whether she tipped off any of her contacts cannot be discerned from the file, but it seems unlikely; she was sharp enough to know that would have meant becoming entangled in plots and counterplots that made academic politicking seem like nursery games.

So England it would be. But it was not until July 1943 that all the paperwork was finally stamped, signed and sorted out and she appeared at the British Embassy in Madrid, asking for the Passport Control Officer, the 'day job' of Kenneth Benton of SIS. Benton's account does not mention – perhaps he did not know – that the previous September the Most Secret Sources had picked up a message from Paris to Lisbon asking them to confect a telegram to support Lily's eventually abortive application for a Portuguese visa; the message had given her full name. So one way or another she was not the 'cold caller' Benton implies. Indeed she had been sent to him by a Colonel Stevens of the US Embassy. She remembers Benton as 'tall, young and slim . . . with thinning red hair' and 'trés Anglais'. When Benton read this comment years later, he noted wryly that coming from her it was 'certainly not a compliment'.

Lily wasted no time in telling him of her Abwehr relationship, but stressed she was volunteering to work for the British. She brought with her 20,000 escudos the Germans had given her, a 'good' secret ink and many instructions from Kliemann which he had told her to memorise but which she had written out in lemon juice on two sheets of note paper. Messages coded via the unbreakable 'one time pad' dotted and dashed over the airwaves between Madrid, SIS Section V, whose Iberian operations were under the suave management of Kim Philby, and Tar in St James's Street.

The wheels began to turn. Benton told her that London felt she could be of great help, that she had handled herself well so far and they would be pleased if she would work with them. He also warned her not to underestimate Kliemann; it was all very well to sneer at his unpunctuality, but he was 'one of the senior men in German intelligence' and if ever he found out that she was betraying him 'I promise you that is one rendezvous he won't be late for.'

She hardly needed a reminder. Just before she left Paris, Kliemann had told her casually that in case the British ever ran a check on her, it was important to leave the impression that far from working for the Germans, she had aroused their suspicions and they were trying to track her down. So he had sent the Gestapo to grill the concierge at her studio and, even more alarmingly, to bring her parents in to answer questions. All had gone well; the concierge knew nothing, and her parents said all they knew was that she had gone to Portugal to see a sick aunt. They pretended to know nothing about any notion of going on to England and 'had been released the same day'.

Lily understood the subtext clearly: we know where your parents are and we can haul them in at any moment. All the more since she knew the Berlin Gestapo had filled many pages of notes with information on her family and its history. Here we find our peripheral vision distracted by yet another of those floaters, like Dassel and the Miller kidnapping which drift tantalisingly on the margins of her story even more than in the case of SNOW. She told MI5 that her mother worked as a part time secretary to Père Patrick O'Reilly, a 'missionary', somewhat improbably employed at the 'Département des Océanies at the Trocadero Museum'. The museum was in fact the Musée de l'Homme, an ethnographical institution which had come to occupy a prominent position in the cultural, political and social life of 1930's France. It was also the centre of one of the earliest Resistance networks, and it is curious that the MI5 file does not go on to make the connection. The unravelling of the network through a French informer, and the execution of its eight main members by a Wehrmacht firing squad on 23 February 1942 after a perfunctory 'trial' intended to show the Germans were 'playing by the rules', were an early milestone in

France's history of defiance and it seems inconceivable that Mariya Sergeuiew would not have come to the Germans' notice during the investigation, something which would surely have added special resonance to Kliemann's threat.

Lily spent two fraught months in Madrid. Though as a Fascist State its sympathies lay with the Nazis who had done so much to help General Franco to power, Spain was a non-belligerent and as the tide of war changed, so too did the sympathies, a process said to have been lubricated by British backhanders of some $20 million to various Spanish generals, channelled by SIS through the Spanish banker Juan March.[4] Nevertheless most Madrileños still bore the fresh physical and mental scars of the Civil War which from 1936 to 1939 had riven the country, its institutions and its loyalties, and large sections of the international community. Rubbed raw by the totalitarian pressures of General Franco's Falange Party, its *Brigada Politico-Social* or secret police and the power of the reactionary Church, these wounds made the city a place in which one trod circumspectly, if not in actual fear, and spoke quietly. Benton remembered that when he arrived in 1941, the men and women he saw on the streets looked cowed and half starved. Supporters of the losing side in the Civil War were by definition unemployable and thus condemned to poverty, and the quiet of dawn was often disturbed by the distant rattle of Falange firing squads settling scores.

Notes

1. King Alexander I, 'The Unifier', of Yugoslavia 1888–1934. Because three members of his family had died on a Tuesday, he avoided any public functions on that day. But diplomatic timetables and the demands of protocol meant that he had to begin his visit by driving through Marseilles on Tuesday, 9 October.
2. See e.g. Vaksberg.
3. Hill, Professor Elizabeth, DBE, 1900–96, a remarkable lady. See also Elliott and Shukman.
4. Foot, p. 121.

32

Lady Of Spain

During Lily's time in Madrid, it was crushingly hot and dusty; air conditioning was a science-fiction dream and the smell of rudimentary plumbing pervasive, even in the better hotels. In the alleyways behind the once grand main avenues, along which rattled rundown yellow trams, it was a city of poverty; those with money and thirsty for a pre-dinner cocktail had to weave their way to a table at the open-air cafés through a pitiful line of ragged beggars drawing attention to their mutilations or nursing wide-eyed starving children.

But like Lisbon, for foreign diplomats and spies, it was an agreeable haven free from occupying troops, from bombs, air raid sirens, searchlights, ration books, ersatz food. They could gorge on beef steaks, fish and fresh fruit that they had almost forgotten existed, and cool down at the country club pool. According to Tar's agent TRICYCLE, Dusko Popov, the Abwehr had a staff of 120 in the German Embassy itself, and as many as 400 other personnel scattered around the city under various forms of commercial and press cover. Based on a 1940 MI5 or SIS analysis, the number seems an exaggeration but is an indication of the seriousness of the German effort and may also explain the Abwehr's dysfunctional disconnects.

Lily was playing the double game in deadly earnest, not via the mail or though the airwaves. There were clandestine briefing meetings and dinners with the Germans, training in microdots, memorising instructions about the times and frequencies for German radio messages, cover addresses in neutral Europe to which she was to send her invisible ink reports, and what those reports should focus on. Between the encounters with the Germans she and Benton met overtly, on the grounds that she was progressing her visa application, and covertly in a series of drive-by pickups, unbothered by Hans, the young Abwehr officer who was supposed to be baby-sitting her, but for whom the distractions of Madrid were more compelling. At one point a maudlin Kliemann asked Lily to hire a private detective to check whether his French mistress Yvonne had been unfaithful to him with a scion of the prominent Espirito Santo banking family when she herself had visited Madrid. The detective reported that she had not. Whether that was the truth, what the detective thought Kliemann wanted to hear, or not improbably, whether the detective had been 'bought off' by the family to avoid any hint of scandal, we are left to guess. That strange sideshow apart, as with Dassel, no hint of romance is to be found in any of the various versions of the story.

Once she was in England, the most efficient way to communicate would be by clandestine wireless. The Abwehr clearly hand-tailored its book of codes to the backgrounds of its agents. Ritter gave SNOW a pulp fiction thriller. The more sophisticated Kliemann handed Lily a copy of Pierre Frandaie's 1910 four act play *Montmartre* and as a fallback a quotation from Racine's bloody 1691 tragedy *Le Songe D'Athalie* – "*C'était pendant l'horreur d'une profonde nuit* . . ."[1] The alliterative link between Athalie and Nathalie may have been an Abwehr in-joke; MI5 had already spotted an Abwehr penchant for 'heavy humour' in its code names.

But until Lily had a set that could transmit as well as receive, she would send her intelligence by mail, written in invisible ink across a seemingly innocuous social message, and sent to a series of cover address in neutral countries; as with SNOW the lesson of Baillie-Stewart had been forgotten. But how to get her radio into the UK?

Fortunately for Dr Hill's peace of mind, Kliemann's bizarre suggestion that it should be mailed to her in Cambridge in the guise of a present to Lily from her aunt, the Mother Superior of a convent in Portugal, was not pursued. In one of their final meetings Kliemann gave Lily a diamond ring and a brooch, for practical rather than romantic reasons, since they could be taken into England more easily than cash, and sold or pawned there. The spontaneous gift of an Omega watch seems more a goodwill gesture of the kind agent handlers are taught to make to reinforce their relationships.

Eventually, the visa came through. In Benton's words Lily then 'exploded her landmine'. She turned up in his office 'made up and dressed to kill' with a tiny French poodle which she said she was taking to England with her. Memory is fallible; though he recalls its name as 'Frisson' it was actually called 'Babs' and Lily's photographs show it was a cheerful dog with terrier traits. But little turns on the name or breed. The dog itself was to be what John Masterman might have called the "*fons et origo*" of the next chapters in the drama.

Benton told her that Britain's rigid regulations about bringing animals into the country, meant that if Babs went to England it would to have to spend six months in quarantine, even though she waved in his face the certificate for Babs' anti-rabies shots. (Much as we might be surprised by the limits on the Abwehr's ability to get paperwork fixed in Occupied France, it seems strange that such a run of the mill, or 'run of the kennel' problem could not have been solved. SIS and MI5 were skilled in smuggling men, women, bombs, guns, gold ingots and cash across borders, and getting the British Customs, the police and even Coroners to play along with their schemes.)

Lily then unleashed a formidable Slavo-Gallic tantrum. Quarantine meant death. Nor could she leave the dog behind in Spain. 'I will not leave Babs to starve.' The answer was clear: she would tell the Germans she was finished, and would stay in Spain. Benton threatened to tear up the visa.

'No, don't do that. You are being horrid with all your stupid rules, but there must be a way.' She remembered that a friend of her father's was an Admiral in Gibraltar, and if she and the dog could get there, he would surely help. 'The Navy are honourable people', she told him pointedly.

'Lily, when you are fighting a war you must sometimes make sacrifices. I will find a kind owner for Babs.' She picked the dog up, whispered to him in Russian and told Benton, 'You shall not have him. Poor little scrap. He knows nothing about your war, all he wants is to be with me.' Benton said that he would do what he could. 'How kind you are,' Lily said sweetly and swept out.

Benton, Section V and Tar quickly saw advantages in taking the Gibraltar route. It took Lily closer to England, and by telling Kliemann she was travelling via Gibraltar he might well be prompted to give her a set of intelligence questions which would show what the Germans did and did not know about its defences. Not least, it passed the Babs buck to their colleagues on the Rock. Kliemann fell for it, and according to Benton his questions showed that the Germans already knew a great deal. (Not that it did them much good. Another Double Cross Committee briefing note from 1943 says the Abwehr's saboteurs targeting Gibraltar, all of them Spaniards, had also been converted, by adroit persuasion and pressure, rather than faith, into British double agents who kept the Germans satisfied with scraps of minor intelligence enhanced by the occasional fake explosion.) As he said goodbye Benton assured Lily that his Head Office would find a way to get Babs through the quarantine, though she was 'still giving me suspicious looks'.

She was right to do so. It was neither the first and far from the last white lie told by SIS in a good cause, and though Lily did reach England, we have for the present to leave Babs behind in the arms of a burly Field Security Policemen in Gibraltar. On 6 November 1943, rebadged with a British passport in the bland name of Dorothy Tremayne, Lily flew into Bristol Airport and was whisked away for a sobering six days at a women's annexe to the London Reception Centre, where as we saw earlier any even marginally questionable arrivals to Britain were screened and questioned by SIS and MI5 teams.[2]

In the gloomy house in Nightingale Lane she told and retold her story to a Captain Ambrose. The record is testimony to her retentive memory, her recollection of small but telling details, her frankness and Ambrose's careful patience and evident knowledge of the background which helped him tease a coherent and evidently convincing story out of a women under considerable stress. Her desire for acceptance did not quite dampen her rebellious streak. One night she challenged the security system by climbing out of a window, walking up and down the lane, and then knocking triumphantly on the front door asking to be let back in. Once Tar had decided she was genuine, helped no doubt by the ability to cross-check at least some of the story against the Abwehr intercepts, she was given the alias TREASURE and put into the capable hands of his colleague, Mary Sherer. We know little of her except that as TREASURE's 'minder' and nursemaid, she showed herself from the records to have been a well-organised officer with tenacity, discretion, imagination and the ability, under Tar's guidance, to 'keep her cool'. Benton, who was a friend of Sherer's thought she had 'a great deal of character.' TREASURE was her first double agent and she was determined that she would make a success of it. Many of the file notes on which we have drawn are hers.

When she told Benton she was making good progress with TREASURE, Benton passed the comment on to a visiting Kim Philby, who remarked : 'Poor girl. She's in for a disappointment. Never trust a Tsarist émigré. They're all as twisty as eels.'[3] It is a chilling thought that via Philby, who needed only to look in his shaving mirror if he wanted to see a real eel in close-up, TREASURE'S real name no doubt found itself with those of most of the other key agents between the cardboard covers of an NKVD file. And though he was a relative newcomer to the secret world, Philby would already have had a feel for Russian émigré intrigue, and his Moscow colleagues' ruthless exploitation of it.

On 12 November, Tar came to see her at the first of several 'safe houses', a two-bedroom flat in Rugby Mansions, then a soot-blackened block of Edwardian-era mansion flats just off the Hammersmith Road in west London, a setting TREASURE strikingly recalled as being 'as gloomy as an old lady recovering from an attack of jaundice.'[4] He wasted no time in telling her she was to play a key part in deceiving the Germans about where the Allies would land in the already much talked of invasion. She was impressed, even daunted, by the importance of the task, but singularly unimpressed with the fact that Tar took all the cash and jewels she had brought from Portugal and told her she would be paid £50 a month. The Germans had paid her £250. 'I would have expected the British to have more pride than to offer me less', though she says she would have refused to take it. As was the case with all Tar's agents she was not told about the Most Secret Sources. Nor would she have been made aware that she was part of a far larger team.

Working from the outlands of Hammersmith, from a rather grander 'safe house' in Mayfair's Hill Street[5] and from the home of Mary Coates a childhood friend, in a village near Bristol, TREASURE's first phase was as a 'secret writer' with Mary Sherer at her side dictating, checking and helping her cope with mood swings and the more serious effects of a kidney infection, for which she refused to have an operation. She was still fretting about Babs – clutching now at the straw that an American pilot she had met in Gibraltar would fly him to Britain clandestinely via Algiers – and at one point went 'on strike' at MI5's failure to ship him over – until Mary Sherer coaxed her back to the writing table. It is hardly surprising that Tar's team found her 'exceptionally temperamental and troublesome'.

Using a small wooden pointer, much like the stick James Bond might expect to find spearing the olive in a dry martini, dipped in a chemical ink that Kliemann fondly believed was undetectable by the British censor, she sent him between the lines of the chatty letters of old friends swapping news, carefully calibrated 'chaff', describing the insignia of troops she had seen, snatches of conversations overheard in trains, all of it creating the impression that Bristol and the West Country, in reality the site of a substantial build up of US and British invasion forces, roads clogged with military traffic 'from dawn to dusk and through the nights', were oases of rural calm.

But letters were not enough. Here, though the Abwehr did not realise it, British and German interests coincided. Time was the real essence of the Double Cross game. The Germans knew an invasion was coming. But when and where? To maintain its credibility in the battle with Himmler's Sicherheitsdienst, it needed to supply its masters in Berlin with up to the minute and purportedly first-class intelligence. So agents in London were vital. In their 'parallel universe', Tar and the D-Day planners needed to feed the Germans with equally up to the minute, plausible deception material and to tap into the crystal stream of those Most Secret Sources to see what the Germans made of it all. For both sides in the game, letters were too slow. TREASURE had to get a wireless somehow. Tar decided that despite the risks, she would have to tell Kliemann she was coming back to Lisbon to collect it.

Notes

1. Act 2, Scene 5.
2. A note in her file shows Tar complaining mildly to SIS who had supplied the passport that the choice of such an English persona for so foreign a passenger had raised suspicions among her fellow travellers and caused problems with Immigration on arrival, since they had been given only her real name, not the alias.
3. Benton, p. 406.
4. The soot has long gone, the block has been much spruced up. A flat there was recently on the market for £875,000. The same address was used by MI5 after the war to debrief the British born Soviet agent Alexander Foote, a member of the Swiss based Rote Kapelle network.
5. Like Rugby Mansions, another MI5 favourite. Used earlier in the war to house CELERY and ZIGZAG among no doubt many others; even today it has a transient, 'sagging lace curtain' feel to it out of harmony with its multi-million pound neighbours. TREASURE was unaware that the housekeeper, whom she knew as Maritsa, was actually the Croat-born double agent THE SNARK.

33

The Dog It Was That Died

TREASURE's new mission came at the bleakest of times. That London was being heavily bombed, and that she was unwell, were nothing compared to the news from her sister that Babs was dead, run over on a dusty Algiers side-street. TREASURE felt 'absolutely alone', and scribbled in her diary that while she admired some of their qualities she found the English – she would have included Tar in the condemnation, despite his Scottish roots and tartan trews – 'cold, undemonstrative and hard to read.'

How was she to convince the Germans why she was being allowed to travel at such a critical time, on a route that was so sensitive from a security viewpoint, on which aircraft seats were a precious and strictly allocated commodity? Similar questions had aroused Ritter's suspicions of SNOW, though Ritter had left for North Africa without sharing his doubts. But a solid cover story was essential. As Tar had counselled SOE, 'it is practically impossible by ordinary, staight-forward interrogation, to break a person who has a watertight and genuine story.'

Tar took Mary Sherer to the Ministry of Information, then occupying the recently completed Stalinist-style white towers of the University of London Senate Building, where a senior Civil Servant agreed to 'employ' TREASURE in the Enemy Occupied Territories section of the Film Unit, which produced documentaries, mostly with an unabashedly propagandistic tone. That still left unexplained how she had got such a coveted job, at a salary of £350 a year, and even a small office to herself in its overcrowded hallways.

According to Mary Sherer's script TREASURE had been introduced by her cousin Elizabeth Hill. But Dr Hill was an unwitting participant in this farrago. She had not seen her cousin since 1937 when TREASURE had foisted herself on her during a holiday in Prague, and proved herself to be 'self-centered, quick witted, smartly clever but shallow'. There had then been those dangerously ambiguous letters. To cap it all, when TREASURE arrived from Gibraltar she took the train to Cambridge and 'floated up on the doorstep . . . full of her usual, semi-flaunting adventurous self'. After one frosty encounter, when TREASURE explained what she was up to, Dr Hill went out of her way to avoid her, telling TREASURE she was 'playing a dangerous game. It is dishonourable to both sides.' That they were related was immaterial: she would offer no help and would not allow TREASURE to stay with her. 'I am committed to loyalty; you don't seem to have any at all . . .'

That did not save Dr Hill from being called to an awkward interview at 'The War Office', no doubt MI5's 'cover address', at which she would surely have dismissed any notion of involvement with TREASURE, 'an inadequate person with no real knowledge of affairs, or understanding of politics and diplomacy' who had behaved towards her 'irresponsibly' and in a 'compromising way'. Though a scribbled archive entry suggests that MI5 had opened a Personal File on Dr Hill, and put a mail interception warrant on her Cambridge address to pick up any letters which might be sent there for TREASURE, her direct involvement in the tale seems to have come to an end.

However to judge from her memoirs from which these quotations are taken,[1] the episode understandably upset her greatly. 'My name was mud.' Had she known that she had been written into Mary Sherer's plot she would certainly have turned her interview into a incandescent fireworks display of outrage in the face of which, even hardboiled 'War Office' questioners would have cowered in terror.

The script was detailed and well-rehearsed. Mary Sherer even took TREASURE by bus from her supposed address in Redcliffe Gardens in South Kensington (alas for poor Dr Hill, it had allegedly been rented from someone she knew), to the Ministry's offices on Mallet Street. There she was taken inside the entrance hall and told about the prices of canteen meals; her mythical office upstairs was described in detail. She was briefed on the Minister and the senior officials, information which included the comment that the Head of the Film Division, Jack Beddington, (in civilian life Shell's Head of Publicity), and TREASURE's notional boss, Sidney Bernstein, (who in another life ran Granada Cinemas and would go on to build Granada TV) were Jewish.[2]

It is hard to see the rationale for including this gratuitous information. The thought may have been that because so many Russians, not least well-bred White Russian émigrés, were viscerally anti-Semitic, (their last Tsar had been heard to lament that the problems of his crumbling Empire could be attributed to the fact that '90% of the revolutionaries are Yids'), it would be plausible for TREASURE to make a point of their racial origin. Like SOE, the Ministry was a wartime creation which attracted much hostile attention not to say jealousy, notably from those in the media who felt they could do better; the often splenetic *Daily Mirror* columnist 'Cassandra', William O'Connor, had attacked it in 1940 as being controlled by 'Assyrian rug merchants',[3] and George Orwell immortalised it in 1984 as 'The Ministry of Truth'.

Earlier in this story, we drew an admittedly improbable parallel between Tar and Alfred Hitchcock, suggesting that SNOW had some of the seedy characteristics of Patrick Hamilton's fictional 'Gorse'. By now nothing in Tar's tales should surprise us, not even a walk-on rôle by Hitchcock himself in TREASURE's cover story, reminiscent of his cameo appearances in his own movies. The story's premise – Hitchcock would have called it the plotline – was that Hitchcock, a name the Germans would know well, was now working for the Ministry. TREASURE had persuaded Bernstein to send her to Lisbon to talent-spot exiles whom she could interview about conditions in Europe under Nazi rule, as the basis for a series of Hitchcock-directed films. Some of the exiles might even be brought to Britain to appear in front of the maestro's cameras. Again following Tar's precept on cover stories, this was not just invention, but had a basis in fact, to be found in a series of interviews Hitchcock gave in 1962 to his admirer, the French auteur Francois Truffaut.[4]

Hitchcock explained that he had moved to Hollywood in 1939 but had come back to England when Bernstein asked him to make two short French language films, *Bon Voyage* and *Aventure Malgache*, as tributes to the Resistance, to be shown in France as the Germans retreated. He told Truffaut 'I felt the need to make a little contribution to the war effort. I was both overweight and over-age for military service.[5] To round off this parallel between clandestine life and cinematic art, Bernstein and Hitchcock went on to create their own production company in Hollywood. One of the first films they made was *Rope* by Patrick Hamilton, creator of 'Gorse'.

Tar himself cleared TREASURE's cover story with Frank Foley at SIS, since their Lisbon Head of Station would be watching over her while she was in Portugal. While there were London turf wars, or perhaps more accurately, skirmishes between St James's Street and SIS, the files make clear just how close the co-operation was overseas. When for instance it was felt desirable to reinforce the Germans' belief in GARBO, SIS in Lisbon was given the delicate task of making enquiries at the cover addresses he used for mail from London, in a way which would come to the Germans' notice and raise concern that he was suspected by the British. Kenneth Benton who saw double agents from an operational perspective in both Spain and in London remarked that 'looking back, it is sometimes difficult to recall who was MI5 and who was Section V. We were in constant touch with Tar Robertson, Tommy Harris and Anthony Blunt and also members of the Double Cross Committee. There was no feeling of rivalry because we were all involved in the same task.' Not quite, might be a fair comment as regards Blunt and Benton's boss, Philby.

TREASURE was not stupid; she asked technical questions about film making and its costs, and asked Mary Sherer for a detailed description of Sidney Bernstein himself.

But was there something else going on, another elusive 'floater'? We go back to the Reichstag fire in 1936 and TREASURE's brush with the Gestapo when she tried to attend the trial of the alleged conspirators. The blaze and its aftermath were seized on by anti-Nazis of all shades, from well-meaning liberals to what Lenin once called 'useful idiots', carefully choreographed by Otto Katz, Moscow's clandestine propaganda puppet-master.

In London the centrepiece of their efforts was a 'Counter Trial' staged before the real event in Leipzig and intended to prove to the world that the fire had been a Nazi plot all along. Among the many luminaries involved and playing leading rôles in the 'The British Committee for the Relief of Victims of Fascism' were Sidney Bernstein and the Left Wing publisher Victor Gollancz. We know from the files that the latter's travels were watched by Special Branch and that, according to the entry on Bernstein in the *Oxford Dictionary of National Biography*, MI5 had advised against his appointment to the Ministry because they thought he was a security risk. Another Committee member, who actually went to Leipzig to attend the trial, was Ewen Montagu's brother Evan, film producer and table tennis ace, who had worked as Hitchcock's assistant on several films and who as a staunch Communist, was himself under MI5 surveillance. It is tempting to look for some buried meanings in the interweaving of all these names and connections, but as so often, it would prove fruitless.

Alerting Kliemann by cable to one of his cover addresses, and after a detailed 'rehearsal' with another of Tar's team on how to answer his questions, TREASURE flew from Bristol to Lisbon on 3 March 1944 armed with a 'cover' introduction to the British Press Attaché. Tar asked her at their last meeting if she was sure she wanted to go. TREASURE told him that though she was depressed, that would pass and she was not afraid.

She found herself again centre-stage in three weeks of risky play acting, tripping insouciantly between the local SIS Section V officers and their opposite numbers in the Abwehr, waiting for Kliemann to turn up. Abwehr staff, among them one Bücking, whom she claimed later – nothing in this story is too implausible, truth is often stranger than fiction – she had first met in the 1930s when he was captain of a cargo boat on which, at the close of her Warsaw adventure, she had travelled from Danzig to Rouen. When he eventually appeared Kliemann gave her another bracelet, an intelligence questionnaire, new codes and a box of cigars for her notional boss Sidney Bernstein in London. They also had time for meals and strolls and TREASURE used her Zeiss camera and its delayed-action shutter, (brought out from England contrary to Tar's explicit instructions), to take a few photographs of them together, an extraordinary trophy for MI5.

She had more time than SNOW, CELERY and BISCUIT to explore Lisbon beyond the synthetic glamour of the Estoril casino and the grand hotels. There were the damp cellars where soulful Portuguese singers tugged at the heartstrings with the doleful melodies of Fado. Or the improbable nightclub with scenes of old Russia painted on the plaster walls, and waiters in Cossack blouses, a scene made even more improbable when a tall ginger-haired Scot named Mackie, said to be a cashiered Guards officer, commandeered the piano and bewildered the audience with his renderings of 'Loch Lomond', 'Annie Laurie' and 'Auld Lang Syne'.[6]

Kliemann also gave her money, though in another fit of almost Chaplin-esque bungling, he first produced it in two large shoe boxes, each stuffed with English one pound notes, saying that this was all the local exchange dealers could provide. When TREASURE pointed out that taking it back through the British Customs might cause her problems, he scurried around to find some notes of larger denominations.

In turn, she gave Kliemann a Dunhill pigskin wallet, bought by Mary Sherer in Bond Street and made to resemble an envelope with the image of a 2½d stamp embossed on the upper right corner. She also got the much coveted wireless set, outwardly an ordinary domestic radio, but with its wiring rejigged by Abwehr engineers, so that it would operate as both receiver and transmitter at the flick of a hidden switch. She told Kliemann it would be best for her to give it to the Press Attaché, telling him she had bought it on the spur of the moment and ask him to ship it back to the Ministry in London. In fact she handed it over to SIS, and unlike poor Babs it reached London safely in the next diplomatic bag, along with a note of the detailed debriefing of TREASURE by the SIS Head of Station. When she had cleared Customs and taken the train back to London and her Mayfair 'safe house', Tar came calling, announced by Mary Sherer's trademark scratching with her fingernails at the flat's front door.

'Well, you're back' he said, shaking her hand. 'Truth be told, we thought we wouldn't see you again.'

'I know.'

'Did you have your doubts too? Anyway, everything's worked out just fine so that's alright.'

It was an exchange that a later French commentator thought sarcastically, demonstrated 'excessive sangfroid' on Tar's part, considering she had put herself very much in harm's way. It certainly smacks more of the terse greeting a spy chief in a John Buchan novel would offer an agent, just back from the bazaars of Baluchistan, than something calculated to resonate with an overwrought Russian woman.

We have long since come to understand the power of those Most Secret Sources but it is still impressive to see that all the German messages about the logistics of TREASURE's visit – where she should go, authorisng Kliemann to give her the cash, explaining more than once why Kliemann had been delayed – were being snatched out of the ether, broken at Bletchley Park and passed back to Tar and SIS. With all this backup, all these insights, what could go wrong? No one thought about the dog.

To make sense of the tensions that arose after she came back we need to remember that this was the run-up to D-Day. Tar, his case officers and the key deception agents were working day and night with General Eisenhower's planners, handily around the corner in St James's Square. As we saw, their task, to which Anthony Blunt also contributed, no doubt to Moscow's benefit and delight, was to create a soufflé of fact and fiction to mislead the Germans about when and where the attack would come, and to continue to deceive them in the period after the landings. One misstep in the mixing, one wrong ingredient, a mistake of one or two degrees in the oven temperature, and the soufflé could collapse. The first sign of trouble came from SIS soon after TREASURE's return, citing an American source in Lisbon who claimed that Bücking had been overheard saying he knew about TREASURE's mission, about which she had spoken far too indiscreetly and that he and she had arranged to stay in touch by mail. The report was initially ignored as being too vague.

But it was soon backed up by a similar account gleaned at Camp 020 in the interrogation of one of Bücking's couriers.

TREASURE meantime was working hard, from 'safe houses' in Hampstead and Palace Gardens Terrace, in Kensington, (not far from the Soviet Embassy), sending at least three messages a day on topics as varied as supposed troop movements, gossip from a drunken General about the Allies' policy on the use of gas, and the fact that gliders would form a major part of the invasion force.

But on 17 May, the ghost of Babs appeared on the scene. TREASURE told Mary Sherer – from the tone of the file note, rather truculently – that while in Lisbon she had agreed with Kliemann a 'check' sequence of letters which, if omitted from a message, would show she was operating under control. She had not told MI5 because when she returned she had been determined to get her own back on them for Babs' death by omitting the check at some point and thus 'blowing' the whole operation. This she had now decided not to do, though she initially refused to say what the check sequence was. Though some in MI5 did not believe her, thinking she was just 'spreading alarm and despondency', it was decided she had outlived her usefulness, though the set and its traffic still had value and would be handled by someone who knew her 'fist'. But they waited a prudent three weeks, until just after D-Day to confront her.

Tar did the job himself on 14 June and his note of the session will again surprise those who knew him only as a genial and unruffled colleague or grandparent. As with SNOW it combined menace and superficial generosity. She was finished. Her deceit over the check signal and the allegation she had agreed a 'back channel' to correspond with Bücking, (which she vehemently denied), had destroyed their trust in her. MI5 would pay her £5 per week, settle her doctors' bills and pay for a kidney operation if she needed one. Tar would also try, without commitment, when 'conditions made this possible' to arrange for her to rejoin her family in Paris or her sister in Algiers. 'I pointed out, however', his note recorded, 'that if I had any cause to think she was being indiscreet or in any way acting contrary to the interests of the Allied cause, I would at once take severe action and would either put her in prison or hand her over to the French authorities who would no doubt deal with her pretty severely.' The weekly payments would also stop. (It is not clear what grounds the French would have for treating her 'severely' unless this is a reference to one of our dimly glimpsed 'floaters'.)

Before leaving her he asked if she wanted to say anything. She did not, except – and one can almost see the pout and hear the foot stamp – that she did not want the money.

'I said that she would take it whether she liked it or not and that she could do what she liked with it.'

Her own memory of the encounter broadly matches Tar's, though with her love of detail she noticed that Tar's eyes seemed even bluer as his face grew ever more red. He had a clumsy darn in one leg of his Seaforth trews, those legendary 'Passion Pants', he needed a haircut and while he scolded her he gripped the arm of his chair so tightly that his knuckles went white. He behaved, she wrote witheringly, 'like a bad actor in a cheap melodrama'. It is hardly surprising he was upset. Though the D-Day landings had gone well, a leak by or through TREASURE could still wreak havoc. And the confrontation came just a day after the fear level of even the most fearless had been notched up when the first of the German V1 rockets, which were to become known as 'doodlebugs', had droned across the Channel and Southern England.

Later the same day Mary Sherer called on TREASURE and in the face of considerable petulance and affronted dignity, succeeded in getting her to divulge the check code.

As the war wound down and tempers cooled – for a while – TREASURE went to Paris to work for the Red Cross and in various liaison rôles for the French Army. By this time Kliemann had been captured and brought to Britain for interrogation. The TREASURE traffic nevertheless continued, to see what the Abwehr might make of it, but with the curious twist that the apparent sender from the British end was actually in Paris while the apparent recipient on the other side of the Channel was locked up in Camp 020. Kliemann's initial questioners thought flattery was the best way to induce him to talk but if he did not respond 'other treatment might be contemplated'. He was clearly in a bad shape mentally, swinging between apathy and tears, which did not deter a later comment when he was felt to be holding back, that if he continued 'he should be given as severe a shaking up as possible'.

However obtained, the reports of Kliemann's interrogation are a mine of information on his background, the Abwehr and its personalities, radio training of agents and the network of shabby individuals he had recruited as supposed 'stay behind agents' after the Germans left France. (Most of them had been supplied with captured British radios as German production had been bombed to a standstill. It hardly mattered since many of the supposed agents had already been rounded up and some even 'turned'.) Kliemann also revealed details of postal censorship, the travel pass system, and not least the shady 'Otto Organization', a group with strong SS ties and protection which, from an office in the Bois de Boulogne, a cluster of warehouses, and its own canal wharf and rail spur 'controlled the black market' from its position as the German's main buying agency in France.

His interrogators were briefed that though TREASURE's name could be mentioned as one of his agents whose name MI5 had uncovered, on no account should they tell Kliemann that she had in fact been working for St James's Street all along. This led him to volunteer that MI5 should run TREASURE and another agent back against his colleagues as doubles and that he would be willing to help. As Guy Liddell commented drily in his Diary, 'He has no idea that they have been run as such over a considerable period and that he himself is the sucker.' In fact the reports show that when Kliemann in blissful ignorance of Tar's triumph, identified Abwehr spies outside France, 'every agent whom he has mentioned seems to be controlled by B1a or similar bodies elsewhere'.

MI5 were professionals with a vital job to do. But in depicting TREASURE as temperamental, self-centred, impulsive and even occasionally hysterical, we cannot write her off nor lose sight of the fact that like SNOW, CELERY, GARBO, TRICYCLE and ZIGZAG, even the briefly seen GWLADYS, she went to face the Abwehr and the risk of exposure, interrogation, and death. Despite her tantrums, she had a clear mind, and was obviously convincingly charming whenever she needed to be. As we shall explore later, the Abwehr may well have been sloppy and gullible but in the middle of a war, they were dangerous folk to cross.

What did the case achieve, apart from much heartburn at the London end?

In the short months she had her radio, GC&CS found the traffic of great benefit in providing points of entry into Abwehr circuits and codes. A file note by John Marriott records a Bletchley Park comment that the TREASURE and BRUTUS traffic had 'absolutely saved the bacon of GC&CS during June, July, August and September'. At an operational level, Kliemann swallowed whole her deceptive written reports on troops movements and conditions in England. And though she never knew it, she actually got herself noticed by the German High Command, for example, with a message on 8 May 1944 that the illusory First US Army as under the command of General Montgomery, and another on 17 May about the Second US Army Division.[7] Perhaps her most striking 'posthumous' triumph was a message sent on her set in October 1944 by an MI5 operator who could imitate her style, on the effects of German V2s.

The intercepts showed it had been quoted almost verbatim in a German High Command communiqué, an acceptance which fuelled the difficult Whitehall debate about what more dis-information about impact points around London should be put across to the Germans to induce them cut back the rockets' range. (Though the details are less well documented than FORTITUDE, the analysis by Sir Michael Howard makes a convincing case that by averting even more destruction and havoc in London, this initiative deserves to be ranked among the major accomplishments of Double Cross.

It may also have given Tar an anxious moment. As we know he had moved Joan and his daughter Belinda down to Tunbridge Wells. Though it was well out of the way of the London Blitz it was on the rockets' flight path, though it seems only to have suffered minor damage from Goering's pilots dropping their remaining bombs as they scuttled homewards.

Nor did MI5 come away empty handed. In December 1944 Sir David Petrie, flanked by Guy Liddell, Tar, three other MI5 officers and Frank Foley of SIS, gave a dinner to honour TRICYCLE, rounded off by fine cigars, a wartime rarity. The 'need to know' principle held good even among friends; TRICYCLE was not let into the secret that the cigars were those given to TREASURE by Kliemann in Lisbon, as a gift for Sidney Bernstein. But the Abwehr too had its little laugh. Of the £10 notes Kliemann gave TREASURE in Lisbon, twenty-seven turned out to be forgeries.

Sadness and frustration run though many Russian stories. TREASURE's was no exception. In September 1945 her sister, Moussiya, who had married a French Count, disappeared while hitch-hiking across the ravaged landscape of northern France. At first a distraught TREASURE, who thought her sister feckless, wondered if she had been arrested by the British, more specifically the 'gangsters' as she called them, of MI5. Moussiya's body was then found in a ditch; she had been strangled. The alleged killer, a Belgian mechanic, said he had been trailing her on orders from an intelligence officer in US uniform 'who looked like a Mongol' and who had actually committed the crime. His story was not believed.

The frustration was Tar's. He began to worry about a book TREASURE had written about her wartime experiences. Had he known she had actually been keeping a diary, in defiance of basic security principles, his reaction would surely have verged on apoplexy. She had been adroit at concealing her scribbled notes from the French, Spanish, German, Portuguese and British customs officials as she criss-crossed Europe.

Although John Masterman had slithered through a legal loophole by publishing his recollections of Double Cross in the US, until well into the 1990s, Tar and his colleagues had chafed at MI5's unwillingness to let them tell their stories, even as more and more material came into the public domain. In 1944, still smarting from his passage at arms with TREASURE, Tar saw things differently, and made strenuous efforts, first to get hold of the manuscript and when that failed, to find backdoor ways to censor its contents. He ran the campaign himself rather than turn it over to Hinchley-

Cooke's legal machinery, maybe because in what seems an unusual oversight, unlike SNOW, TREASURE had not signed the Official Secrets Act or any other agreement to allow MI5 to have a say over what she published.

Mary Sherer and an MI5 colleague Susan Barton were asked to tug on the ties of feigned friendship to get a 'sneak preview'. Writing to 'Dear Mrs. B' in November 1944, Tar made no secret of his views about 'this wretched woman' who would 'always be a source of trouble to us, no matter what restrictions we impose on her – short of imprisonment for life'. Maybe Sue Barton could offer to help with the editing 'and advise her in connection with possible prosecutions which might arise as the result of published indiscretions'. But she risked being condemned by TREASURE as one of his 'gangsters'.

When that attempt failed Tar enlisted the help of Malcolm Muggeridge – 'Dear Malcolm' – who was then stationed in Paris as an SIS officer. One of his tasks there was to investigate the innocuous but inevitably controversial broadcasts made by the British humourist P. G. Wodehouse while in German hands during the war. Tar apologised 'for bothering you with this seemingly trivial matter, but I attach a certain amount of importance to it'. Muggeridge, whom we met first casting a cold eye on the early American arrivals in SIS' 'intelligence brothel', did not get the manuscript either but did succeed in getting the French Security Police to give TREASURE a stiff warning, which she was required to acknowledge in writing, backed by their private assurance to SIS that if she did try to publish in France, they would see to it through the publishers that London had sight of the manuscript in advance.

TREASURE then married an American and moved to Detroit, prompting an undaunted Tar to lean on the FBI via its 'Legal Attaché' at the US Embassy in London to get hold of the manuscript. They replied blandly that they had no power to intervene or even interview her unless she was in breach of any undertaking she had given the British. The book eventually appeared in France in 1966, and in a slightly amended English version in 1968; the French publishers' note says she died in 1950 after a long illness; the English edition attributes her death to 'an illness contracted during the war'.

Neither version is inconsistent with the debriefing report so carefully teased out in Nightingale Lane by Captain Ambrose and apart from her sniping at Tar, there seems little or nothing to which he could have taken serious offence, or which would have breached the security bulwarks. Whether the long delay in publication was the result of continuing background pressure which toned down her first version, or simply publisher disinterest, we do not know, but its eventual appearance seems to have caused no publicity ripples or official disquiet. Nor do we know whether Tar ever troubled to read it, though all those years later a favourable newspaper review, to which an unknown hand has added an exclamation mark, was duly added to her file.

Poor Babs was just an expendable furry pawn in the Great Game, broken-backed in an Algiers gutter. Had TREASURE gone through with her threat, blown the operation, and changed the course of history, Babs might have been memorialised in bronze on a plinth in the Unter dem Linden in Berlin, unveiled to the oompah-pah melodies of a Prussian brass band. As it was all he heard was the squeal of brakes. He is surely the only dog commemorated by his photograph in an MI5 file.

In 1995, another mention of TREASURE revived memories of those deadly prewar events in Paris. V.V. Popov, the one time Soviet Ambassador in London, tried his hand in retirement at a history of the Blunt case. To judge from the text[8] and the absence of source notes, he was allowed to put questions to the KGB archivists, and to interview at least one of the controllers of the Cambridge 'Ring Of Five', but was not given direct access to the files. He claims in a rather throwaway paragraph that TREASURE was in fact a Soviet agent, recruited in Paris by the treacherous Skoblin, betrayer of her uncle, General Miller, and that while she was working for Tar in London, Blunt helped her maintain contact with Moscow.

Leaving aside the lack of attribution, it is hard to see how Blunt could have had much contact with her, or quite what it was that she passed back to the Centre. If there is anything to the story, it is more likely that Blunt played back to Moscow all he knew about TREASURE, (to add to what Philby had undoubtedly also told them), and also her FORTITUDE traffic. An unsubstantiated claim made by Lauran Paine, that SNOW too, was a Soviet asset code-named 'Mr. BROWN' seems even more implausible, even for that epitome of implausibility.

Susan Barton deserves more than a brief mention for her rôle in trying to get sight of TREASURE's manuscript. Long before the emotional Russian came on the scene the files show she had alerted Tar to anti-Semitic comment in traffic sent by some agents. At the time, one of her jobs in Section B1a was culling the home and foreign press for material which could be used to add flavour or fact to agents' messages. To guide her, she also saw the agents' outgoing traffic, and she pointed out to Tar rather firmly that MUTT had been allowed to comment to the Germans that anti-Jewish sentiment in Britain was growing, while BALLOON – notionally an accomplice of TRICYCLE – had referred to 'the dirty Jews'. She told Tar that while there were indeed signs of negative public sentiment towards the Jews, fuelled by press reports of 'food racketeering', this was a dangerous and harmful line for supposedly well-placed German 'agents' to feed their masters. It would allow William Joyce, the renegade Fascist who broadcast to England for the Nazis, whom his British listeners had scornfully nicknamed 'Lord Haw Haw', to claim that Germany had been right in its treatment of the Jews and to argue to his British audience that the war would go on 'as long as it suits the Jews'.

Tar consulted Charles Cholmondeley and John Masterman and sensibly, as usual, commented not on the substance of the point but on the wider issue that Section B1a lacked a mechanism for clearing information of a political nature, which he felt this was, to be put across by their agents. He had understood the arbiter was Victor Cavendish Bentinck at the Foreign Office 'but we have never got any nearer him than Major Cowgill'. He also suggested John Masterman use his contacts to find out about the remit of the new Political Warfare Executive, (he refers to it in error as the Ministry of Political Warfare), the organisation initially part of SOE but soon hived off into a separate structure generating overt and covert propaganda.

As we learn from Christopher Andrew,[9] Susan Barton worked as a 'casual agent' for MI5 for several years before the war, providing information on the German community in Britain; she may well have been an émigrée. She moved to The Hague where she caught the eye of the German naval attaché. London hoped the relationship would lead to intelligence opportunities, but after the Germans captured the two SIS officers at Venlo, there was too great a risk her identity would become known, and she was pulled back to Britain.

Evidently another capable multi-tasker, she also appears in the GARBO story. To provide a commercial veneer for GARBO's activities in London, Tar rented a small office off Piccadilly as the base of a company called – rather disingenuously – Tarlair Ltd and provided him, as GARBO later reminisced, with 'a secretarial gem . . . without whom I would have been lost. She mixed my invisible ink and prepared code messages and the drafts of letters to be sent to my mail drops'. Her name was Susan Barton.

Notes
1. Stafford Smith, pp. 227–8.
2. Bernstein, Sidney Lewis, Baron, 1899–1993.
3. Casson.
4. Truffaut, François, 1932–84, film producer, director, screenwriter and actor, one of the founders of the 'New Wave' in French cinema.
5. Truffaut, p. 158.
6. See e.g. Seligo.
7. See e.g. Hesketh.
8. Popov, p. 91.
9. Andrew, *Defence of the Realm*, pp. 242–3.

34

Game Set And Match?

To judge by the style, Hugh Trevor-Roper was the anonymous reviewer quoted at the outset about the British talent for deception.

He went on to savage Tar's opponents in the Abwehr as '. . . the most inefficient, credulous gang of idlers, drunkards and turncoats as ever masqueraded as a secret service'.

There are individual Abwehr officers, especially those luxuriating in neutral capitals, against whom one or more of these barbs can be fairly directed. But do they smack rather of the triumphant jibes of a victor? After all, intelligence and security services across the world and the span of history, the British, American and Russian not least among them, have let their guard down, falling prey to all of these weaknesses and more besides.

Like MI5, the Abwehr has intrigued many researchers, notably David Kahn's groundbreaking study, though the lack of archival records is an obstacle. It had its roots in the sub-rosa stirrings of German rearmament after the First World War, and was eviscerated by the Nazis in 1944. Also about Admiral Wilhelm Canaris, who became its head in 1935. But in the run up to the Second World War, Tar and his colleagues knew very little of the organisation they were fighting. So how and why did they come out on top? We have seen enough of the subtlety and detail of Tar's operations, the Most Secret Sources and the broad and complex supporting infrastructure to understand the power of the machine. But though unlike the British, the Germans were not able to trace an intelligence tradition going back to the time of the first Queen Elizabeth, they were not amateurs. As Colonel Woolrych of SOE commented ruefully, he had found a briefing by Tar on the Abwehr's weaknesses, 'deeply disappointing for one anxious to learn all he can professionally from an enemy who can usually teach us so many lessons.' Our own necessarily brief review begins with twenty-two single-spaced 'Top Secret' pages headed THE GERMAN INTELLIGENCE SERVICE AND THE WAR, also written by Trevor-Roper at the end of the Second World War. It came to rest in the Cabinet Office files, rather than those of MI5.

It is a harsh indictment, but more even-handed than the book review from which we quoted, giving credit to the Abwehr for some of its notable victories, not least against SOE in the Low Countries. Its Belgian networks were wholly compromised and in Holland, in an operation which Tar described after the War as 'brilliantly handled', two Abwehr officers played the radio game with such deadly efficiency that over an eighteen month period they lured SOE in Baker Street into sending forty-six agents into German hands, as well as container loads of arms and supplies; SIS lost four agents in the same trap. Occupied France too was another clandestine battle-ground on which the Abwehr and its agents used penetration and duplicity to inflict significant damage on some key SOE circuits, and again get their hands on weapons, ammunition and large amounts of money dropped into their eager hands by a hoodwinked London.

The Germans could also claim credit for rolling up the Soviet 'Red Orchestra' espionage ring, the purloining of Top Secret papers from the British Embassy in Istanbul by the Ambassador's valet, codenamed CICERO, and the coups of SNOW's case officer Ritter in the US. Though sloppy tradecraft left his network, by one account extending to thirty-five agents, and known later as the Duquesne Spy Ring, exposed to rapid FBI penetration, its successes with the plans of the top secret Norden bombsight and the Sperry gyroscope were of major benefit to the rapidly rearming Luftwaffe. Ritter's recruitment of the Hungarian adventurer and explorer Count László Almásy[1] to lead an espionage mission across the Libyan desert to the Middle Nile, was an operation put together with élan, though it ended badly.

The 'Bureau Klatt' in Bulgaria, run by an Austrian Abwehr officer named Kauder under an alias, was apparently a valuable source of high-grade intelligence on Russian matters and to some extent the

Middle East, though the balance of opinion seems to be that its main sources, one an émigré White Russian Prince, were being fed with information by the Soviets. (Its activities were being tracked in London by GC&CS, MI5 and SIS; the latter's representative on the case was Kim Philby, another of the ambiguous short-circuits which dot the files.)

Abwehr surveillance of the SIS Station in The Hague had led to the well-exploited kidnapping of Stevens and Payne-Best. Less well known is that by bribing a junior officer in the station they also got their hands on Otto Krüger, a prominent businessman who had been a valuable SIS source inside Germany since 1919.[2] Spain was the Abwehr's trump card. Through Admiral Canaris' long-standing ties with the Franco régime, (a signed photograph of the Generalissimo had pride of place on his office wall), in the early years of the war his service was able to add a pro-German bias to Spain's supposedly non-belligerent stance and provoke sabotage against British shipping and Gibraltar itself. In one of its better initiatives, it even built a sophisticated monitoring station to track Allied shipping movements though the Straits, (though British pressure on Franco soon led to it being shut down). Franco's Chief of General Staff Intelligence, General Martinez Campo looked forward eagerly to his annual 'Christmas Box', paid out of Abwehr funds and as Trevor-Roper noted, Spanish police, coastguards, Customs officials and army officers acted for the Abwehr with the approval or connivance of their superiors.

Looking first at the higher-order weaknesses, Hugh Trevor-Roper saw the root causes of the eventual downfall of Canaris and his service as the Nazi system itself and the Admiral's personal failings. One of the régime's characteristics – it had been bloodily evident as the Nazi Party rose to power – was that though the world saw and feared it as a structured pyramid with Hitler at its head, the latter's guiding principle, if we can use that word of a genocidal maniac, was 'Divide and Rule.' Much like a mediaeval court his satraps schemed and fought for each scrap of power – since power brought wealth and booty, as well as the Fuhrer's ear – and Hitler, often deliberately unwilling to decide between rival claims, letting the rival groups fight out their battles in what Trevor-Roper called 'a vortex of competing personal ambitions'. So it was with intelligence, where the Abwehr had to compete with the *Sicherheitsdienst* or SD, controlled as part of the SS and Gestapo empire by Heinrich Himmler through thuggish lieutenants like Ernst Kaltenbrunner, Reinhard Heydrich and Walter Schellenberg. The kidnapping of the SIS officers at Venlo was a rare example of co-operation between the two organisations; the Abwher did the watching while the actual 'snatch' was carried out with some bravura by the SD.

In a move with which their opponents in London would have grudgingly empathised had they known, as early as 1935 Canaris and Heydrich had to try to resolve their demarcation disputes formally but only temporarily, through what became known – oddly in that wildly ungodly regime – as 'The Ten Commandments'. But there were other players on the intelligence field. Goering's *Forschungsamt*, which tapped phone and teleprinter lines, especially of foreign diplomatic missions, and thus provided Hitler with valuable insights as he bullied and bluffed his way through the 1930s. The Wehrmacht's signals intercept service monitored the lower-level operational traffic of Allied forces, with some success, notably in North Africa. The Nazi Party's overseas *Auslandsorganisation* hoovered up commercial and technical intelligence from sources in expatriate communities, while Foreign Minister von Ribbentrop jealously guarded the activities of his own Political Intelligence Bureau. Goebbels used the various German news agencies controlled by his Propaganda Ministry to gather intelligence and spread disinformation.

Unlike in Britain, interception and codebreaking were not centralised, so that its products and its opportunities were not assessed centrally, nor was any one body responsible for the investment in intellectual and technological firepower which created RSS, the deciphering 'bombe' machines, and built Bletchley Park into a lynchpin of the war, all operating under a well-oiled co-ordinating machinery encompassing Whitehall and the armed services, something the Germans never had. Their intelligence, in Trevor-Roper's words, 'stagnated in private pools'.

Trevor-Roper also points the finger of blame at Canaris himself as 'a bad judge of men and himself a professional intriguer rather than an organiser. As a consequence of the first fault he chose worthless officers and in consequence of the second he gave them practical independence. In effect the operational officers of the Abwehr sat in Paris and Athens, in Biarritz and Estoril enjoying the opportunities for self indulgence provided by these resorts undisturbed (owing to a complete lack of centralisation at headquarters) as long as a quota of reports was sent in.'

Canaris rarely fired any of his 2,000 or so officers, whatever they did or failed to do, and despite his preaching that 'modesty was the way to good fortune' and that his colleagues should exercise moderation in their consumption of alcohol. 'Excessive spending and celebrations' were to be avoided, and, reminding us that he was a man of Kell's generation, female employees were to avoid too much 'dressing up, painted lips or fingernails'. On no account should a woman have the keys to any Abwehr safe. We have spoken of the Kell era MI5 as 'a family firm'; some on the German General Staff spoke sarcastically of the Abwehr as 'The Canaris Family Limited' because of the large number of the admiral's relatives on the payroll.

We do not know the names of all the Abwehr men SNOW met in Lisbon but it seems certain that one of them would have been its Major Kremer von Auenrode, also TRICYCLE's case officer, whom he knew as 'von Karsthoff'. In the Spring of 1942 an investigating officer told Canaris that von Auenrode and some of his staff should be dismissed for 'palpable corruption'. Canaris refused to listen.

Nor did it matter much whether agents' reports were true or false, since there was no central point where they were evaluated, and at least as long as the Wehrmacht was advancing, veracity was unimportant. Quantity counted more than quality.

Trevor-Roper writes: '. . . it was equally unimportant whether agents were controlled by the Allies or not'. 'It was better to have one controlled agent than none at all,' observed one cynical officer when it was suggested to him (correctly) that his principal source of information was under Allied management. And another officer when a similar suggestion was made about another agent (again correctly), raised his hands in horror at such an indecent reference to these undisputed but irrelevant facts of life. 'If he were to admit that to his chief', he said, 'he would be shot for defeatism'. There were no other agents producing information of similar value and the [Abwehr] could not afford to admit that it had no genuine agents in Britain.

The *reductio ad absurdum* of this system came when it was realised that if truth and falsehood were irrelevant, it was a waste of money to pay real agents. By the end of the war there were several officers or head agents who were regularly inventing (and being paid for) both their agents and their agents' reports. As Trevor-Roper concludes even those Abwehr officers 'who were intelligent enough to see the need for central evaluation were corrupt enough to see the necessity of preventing it.' The point was made in another way by an elegant former Abwehr secretary interviewed for the BBC's *Timewatch* TV programme who saw agent running as 'a matter of prestige'. The more agents an officer ran, the higher his standing amongst his peers, and an agent in Britain counted for more than one in, say, Switzerland.

Conversely, as several observers have pointed out, if case officers owned up to the reality that they had no spies, or that the bona fides of those they did claim were open to doubt, they ran the risk of a rapid transfer to the Russian front.

Any Abwehr officer could recruit an agent and once that was done the agent was his rather than the Abwehr's. Our brief notes about the supporting cast of lesser known but in their way equally valuable agents bear this out. Some were recruited from Germany, some in Lisbon or Madrid, some were run from there, others from Bremen, Oslo, Hamburg, Paris or Nantes. The centralised disciplines, the cross-checking, the vigilant well-briefed interrogations at the London Reception Centre, the co-ordination with other services, the constant vigilance, close to mistrust, which were London's hallmarks, were notable by their absence on the German side. At the same time such efforts as the Abwehr made to keep its various offices informed of agents' movements, training and cash needs, meant the multiplication and repetition of messages, valuable grist for the mills of Bletchley Park. The grist also served to reinforce the confidence of Tar and his colleagues that the Germans were swallowing their scripts, all crafted with the attention to detail of a Robertson embroidery needle.

Another aspect of Trevor-Roper's point about poor management again comes from our own narrative, in the way Ritter and Kliemann scurried around Europe, the Balkans, the Middle East, like White Rabbits always late for an important date, clearly without any time to really reflect, let alone consult with colleagues. This may be a more practical explanation of John Gwyer's conclusion after his postwar interrogation of Ritter that 'his handling of the cases under his control was, from the outset, extremely slack. When he could leave a case or part of a case to some other section . . . he did so. As a result his own knowledge, even of the SNOW case, is strictly confined to those parts of it which he handled personally. Of the rest he remembers very little and never even at the time, knew very much.'

Nevertheless Ritter would have been flattered to know that based on RSS analysis of Abwehr radio traffic, Trevor-Roper concluded in 1941 that Ritter was 'obviously a man of great importance . . . he seems to be the highest personage we know of in the whole Hamburg system . . .' Indeed '. . . Ritter, more than anyone else, is the Hamburg system . . .'

He had been an enigma to MI5 since his name first surfaced in the SNOW case and the files contain notes and cables from almost every senior officer – Tar, Masterman, Dick White, Marriott, and 'Buster' Milmo, to any source which might throw up a lead and better still identify a photograph – 'Tin Eye' Stevens down at Ham, the FBI, SIS, and the Governors of Dartmoor and Aylesbury Prisons. (The photograph that fluttered from hand to hand, and which remains on the file, is almost certainly not Ritter.)

Ritter worked hard and was not a 'bad man' but again we can criticise the Abwehr for making him responsible for the British target, about which he knew demonstrably little, instead of leaving him in place under non-official cover in the US, which he knew well.

His misapprehensions about Welsh revolutionary fervour, his unquestioning acceptance that SNOW had a Welsh friend who would give him access to a trawler in the middle of a war, suggest a lack of understanding of his target country. And his assessment that a potential agent, an Oxford educated German who wore tweeds, smoked a pipe and 'often sported a deerstalker hat' would blend in to British society as a source of intelligence seems wide of the mark, even by 1930's sartorial norms.

In the same vein his plan to infiltrate the glamorous Vera Schalburg into Britain to add to the attractions of a 'salon' run by the Duchesse de Château Thierry, (a lady whose title was grander than her provenance), which would act as a magnet for nuggets of society and political gossip seems to have been based on a reading of bad translations of Michael Arlen and Evelyn Waugh.[3]

Abwehr counter-intelligence operations did better in territories, such as France, controlled by the German army and a sharp-eyed Gestapo, such as France, with a largely subservient local police force and bureaucracy, and a cowed population, some elements of which were always ready to collaborate overtly or covertly, or to inform on their neighbours to curry favour, or extricate themselves from trouble. Hitler had made no secret of his ambitions and the Abwehr had time to lay its groundwork, and to cultivate and suborn biddable officials, businessmen with an eye out for contracts, and right-wing or Fascist sympathisers. But even in occupied Amsterdam, so a postwar interrogation report claimed, the Abwehr chief had used his office 'less for intelligence purposes than to bed his mistress and to conduct his Black Market activities'.[4]

By contrast, as Dick White conjectured in his lecture, Britain was treated for too long as a country which might be cajoled out of war, which meant that the Germans made almost no effort to create networks and put agents in place, a perverse credit to those in high circles who in the 1930s encouraged appeasement of Hitler and Mussolini by allowing them to satisfy their territorial appetites.

Support for this is found in the postwar reminiscences of a senior Abwehr officer Paul Leverkühn who wrote that until 1936, Britain was 'off limits' to all German intelligence. The prohibition was then relaxed but only to the extent that while 'a certain degree of observation' was permitted, deployment of active agents was still prohibited. It was not until the autumn of 1937 that the restriction was lifted, and the Abwehr was allowed to target not just the UK but its naval bases and garrisons overseas. 'It was terribly hard to find people for this extended mission' and while some success was achieved the best results – and even those were not comprehensive – came from efforts against French naval bases. When war came, Britain was ready, thanks in large part to MI5, to go into what twenty-first century journalists would call 'lockdown', protected behind its maritime moat, with tight border controls, an alert police force and not always dozy Home Guard, its people xenophobic and nervously alert; in Leverkühn's words 'at all levels of society the British have a remarkable passion for playing the detective . . .' As we shall see later, so did Leverkühn.[5]

The agents who were hurriedly recruited across the Continent were unprofessional, unfit and untrained. They had flimsy cover stories, defective identity papers and foreign accents. Above all their impending arrival, and often their earlier movements had been signalled by those Most Secret Sources.

More broadly, there was none of the central command and control exercised by Liddell and Tar and no 'tea parties' to chew over what to do next on tricky cases.

Notes
1. A larger than life character who, improbably, spent some of his childhood in Eastbourne; he was the model for the eponymous English Patient in the 1992 novel and the subsequent film.
2. Brammer, p. 71.
3. In any event the plan failed when Vera and two other agents were caught soon after a flight in a seaplane and a less comfortable ride in a rubber dinghy had brought them ashore in Scotland. The agents were executed but rather than being 'doubled', Vera, born in Siberia and in earlier life a Soviet intelligence 'asset' was described in one MI5 note as 'an interesting type quite capable of extracting information through intimacy with men'.
4. Hoare, p. 364.
5. See e.g. Leverkühn, p. 67.

35

Gullible's Travels

We need only to look at SNOW, GARBO, TRICYCLE and so many of Tar's other cases to understand 'credulous'. The Abwehr swallowed everything thrown its way, like a Medan crocodile. It was not just the diet of deceit fed to them from London. Until the end of the war the Abwehr classified as 'correct without qualification', intelligence fed by fabricators, notably the inventive Czech they codenamed OSTRO, a 'businessman' based in Lisbon. His reports were based on diligent reading of the local, British, US and neutral press, trade directories and journals, and railway timetables, souped up by a creative imagination bordering on genius.[1]

His reports were so close to the mark that when his traffic was first picked up in London, it raised concerns that he might be running a genuine network in Britain. Even when that idea was scotched, his reports on troop movements in the run-up to D-Day were so uncomfortably accurate that they threatened the FORTITUDE deception; we have already noted Liddell's rather chilling aside that MI5 and SIS were debating whether OSTRO should be 'torpedoed' in some way, '. . . the present suggestion is that we should try to buy him up or bump him off.'

An even better example of gullibility compounded by crossed wires is the fabricator and double agent known to MI5 as HAMLET, and to the Abwehr as Doctor Koestler, notional head of the chimerical Lisbon-based KOHLBERG organisation. Starting with John Masterman, there are several versions of a tale which far outrivals SNOW and CELERY in its ambiguity and complexity. It also has a different flavour – literally, since one of its consequences was that Section B1a found itself in the lemonade powder business. Space does not permit more than a brief glimpse of Koestler –

described in an MI5 file note as 'an Austrian Jew, the son of a family of well to do lawyers and bankers' and 'an industrial chemist of some ability', who walked the tightrope of deception with cool agility. He makes SNOW seem a rank amateur. Round his genuine 'Sociedad de Productos Exclusivos', he built a fictional intelligence network which Major Brinkhaus of the Brussels Abwehr embraced with fervour and cash as the Kohlberg Organisation. He was excited as it blossomed into spurious life, first with local subagents and, as the fantasy fed on itself, six imaginary Polish agents, some of whom had allegedly been sent to spy in Britain, some to the US, while one was being trained for work in North Africa. By February 1943 Koestler had sent 138 reports to Brinkhaus in Brussels; like the chalked boast with which London's now vanished pavement artists appended to their multi-coloured drawings, he could have signed them 'All my own work'. He had the sense not to.

But Koestler had another secret harmony to play. He turned to London, first with the story that he represented a group of senior Wehrmacht officers who favoured a negotiated peace with Britain, and that if Whitehall could provide him with some 'judicious propaganda' suggesting Britain might be receptive to such an approach, Koestler would pass it on to the officer group to encourage them. An MI5 agent designated MULLETT was ordered to keep the contact alive. He became a frequent flyer between Lisbon and London on those dangerous flights with their dangerous passengers. he even took on the rôle of Koestler's notional business representative in London according to a move which later, Masterman 'compelled B1a to embark on considerable business activities connected with soaps, impregnated paper, and degreasing patents, as well as lemonade powder'.

Koestler then disclosed that the officer group did not exist. Nor did the Kohlberg Organisation. What he really wanted was British help in supplying more intelligence that could be fed to the Germans and keep his supposed organisation in play. MI5 understandably wondered about was driving him. As an Austrian refugee and Jew, who might or might not have spent time in a concentration camp, revenge against the Germans must rank high. There was a commercial advantage for him to stay in Lisbon and continue to build a successful business outside the German orbit. A 'substantial motive' for wanting to 'stand well with the British authorities' was that his two children were in Britain. (According to Masterman he had asked MULLETT to carry jewels back to London to be sold for the children's support). Whatever the real reasons he 'placed himself entirely in our hands and was even willing to provide us with such compromising material as copies of the letters which had been exchanged between him and Brinkhaus.'

The story, on which as the files show Tar kept a careful eye, and in which SIS played an active rôle, has many more twist and turns, but our purpose in thus summarising it is to highlight another of the Abwehr's weaknesses, a propensity for internal 'turf wars'. Koestler was run from Brussels, his home after he left Austria, and though he was now based in Lisbon, his 'organisation' operated quite separately from the Lisbon station. The station's Head, Kammler, became apprehensive about the scale of Koestler's activities and made a bid either to get it under his control and 'put some check upon its operations'. This was not easy. Not only was he trespassing on Brussels' turf, but also – in another example of the Abwehr's dysfunctional structure – on that of Cologne, which claimed some authority over another of the agents involved. Officers from the three Stations met, debated, and on the face of it, Cologne and Lisbon withdrew their claims, leaving the field to Brussels. But in a gesture interpreted by MI5 as a bid to deter Koestler from returning from a visit to Madrid, Kammler reported to Berlin that his heavy involvement in currency and gold smuggling had come to the notice of the Portuguese police who were going to arrest him on his return. Nothing seems to have come of this, either because it was a falsehood or because the nimble Koestler wriggled his way out of whatever the problem was.

HAMLET severed his Abwehr links in April 1944. Masterman's summing up[2] was that while the case had considerable potential, MI5 did not draw 'a proper dividend'. He suggests that one of the reasons, alongside lingering suspicions of HAMLET's motives was that perhaps because of those peace feeler aspects there were other

Whitehall players on the field, one of them presumably SIS. As he puts it elliptically '. . . the opportunities which it offered to other departments made us chary of using the case fully for our own ends'. To judge from the file these included not just SIS, interested in undermining the Abwehr, but also the Foreign Office and the Ministry of Economic Warfare, busy fighting the wolfram battle.

The Abwehr's wide-eyed, unquestioning appetite for intelligence stemmed from the fact that they saw their primary rôle as gatherers of information, to be assessed on quantity rather than quality, leaving to others higher up the military chain of command the responsibility for collation and evaluation. As Frank Foley of SIS wrote to Masterman in 1943, '. . . the Abwehr are receiving an immense amount of contradictory information which they are religiously feeding to Berlin. If the German General Staff read it, it must be either giving them a severe headache or destroying their faith in the Abwehr, if they still have any left.'

Even so, the healthy if not always justified respect in Europe and indeed elsewhere for the deviousness and cunning of the legendary 'British Secret Service' ought to have put them more on the alert for trickery. Instead, doubts and disbelief were miraculously suspended. One reason was that high-level sophisticated deception was not a mainstream Abwehr strategy. Its success in playing back of SOE radios was considerable, but essentially operational rather than strategic and probably not widely shared across the disjointed Abwehr organisation.

Even before the war, reverting back for a moment to SNOW's early involvement with SIS, the one Service which did attempt to generate deceptive material was the Kriegsmarine, the German navy. Once the war started all the German armed services were extremely reluctant to release even scraps of information to be passed to the enemy. The Abwehr thus had no conception of the myriad shapes deception could take, like the mutations of gods and monsters in mythology, even less the boundless imagination and scale of the organisation ranged against them from St James's Street and Bletchley Park. Though the Kriegsmarine was instinctively suspicious of the security of its Enigma machines, especially when the

Royal Navy and RAF seemed to be having uncanny success tracking down its U Boats, painstaking investigations and multiple bouts of intense analysis[3] concluded that the British could not possibly be reading its signals traffic and that the answer lay in Britain's technological lead in Radar and direction-finding.

'Idlers and drunkards' are again rather subjective jabs, though there are enough descriptions of the dolce vita in the neutral capitals to suggest they are hardly unfair. Keith Benton tells of one Abwehr officer in Lisbon who welcomed the chance to visit Madrid since he was a great fan of pornographic movies. Salazar's ascetic régime frowned on such things whereas Madrid had at least two movie theatres specialising in the genre, known as 'cinés cochons'. And we know from CELERY that he found several Abwehr officers and diplomats subsisting on a mind-blurring diet of what today would be called 'uppers' and 'downers'.

As for 'turncoats', there were several important Abwehr defections, most publicly the anti-Nazi Catholic Eric Vermehren and his aristocratic wife.

Without discipline and accountability fraud was unavoidable. Case officers 'skimmed' some of the money destined for their agents or dabbled profitably in illegal currency exchanges. At a more senior level one high-ranking official was found to have used his official position to help seven wealthy Jewish families to flee into Switzerland. He had some difficulty in explaining why if they were there, as he claimed, so that some could act as agents, the move was accompanied by the transfer of $100,000 from Abwehr funds to his personal account with a Swiss bank. And though the facts are as so often, murky, the Abwehr officer central to the TRICYCLE case, his old friend Johnny Jebsen, was himself involved with TRICYCLE's brother in a number of currency arbitrage and money laundering schemes, 'financial rackets', in the words of the MI5 file, for his own and colleagues' benefit.

TRICYCLE tells us that in pre-war Yugoslavia, Jebsen had been 'an indefatigable businessman' whose friends had coined the word 'Jebseniade' to describe 'some business proposition or a clever trick'. His lifestyle as an Abwehr officer in Lisbon[4] was bound to ring alarm bells all the way back to Berlin, and lead the Abwehr's many enemies in the Nazi system to wonder what he was really up to. He 'maintained a luxurious villa [in Estoril], with four servants. Johnny's Rolls Royce Silver Ghost was like a chariot of Eros ferrying the most beautiful women . . . with special emphasis on the useful secretaries of the German Embassy to candlelit dinners at the villa'. It was his illegal currency transactions rather than the fact that he had turned his coat and become a Double Cross agent known as ARTIST, which cost him his life when the Gestapo caught up with him.[5]

Notes

1. A detailed study of the potential sensitive information available in the public domain in those years would be interesting. A casual glance at *Flight* magazine, as a random example, suggests that the British censors, always on the lookout for even minor indiscretions in day to day letters, could nod when it came to technical matters.
2. Masterman, p. 119.
3. See e.g. Ratcliffe.
4. Popov, D., p. 217.
5. It is an episode well told elsewhere (e.g. Hesketh). By comparison, TREASURE's threat to blow the whole operation was a minor diversion. ARTIST's arrest had Tar and his colleagues seriously worried that if he were broken, or revealed all to save his skin from the corruption charges, it would fatally compromise all their careful planning. He wasn't and it didn't.

36

End Game

But even darker clouds loomed on Canaris' horizon. In the 1960s John Osborne, in his way as much an *enfant terrible* as Trevor-Roper, built a controversial play around a question the Austro-Hungarian Emperor Franz Joseph is said to have grunted, when told that a rising young officer was a true patriot. 'Yes but is he a patriot for me?' In the marble corridors of power of Hitler's Germany it was a question often asked about the Abwehr and Admiral Canaris, at first *sotto voce* and later as its lack of success became more evident, with increasing stridency. The Abwehr had its share of wins. But these might be classed as operational, rather than strategic. When it came to anticipation of major Allied initiatives such as Operation Torch or Husky, or key developments such as the overthrow of Mussolini, they failed dismally, feeding the paranoia of those who felt the Abwehr, like the senior echelons of the Foreign Ministry and many in the General Staff were not 'patriots for the Führer'.

Many Abwehr officers were certainly at best ambivalent about the barbarity of the Nazi régime, though initially they trod a cautious line, exemplified by a speech Canaris had made to some of his officers in December 1941. He told them the Abwehr had nothing to do with the persecution of Jews, who were to be treated in a humane, respectable, correct and 'cultural' manner. On the other hand while 'activity against the Jews' was to be avoided, it was not to be criticised. Writing long after the Second World War, Leverkühn tells us that the Abwehr also opposed the policy of taking and shooting hostages in reprisals for Resistance attacks in occupied territories. He and his colleagues felt, as he later wrote this was not 'justifiable' under international law and more pragmatically only served to escalate the cycle of violence.

Judging from the historical record, these *post facto* views were not expressed loudly at the time. But it was no doubt free discussion between Abwehr officers themselves on such delicate topics that, after eighteen months, led it to unplug microphones buried in the banquettes of a popular restaurant near its Hamburg headquarters, 'to avoid the risk of court martial and damage to the Abwehr's standing with its peers'.[1] Testifying at the Nuremberg Trials, one of Canaris' close colleagues[2] described his Chief as 'a pure intellect, an interesting, highly individual and complicated personality who hated violence as such and therefore hated and abominated war, Hitler, his system and particularly his methods. In whichever way one might look at him, Canaris was a human being.'

In 1939, just before Germany's invasion of Poland, Canaris had, he told the Tribunal, 'expressed scruples' about the planned bombing of Warsaw, because of the likely repercussions abroad, and 'protested vehemently' to Foreign Minister Ribbentrop, and Wehrmacht Generals Keitel and Jodl, against Hitler's orders that the 'Polish intelligentsia, nobility, clerics and Jews' were to be exterminated. Keitel had told him this had been decided by the Führer, with the comment that 'if the armed forces did not want to have a part in it they would have to be satisfied with the SS coming into the field to carry out the measures'. According to Lahousen, Canaris had also manoeuvred adroitly to thwart Hitler's demand for the assassination of the French Generals Giraud and Weygand.

Men with silver Deaths Head badges in their peaked caps had no time for scruples, and also suspected Canaris, perhaps rightly, of backstairs peace dialogues with the Allies. When Franco, sniffing the political and strategic breezes across the Pyrenees switched his stance from 'non-belligerent' to 'neutral', and heavily underlined the move by refusing his quondam friend Canaris a visa to enter Spain, the ideologues smelled blood, and the 'the Old Fox's' slide towards the scaffold began. By February 1944 the long run of failures, the growing tales of venality and the ideological doubts, amongst them its employment of Jews such as Kauder and Koestler, forced Canaris towards retirement. One of Himmler's acolytes mocked the Hamburg office as staffed by 'jazz Jews'. But according to a biography of the Nazi police chief Kaltenbrunner,[3] it was an Abwehr operational mistake in Spain which finally drove the ever vacillating Hitler to act.

Because the Franco relationship was so important and so fragile, he had ordered that it should not be put at risk by any sabotage within Spain. The Abwehr Madrid Station – unheeding, glory-hunting, trouble-making, we shall never know – nevertheless arranged for explosives to be loaded in a cargo of Spanish oranges being shipped back to England on a British freighter. Hitler's fury led him to decree the Abwehr's end. Declaring the very name 'Abwehr' to be 'un-German', (it is generally translated as 'defence'), Himmler took over what one of his aides excoriated as 'the whole box of junk'. In a speech he made to revel in the takeover, Himmler prayed for an immediate invasion so that the 'plutocratic West' could be 'drowned in the stream of their own blood'. 'By 1945', he prophesied, 'the Russians would be driven beyond the Urals and a Chinese Wall built by Russian slave labour to keep them from ever returning.' He was wrong as well as barking mad.

It was too late. Even if his new 'masters of the universe' in intelligence had produced valuable insights, Himmler's control over the product meant that, in Trevor-Roper's words, it was 'withdrawn from rational evaluation and subject to somnambulist interpretation'. It then had to be chewed over in the febrile atmosphere of decision making at Hitler's HQ, and there subjected to 'the arbitrary whims of a group of ignorant maniacs'.

Short months later, the Wehrmacht plot to assassinate Hitler had failed. Several Abwehr officers were directly implicated, most of them executed cruelly and in short order. Canaris, against whom there was initially no direct evidence of complicity, was left in nervous retirement, but when the Gestapo unearthed some allegedly compromising diary notes he was taken to Flossenburg Concentration Camp in Bavaria and hanged, naked, on Himmler's direct orders.

Though each of these factors was another weight loaded onto the scales against the Abwehr, the post-war analysis emphasises the importance of those Most Secret Sources, 'impersonal information against which the reliability of intelligence from personal sources by which the success of penetration could be measured and in accordance with which the policy and tactics of deception could be modulated'. The Abwehr did not have the same advantage, 'a failure for which some excuse can reasonably be made'.

But someone had to do the measuring and the modulating. We have seen enough of the London system to know that while not everything ran smoothly, and there were wrangles over demarcation lines and sharing of intelligence, the overall organisation, the co-ordination and the integrity of the case officers (if not invariably their agents) were markedly different, immeasurably better than on the German side.

For Tar and his colleagues, other than the sporadic tussles with Cowgill at SIS, office intrigue and hierarchical distinctions seem not to have existed, allowing that talented, loyal, hard working group to give complex and critical issues the unique blend of free-thinking, psychological insight and meticulous care that gave them the win. Like the charismatic post-war London banker Siegmund Warburg, they would have regarded catchphrases such as 'we'll cross that bridge when we come to it' or 'no use crying over spilled milk' as anathema. Like Warburg from the austere elegance of his City office, and unlike the Abwehr, before any major business operation was launched, every nuance, all possible or even barely plausible out-comes, all conceivable moves and countermoves, any hint of risk, was something to be picked over, debated, and if necessary discarded.

If despite the planning something went wrong and milk – or in a wartime context blood – was spilled, the failure had again to be held up to the light and analysed from all possible angles, damage limitation measures put in place, not least a careful massaging of the press, a detailed list made of the lessons to be learned, and anyone at fault would need to face up to error.

And while Tar and the team had access to the Sources (subject at times to Felix Cowgill's petulant protectionism) they and the wider system took the greatest care to guard them, their existence and their content, from their agents and from the outside world. One leak could so easily have undermined the entire edifice. There were occasional lapses outside St. James's Street especially in war theatres, but by and large the secret was well kept. As an example in a note to 'Tin Eye' Stephens at Ham in 1941, Tar pointed out that copies of the messages sent by his agents were filed securely and separately, not in Section B1a's own registry '. . . and certainly not' at Blenheim.

Another puzzling aspect is failure of the Abwehr and the Wehrmacht to heed the maxim[4] that 'those who cannot remember the past are condemned to repeat it.' Greek, Roman and Chinese military histories are replete with sagas of deception. But the Germans did not even have to look back that far. They had seen all this before from the British in the First World War. Admiral 'Blinker' Hall had made fruitful use of double agents, and as we have noted in his First World War Palestine campaign, General Allenby and his intelligence chief Archibald Wavell had used elaborate deception, to wrong foot the Turks and their German allies at the Third Battle of Gaza in 1917.

Part of the answer undoubtedly lies in the earlier comments; for many in the Abwehr there was no reason to question 'a good thing' when it provided so many creature comforts and a boost to personal cashflow. They did not have to look far for a reason to question: their colleagues in France and the Low Countries had done considerable damage to SOE by playing the radio game; it is almost astonishing that the corollary of their success – that the British might be doing the same – seems never to have crossed anyone's mind. One reason may be that at the Wehrmacht staff level, where the flow of intelligence material should have had its first objective evaluation, the officers responsible were not generally well respected, seen as in the words of one commentator as *die Mädchen für alles*, ('maids of all work'), who also had to deal with keeping the war diary, watching morale, censoring troops' mail and orchestrating unit propaganda. (In his post-war interrogation Kliemann told the British most of his Abwehr colleagues were officers who did not fit in elsewhere, and that the brightest elements of his service were to be found among the NCOs.)

And their more senior officers knew only too well that Hitler, who believed in his destiny rather than intelligence, only wanted to hear what fitted in with his manic vision. Doubters were not welcome in the Wolf's Lair or the Führerbunker and Field Marshal Keitel, over whose desk many key Abwehr reports passed, often refused to pass them on to Hitler, dismissing them as 'fantasies and pipedreams'. Ritter suggests a deeper rooted cause, that 'teamwork' was simply not part of the German psyche. He even uses the English term to underscore the point, claiming that there is no authentically German word to express it. A dictionary[5] suggests that the language has evolved since his day . Though it offers the hybrid 'Teamarbeit', it also gives the more Germanic 'Gemeinschaftsarbeit' and 'Zusammenspiel' as alternatives.

Perhaps the most extreme interpretation for failure is that conceived by David Mure, an officer in the A Force military deception organisation in the Middle East. Mure, who after the war became an author and carpet dealer, believed the Abwehr's dire performance in Britain could only be explained by the fact that it was actually complicit in the entire Double Cross scheme. As John Campbell puts it 'this infidel-in-the temple interpretation has made little or no academic or historiographical impression, having been all but ignored by scholars'. The debate will go on.

Based on the story we have told so far, the simple answer is that the best team won and that as Brammer soberly concludes, the German intelligence service simply did not meet expectations. 'It was of no decisive importance in Germany's conduct of the war.'[6]

Tar's own summing up delivered many years later,[7] was characteristically modest: 'The war was won by ULTRA and lost by the crass stupidity of Adolf. B1a and A Force were just pawns, important ones, on a very large chessboard'. But rather like another Anglo-German encounter at Wembley in July 1966 there was still some extra time to be played.

Notes

1. Brammer, p. 132.
2. Lahousen, Colonel Erwin, Trial Record for 30 November 1945 and *The Times*, 1 December 1945.
3. Kaltenbrunner, General Ernst, 1903–46, overbearing Austrian-born war criminal, convicted at Nuremberg.

4. Variously attributed, but credited by the *Oxford Dictionary of Quotations* to the Spanish sage George Santayana.
5. *Oxford Duden*, 1999 edition.
6. Some lessons were learned for the future; the East German Stasi became the most effective spy service in the Warsaw Pact bloc, 'better than the KGB' in the words of former KGB officer Oleg Gordievsky based less on terror, though there was no shortage of it, but on telephone, radio and cable interception of an extraordinary level of technical ingenuity and sophistication.
7. Mure Papers.

37

The War Room

Long before the D-Day invasion became a plan, let alone a reality, Tar and his team encouraged the Whitehall machine to think about how they and their agents might serve the larger FORTITUDE scheme. By 1943 they were looking even further ahead. What would the intelligence and counter-intelligence needs be once the Allies landed and began to push across the killing fields of Europe? What should B1a's rôle be?

The tasks they identified were a mix of defensive and offensive. First they would have to sort the wheat from the chaff, to pluck out of the shabby flow of apparently humbled prisoners claiming to be regular Wehrmacht or Luftwaffe officers, Abwehr or SD men hastily rebadged as artillerymen or engineers. And who among the Frenchmen, Belgians and Dutch claiming to have been ardent resisters from the start of the war, or the Poles, Russians and others displaced from across Europe were the genuine article? Some were more ambiguous figures who may well have collaborated or informed. Some as Kliemann's interrogation had demonstrated, had been recruited by the Germans as 'stay behind' spies or even sabotage agents.

A carefully culled minority could be persuaded or pressured into working as double agents. Others might be used to penetrate the German lines and collect battlefield intelligence or spread deceptive 'news'. German agents who had radios were especially valuable since 'playing the wireless game', while perhaps less important in yielding hard intelligence, would help GC&CS keep up to date on German codes and signals procedures. Early on in the debate Tar, always a man for commonsense rather than empire building, opined that double agents in the field could not be run from London. Case officers needed intimate knowledge of the individuals and the continuously evolving scenarios. By contrast over at SIS, Felix Cowgill yet again threw in the argument that anything of this kind outside the Three Mile Limit was SIS' exclusive preserve. What emerged from the debate and the exchanges of sometimes snippy memoranda was a structure which made sense, and which though heavily reliant on secondees from both MI5 and MI6 was officially part of the Allied Forces command structure. Indeed to play his part in it, Tar had to transfer from MI5's payroll to the Army General List. (He was luckier than some of the non-commissioned support staff who found themselves out of civilian clothes in transit through Chelsea Barracks and subject to a military timetable of 'Reveille', 'Tea' and 'Dinner' and told that their laundry and boots for repair were to be handed in each Wednesday 'tied and labelled in accordance with Barracks Regulations'.)

The structure had two interlinked halves; the teams in the field, known as Special Counter-intelligence Units or SCI's, and back in London, what was styled rather dramatically the War Room. Tar was appointed the latter's Director with Robert Blum, one of Muggeridge's 'jeunes filles en fleur' from the OSS as his deputy.[1]

The SCIs were staffed by a mix of MI6 and MI5 officers, supported by OSS specialists for whom Tar had arranged a short course in intelligence work. Christopher Harmer was the first officer sent out from London, initially to Paris and then to Brussels, (the latter preferred because operations there did not have to involve the French intelligence services). The Paris office was in rue Petrarque, a bland street in the 16th Arrondissement 'where Lord Rothschild is based'. The Brussels office was in the far grander Avenue Tervuren with an 'outstation' in a nearby nine storey apartment block. Nicknamed 'Wuthering Heights', the latter housed with apparent disregard for security, the unit's radio station, its interrogation rooms and also served as a rendezvous for agents' meetings.

The files give little or no details on the cases which were run, or their success though some of Tar's comments to Harmer suggest that the latter did produce results. But after Dick White, now seconded to Allied HQ as a Brigadier to advise on counter-espionage, had visited Paris in October 1944 he wrote to Guy Liddell that the SCI 'was the absolute model of a joint MI5/MI6 collaboration'. He asked Liddell to make sure that this was appreciated by Sir David Petrie and Sir Stewart Menzies 'as I feel it offers a pattern for the future . . . whatever the decision of the powers that be about the future of MI5 and MI6/ V[Section], both the force of events out here and the extremely friendly attitude of the [attached MI6 officers] has already turned SIS activities into a joint MI5 and MI6 concern. I can only hope that the force of events will continue in the same direction and bring about the necessary amalgamation at all levels.' (White was reflecting a 1942 initiative by MI5, skillfully deflected by Sir Stewart Menzies, to merge SIS Section V into MI5. Though White later became Chief of SIS, his hopes were not fulfilled though anecdotal evidence suggests that at least in the area of counter-terrorism, the collaboration is nowadays close.)

But the units in the field could not work in isolation. To be effective they needed real-time access to the data built up in the earlier years of Double Cross and the Most Secret Sources, all the facts and fragments so carefully 'carded', cross-referenced, collated and filed by the hardworking girls at Blenheim during the earlier war years. There also was new input from GC&CS and the continuing interrogations at Ham and the Bad Nenndorf mud baths, and information streaming in from one or other of the SCIs which had to be shared between them. What would nowadays be called the 'flow charts' which set out how the data would be channelled to and fro, were an intricate maze and even if Tar did not draw them up himself they demonstrate that as Director he was in charge of a complex piece of clearing house machinery, a 'Clapham Junction' of clandestine communication.

Statistics tell only part of the story, but it is worth noting that during its relatively short life span Tar's War Room generated for the teams in the field some 4,200 'pink cards' with brief details of Abwehr officers and agents about whom there was information on the London records, 2,000 personal files and four hundred subject files. Quite where the data passed to SIS by the French fitted in, is one of so many unknowns. Paillole claims they handed over the names of 3,000 Abwehr staffers and 5,000 'suspects'.

The picture the War Room conjures up for the present author is of Reuters news agency's Fleet Street HQ in the 1960s, a 24 hour smoke-filled blur of clattering teleprinters bringing reports from its correspondents, and sending them out to the world's press, shirt-sleeved men barking down chunky Bakelite telephones or banging on typewriters, a sense of urgency and deadlines, though Reuters trafficked in open news rather than enciphered secrets.

The War Room was another combined MI5 and SIS operation, with a US contingent, and after some initial reluctance on the British side, a small French presence. Tar was supported by Hugh Trevor-Roper and 'Buster' Milmo, the latter responsible for liaison with Camp 020. Amid the hurly burly there was at least one echo of the past, in the shape of Niklaus Ritter. We opened our story with the image of the two adversaries on opposite sides of the war and the North Sea, unknown to each other, seeking to bring the trawler ploy to a head. Their paths crossed again when a message came in to the War Room from Germany reporting that Ritter was in Allied hands, and asking London for an interrogation brief. Less interested in gloating, than in current opportunities and risks, Tar's guidance was that the interrogators should focus on identifying potential agents Ritter had recruited, but who for one reason or another had not been sent into action. It was also important not to let Ritter know that any of his agents had been 'doubled'.

In the Birthday Honours List of June 1944 Tar followed in his father's footsteps, receiving the Order of the British Empire. In the circumlocution of the time he was officially gazetted as 'Civil Assistant, War Office'.[2]

The war in Europe ended on 8 May 1945. The War Room too. Fighting in the Far East would roll bloodily on until mid-August when the atomic bombs dropped on Hiroshima and Nagasaki forced the Japanese to their knees.

It is impossible for those who did not live through it to recall the mix of emotions with which victory was greeted. Relief, jubilation, the ringing of long-muted church bells, red, white and blue bunting, street parties, victory speeches by the King and Winston Churchill, a message from the King handed out in primary schools up and down the land, grief for those who would not come home, and the women and children killed in their homes and shelters by Luftwaffe raids and flying bombs. Many British cities were scarred, some beyond recognition. So were so many families and marriages. As the cheering crowds trudged back home to take down their blackout curtains, they faced up to the reality that the austerity and shortages of food and fuel, which the war had imposed on the British, still gripped the country. The Ministry of Food announced that victory would be marked by extra shipments of potatoes, a special allocation of sugar for school canteens and of concentrated orange juice for children, and a reduction in the price of rhubarb.

An official advised housewives to 'get what potatoes you can. Keep a few pounds apart. Dried eggs and sardines will make a wholesome emergency breakfast. Spend seventeen points (of the food ration allowance) on a tin of luncheon meat or sausage meat for dinner and three on a tin of peas. These should see you through as iron rations.' More nostalgic souls who might have remembered jugs of refreshing Robinson's Lemon Barley Water at the Healing family's pre-war cricket games, had to make do with the suggestion from its makers that until supplies resumed, they should buy their 'Patent Barley' instead and flavour it with the juice of stewed or tinned fruit, or jam.

But even the glummest could not have envisaged amid the euphoria that Britain would live with various rationing régimes until the mid-1950s, nor indeed that the victory was just a watershed; once the tumult and the shouting died, and the captains, kings and lieutenant colonels had departed, the days of Imperial glory, power and national wealth had faded into history.

None of the arms of the British secret state had much time for rejoicing or reflection. SOE, as we saw, was summarily shut down. In St James's Street the academics and business men who had contributed so much to the Double Cross effort were looking forward to a return to civilian life.

As in Roman times and indeed after every British victory across the centuries, honours and medals were handed out. Tar's 1944 OBE seems with hindsight, an accolade which might have merited an upgrade, a view with which Trevor-Roper for one elegantly agreed. Replying to a letter from Tar congratulating him on his peerage in 1979 he wrote: 'The fountain of honour is an erratic instrument, and although it is pleasant to feel its sudden spray, one naturally thinks of all the more deserving people whom it has missed. I consider that your work in the war has never been properly recognised . . .'[3]

The OBE was not Tar's only recognition. Ever since Gilbert & Sullivan impresario Richard D'Oyly Carte, already owner of the Savoy, took it in hand in 1893, Claridges Hotel in Mayfair, a ten minute stroll from the anonymous offices in St James's Street from which Tar had fought his secret war, has been the home away from home for European and Middle Eastern Royalty, film stars, war correspondents, Greek ship-owners, arms dealers, and, in bull markets, generations of the more patrician breed of Wall Street investment bankers, alas now a vanished species.

Towards the end of the war, the Royal Suite, on the half-landing to the right as the unfamiliar visitor ventures hesitantly into the marble-floored front hall, was the pied à terre of the exiled King Peter of Yugoslavia. Though he is vague on the date, history suggests the closing days of November 1945 as the time when, as Ewen Montagu relates, he and Tar found themselves waiting in the Suite's sitting room to be invested with the Order of the Yugoslav Crown, or at least the ribbon; the actual medals were still in a Belgrade vault. They were outranked by Sir David Petrie, Sir Stewart Menzies, and flanked by Masterman and another case officer. The awards were in gratitude for a by-product of the TRICYCLE case, in which several Yugoslav officers had been exfiltrated by the British from their Nazi-occupied country on the pretext that they were to work for the Abwehr. In fact they became double agents.

Montagu remembers two offbeat aspects of the ceremony. First when they left the hotel, he saw that the newspaper sellers' placards outside the hotel carried the hastily scrawled news that Marshal Tito had become Yugoslavia's Communist ruler. Peter was now the ex-

King in an ex-Royal Suite handing out ex-Royal awards. Second, he claimed the medal ribbons they received were at first glance not dissimilar to that of the infinitely more prestigious British George Cross. The unnamed case officer had later added his to an already impressive display of tabs on his uniform but, as was *de rigueur* for a foreign award, at the tail-end. When a little later he visited his club, a bastion of 'Blimpish' attitudes across the road from the St James's Street office, he was berated by a short-sighted senior officer for not giving his 'George Cross' the appropriate precedence. 'If you have it, you should be proud of it!'

'It's alright, Sir,' the officer replied. 'You see, I won it posthumously.'

This was not the only post-war award handed out in a less than formal environment. Dusko Popov, TRICYCLE, received his MBE not from the King amid the pomp and circumstance of a Buckingham Place investiture, but from Tar in the bar of the Ritz Hotel. Nor was it the most bizarre, since in one of the most eloquent testimonials to German gullibility, GARBO, TATE and ZIGZAG each received wireless messages telling them that they had been awarded the Iron Cross at the recommendation of their Abwehr controllers.

In 1946 Tar was awarded the US Legion of Merit. The citation signed by President Harry S. Truman recognised his rôle in Allied 'special operations'. In a macabre twist of fate inspired by Cold War politics, Tito's rival for power in post-war Yugoslavia, Drazha Mihailovic, who had thrown the support of his Cetnik resistance fighters behind King Peter, and some claimed, behind the Germans, in the guerilla campaigns of the Second World War, and whom the Communists hurriedly executed on a Belgrade golf course in 1946, was given the same recognition in 1948, posthumously.

File glimpses of Tar in his closing years of service show him as the supportive friend. Much as he had gone out of his way to try to get CELERY an RAF commission, Tar worked hard as the war ended to help TRICYCLE, Dusko Popov, try to track down his Abwehr friend Johnny Jebsen, who had been hauled away to Germany by the Gestapo. Sadly he could not be found and on all evidence, had been executed. Tar then went to considerable lengths to help Jebsen's wife, an actress, find work in a still shattered Germany, where theatres were few and far between. He also spent time sorting out – via SIS, sometimes through Philby himself – the various assets and liabilities TRICYCLE had left in his wake after his abortive spell of high living in New York.

Even SNOW was not cast into outer darkness. When the time came for his (and his son's) release in August 1944, MI5's attitude was hardly that of an organisation which felt itself betrayed. Tar sent John Marriott down to Dartmoor to bring SNOW back to London, find him a place to live and arrange for an identity card and ration book. Tar set about trying to get him a job and arranged a small allowance. MI5 had given an undertaking to the Home Office that it would be responsible for his support. By January 1945 no job had been found and Tar suggested the time had come to draw a line. If they went on supporting SNOW he would never try too hard to find work. In any event he was virtually unemployable. The only rôle for which he was qualified was that of an agent and 'for this for a variety of reasons he is no longer suitable'. Tar suggested a terminal payment of £500. He backed this with an interesting 'balance sheet'.

'The intelligence dividend we received . . . is impossible to express in terms of money but it was a large one and in addition . . . put into our hands the sum of £13,580. We do not know with accuracy how much money SNOW retained for himself by direct appropriation from sums passed to him by the Germans but the payments and expenses we made [sic] amounted to less than £4,000 with the result that on a purely financial basis . . . the case has been profitable to us.' (We have suggested that money was one of SNOW's driving motives. Perhaps the most telling indication of this is a note by Tar in March 1941 recording that SNOW would be paid £50 a head for any agents who came to MI5's notice through his efforts; true bounty hunting.)

Tar's suggestion was agreed and on 6 March 1945, Leonard Burt, one of the Scotland Yard men brought across to MI5 by the ephemeral William Crocker handed SNOW his cheque and reminded him of the penalties under the Official Secrets Act if he 'should be foolish enough to write his reminiscences or discuss his work with any unauthorised person'. SNOW was delighted; he had not expected this and 'in all the circumstances he felt he had been generously treated'.[4]

(Ritter wrote in 1972 that he had lost touch with JOHNNY but had been reliably informed that he was living incognito in Ireland with Lilly and 'their children'. The consensus seems to be that he died in 1976. If indeed Ireland was his last home, it is nice to imagine that Fate might have arranged for SNOW, then using the rather whimsical alias of 'White', and Norman Baillie Stewart to sit unknown to one another in opposite corners of a craik-filled bar, each sipping a glass of draught Guinness, each wrapped in his own thoughts about what might have been.)

Stories like these never have a clean ending, let alone a neat plot line, as exemplified by CELERY. The files show that after the Sessler adventure he was considered for work as an SOE agent in France but then shipped himself off to Brazil where, as he blarneyed to an unidentified British firm, he could leverage his friendship with a Portuguese diplomat to commercial advantage. David Petrie agreed to give a £500 guarantee to his employers, a wise precaution on their part since the past still dragged like a ball and chain.

In January 1949 Walter Dicketts, giving an address in West London's Holland Park, surrendered to the Metropolitan Police to answer charges laid in 1944 of obtaining money by false pretences from two business men in 1943 and 1944. He pleaded 'not guilty' and the outcome is not recorded. We are in the realm of speculation but it is quite likely that MI5 concluded that while in a post-war world they could not have the charges expunged, for CELERY to tell his full story to the world from a courtroom dock was not the ideal outcome. Thus there may well have been some quiet arrangement, as with the Birmingham episode, that if he pleaded guilty he would get a token sentence; he had after all given himself up and had more than repaid what in the cant phrase was known as 'his debt to society'.

That something was done behind the scenes is suggested by the unusual fact that the magistrate before whom the 1944 charges had been laid, was brought out of retirement for the replay on the grounds that, according to the press report, he was best placed to understand the background. The next sighting is an official notice in the London Gazette in November 1949 that Dicketts, by then of 'HM Prison Wandsworth, London SW' and 'otherwise known as Charles Stewart Pollock' had been declared bankrupt. The sad coda is an anonymous notice in the Personal Columns of *The Times* in December 1975 asking for information from anyone who might know of his whereabouts.

Ritter too has a postscript. Though the chronology is hard to follow it began with his volunteering for a posting to Rommel's Afrika Korps without troubling to share with his colleagues his last exchanges with SNOW and CELERY or any concerns. It was here he joined up with the Hungarian adventurer Almásy, and they agreed to take two aircraft into the desert to pick up several of the latter's agents and drop off two more, 'an Egyptian' and 'a Jew'. But in a welter of inexplicable bruised Magyar sensibilities the Count declined to go, leaving Ritter to fly off on an abortive mission which ended when his plane came down in the sea just off the coast, luckily for him still under German control. He spent nine hours adrift in a rubber dinghy before being rescued, and a splintered arm kept him in a Berlin hospital for five weeks. What neither Ritter nor the Abwehr knew then or for many years after the war was that the Most Secret Sources had been tracking the mission every step of the way, including the plane crash, and the use of a Hungarian Priest in Cairo as a 'dead drop' for one of the mission's radios. Reading the record through modern eyes it was as if the British were following a German precursor of 'Twitter'.

In his Berlin hospital, Ritter found himself under heavy questioning by colleagues, focussed not on his English misadventures but the failure of his US network. Its highly publicised implosion had political repercussions for German-American relations, and like the RSS affair a scapegoat was needed.

He resigned from the Abwehr to join the Luftwaffe's 'Hermann Goering' Tank Division in Sicily and later found himself commanding the anti-aircraft defences of Hanover, a key road and rail communications hub. He told his post-war interrogator John Gwyer that just before the last great saturation bombing raid in April 1944, he had looked carefully at the radar and ground observers' reports and decided that the various small-scale British and US sorties over Germany that night represented the most the Allies would attempt for the time being. So he ordered the Hanover air defences to stand down. 'Precisely six minutes later . . . 1,500 bombers arrived over the town . . . Ritter then withdrew into civilian life', Gwyer noted sardonically.

When the war ended Ritter was briskly processed into Bad Nenndorf, and after some months out again, but only into a series of holding camps. He spent two years behind bars and barbed wire before beginning gradually to rebuild his life. His comment that while he scratched for a living, his wife earned 300 marks a week as secretary to a lawyer, at a time when a loaf of bread cost eighty marks, evokes a moment's sympathy which fades quickly when measured in the context of the far greater post-war sufferings of so many millions of others. The archives, but not his memoirs, tell us that part of the time he worked as a 'consultant and translator' for the Allied authorities, work for which he was given a valuable written endorsement from US Air Force's 'Air Defence Investigations' Unit.

He then began to travel the world as a salesman, before settling down in 1954 as Managing Director of the '*Deutsche Hilfsgemeinschaft*', or 'German Aid Association', in Hamburg, a city backed group which provided and still provides free holidays for needy children and young people. Were he alive today he might find some amusement in the fact that a Norden bombsight, one of the main targets of his US espionage efforts, was recently entered in an auction, expected to realise between $250 and $500.

Even Sessler, the sporty Abwehr officer whom Dicketts tried to suborn, has left a paper trail. At the end of the war he was found living uxoriously in Villa Benvenuto in San Remo with 'the young Countess la Rocca', a rather more congenial billet than the Russian front. His evidence at the War Crimes Tribunal led to the execution of German General Anton Dostler for the shooting of fifteen uniformed US soldiers captured when on a sabotage mission near La Spezia.

We make no excuse for introducing into Tar's story another of those 'floaters' crying out for fuller explanation. It may be coincidence. It may be a reflection of those murky Berlin-Moscow ties, some of the records of which, Dassel was sent to Paris to retrieve. From her emergence from nowhere in the 1930s, claiming to be the Tsar's supposedly murdered daughter, Anastasia, Anna Anderson had been represented by two Hamburg lawyers. One was Paul Leverkühn, whose memories of Abwehr service we have quoted above. His partner was Kurt Vermehren. It was the latter's son, an Abwehr officer himself, who defected to the British in Istanbul. In line with the Nazi principle of family guilt, Kurt Vermehren and his wife were sent off for an unpleasant but non-fatal spell in a concentration camp.

After the war, the two lawyers continued to press Anna Anderson's case. One of their 'star witnesses' was Richard Dassel who, from his deathbed in Wiesbaden, reaffirmed his often-told story that, while convalescing in a small hospital for well-bred, wounded officers in the grounds of the Imperial Palace at Tsarskoye Tselo, he had often been visited by the Tsar's younger daughter, and 'swore blind' that he recognised the 'real Anastasia' in Anna. The latter still lost her case but the story does have intriguing 'small world' characteristics.

In another unexpected link, when Erich Vermehren[5] and his wife were exfiltrated to London, they were first lodged in the Drayton Gardens flat of Kim Philby's mother. When debriefed by her son in his official rôle, they gave him the names of prominent members of the German Catholic underground. When British Intelligence sought to reach them after the war, they found they had all been liquidated.

Notes

1. Blum, Robert, 1911–65. Like so many other Second World War US recruits into intelligence, a Yale academic. His tracks can be seen in many documents relating to planning special operations and psychological warfare strategies for the emerging CIA in the late 1940s and he was later glimpsed as a member of what seems to have been a CIA sponsored mission looking at Indo China in 1950.

2. Philby, similarly honoured in 1947 no doubt to the distant accompaniment of vodka toasts in Moscow, was said to be 'Employed in a Department of The Foreign Office'.
3. Personal papers.
4. GARBO was one of the most outstanding double agents in terms of his imagination and his unremitting contribution, especially in the D-Day deceptions. But here too there was a real, as well as an intelligence dividend. The Abwehr paid him a total of more than £31,000 for his work and that of his 'network' of fictitious agents. He was allowed to retain around £17,500, leaving St James's Street handsomely in profit at the Germans' expense.
5. *The Observer*, obituary of Erich Vermehren, 3 May 2005.

38

The New Broom

The British clandestine Services knew well before the end came that with the Axis Powers defeated, the wartime 'honeymoon' with the Soviet Union, once 'our gallant Allies', would end abruptly and world Communism would become, once again, 'the main adversary'.

Displaying an adroitness in office politics as well as treachery, Philby had manoeuvred himself into the rôle of Head of the SIS Section focusing on the new Soviet challenge, a triumph capped when he was appointed to the 'Committee of SIS Reorganisation', charged with taking a fresh look at the Service's structure, manpower needs and methods in the 'brave new world'. Moscow Centre can scarcely have believed its luck.

On the other side of St James's Park, MI5 were still blissfully unaware of Blunt's rôle as the worm in the apple – in September 1945 he was put in charge of 'Diplomatic and Far Eastern matters', thus presumably continuing his work on rifling diplomatic mail – but inside the office and in Whitehall the need for a shift in strategic focus was evident. It would not be long before the need became pressing.

In May 1946 Sir David Petrie was replaced by Sir Percy Sillitoe,[1] once a St Paul's Cathedral chorister who had gone on to become an 'iron hand in iron glove' Chief Constable with considerable overseas experience. (Whitehall's penchant for secrecy died hard. When Labour MPs pressed in the House of Commons for details of his job, their knowing questions were swatted away by their Prime Minster Clement Attlee with the bland response that Sillitoe had been appointed 'a Director at the War Office', at a salary of £3,000 pa. and was employed on 'special duties'. Though most MPs and journalists knew full well what his real rôle was, it seems not to have been until around 1950 that the London press began to identify him as 'head of MI5'.)

From the delicate comments of Sillitoe's obituarist, Antony Simkins, who joined MI5 in 1948 and in 1965 became Deputy Director,[2] Sillitoe's arrival seems to have had much the same effect as that of Swinton and William Charles Crocker several years earlier. Tar and the senior staff, who thought the job should have gone to Guy Liddell, 'resented the choice of an outsider whose career had tended not to develop the particular skills which the post required. A rift developed at a high level which was never closed.'[3]

Sillitoe himself wrote that he found himself confronted by the stark contrast between the 'unquestioning obedience to rules' and 'scrupulous respect for discipline' which had been hallmarks of his police experience and MI5's 'highly intelligent but somewhat introspective individuals who gave me an initial impression they were working in a rather withdrawn isolation, each concentrating on his own especial problem'. Elsewhere he dismissed them as 'book-learned intellectuals', an epithet which would not have applied to Tar, though to his family the latter made no secret that he and Sillitoe did not get on. As Dick White later commented, 'One did not need to know Sillitoe well to dislike him'. But after thinking seriously about leaving, White accepted the post of Director of B Division, taking charge at the start of a period which, to borrow a phrase from seventeenth century Russian history, might well be called '*Smutnoye Vremya*' or '*The Time of Troubles*', an apposite borrowing since the agonies of the Service and the ecstasies of its many critics were very largely a delayed action effect of Moscow's making.

Spy scandals exploded – names such as Nunn May and Fuchs dominated the headlines, the former on the day Sillitoe took over. Politicians scrambled for cover as the extent of Soviet penetration, and the failure to spot it, became ever clearer, a rumbling row which reached its first peak – more were to come – in the defection of Burgess and Maclean, (names as indissolubly twinned in history as Abbott and Costello or Swan and Edgar) and the early and initially unsuccessful attempts to 'name and shame' Philby as the Third Man.

When Dick White returned from Europe to take over as Head of B Division he found a Service which as Tar told him 'was just ticking over'. A contemporary file note, probably by White himself, lays out the Division's organisation, with Tar heading Section B4 responsible for 'Production and Coordination of Aids to Investigation, etc.' and at the same time and importantly, directly in charge of 'Agents and Informants'. An explanatory memorandum suggests the Section was to have a broader reach than its headline title implies. 'It would make enquiries or show how and when they should be made'. It would act as liaison with RSS and GC&CS and operate a planned new 'central listening post' which would take over all telephone tapping tasks. Reaching even further it was also supposed to 'arrange and supervise the training of newly joining officers'. Then in October 1947 a circular from the new Director General designates Tar as Head of the Section tackling 'Russian and Russian satellite Espionage' with John Marriott as his deputy.

But by July 1948 things had changed. Borrowing an earlier career analogy, if the October Circular can be seen as a move up the Ladder, another undated paper on the file suggests it was soon followed by a slide down the Snake, no doubt a consequence of Tar's strained relationship with Sillitoe. In it his rôle is redefined as in charge of B3, responsible for 'Co-ordination of Overseas Intelligence, Liaison with Overseas Stations on intelligence. Special subjects as directed.' There were two sub-sections, one concerned with the Middle East, Africa, Malta, and Gibraltar and the other 'the Far East, the Carribean [sic] and Ireland'. A much less interesting job description, and one which explains Tar's terse comment to his family at the time that life at MI5 had become 'dull and routine'.

It was all a far cry from the bravado, camaraderie and 'bags of swank' of the war years. He had spent his days, and often his nights, assessing, cosseting, manipulating and bullying an extraordinary cross section of people, coordinating their scripts, and watching hawk-like over the German reactions. So many adrenalin shots, anxieties, and triumphs, so many important Whitehall meetings, so much deft politicking, all as part of a real war with a visible enemy who bombed and exterminated. Now the old enemy had quit the field. A new one, or rather an old one who had confusingly become an ally in the Second World War, and off limits for counter-espionage, had to be understood, a gap which as with the Germans before the war, MI5 would have to work hard to fill, without the magic of the Most Secret Sources. And if we follow the second undated circular, work in which his contribution would be far from central.

No more dead tramps marinating on ice. No more commandeered trawlers, night-time parachute drops or faked explosions. No more Most Secret Sources. No more second-guessing the Germans. The sharp-witted intellectuals had gone. No more 'High Table' talk, no more free-wheeling flights of imagination, Latin tags, acid-drop jokes from Malcolm Muggeridge or feline barbs from Trevor-Roper.[4] It must have been rather like finding oneself running a pier-end show in Worthing after five years as Artistic Director of the Old Vic.

So it comes as no surprise to see on the file in July 1948 – just a month after the start of the Soviet blockade of Berlin signalled a major ratcheting up of East-West tensions – a circular to 'All officers, Home and Overseas' announcing among other moves that Tar 'resigns at his own request on August 31st 1948' with John Marriott stepping into his shoes. Looking at the terse note through a linguist's loupe may be misleading but 'at his own request' catches the eye and ear as one of those clichés favoured by drafters of contemporary corporate announcements – 'to pursue other interests' or 'to spend more time with his family'. One might also have expected to see some expression of regret, of appreciation for a job well done, an unparalleled contribution to the Service, and the like.

Be that as it may, his departure in the wake of the 'brain drain' of academics and lawyers, must have left a large gap in skills, knowledge, judgment, not to mention morale; he was one of those rare characters, a 'life enhancer'.

With echoes of his interlude with the Birmingham Police, he

applied for the job of Chief Constable of Kent, bizarrely the position vacated by Percy Sillitoe when he was tapped to run MI5. In the event Tar did not get the job. Whoever made the decision was right – Tar would surely have been just as much a 'fish out of water' in the rôle as Sillitoe was in his. Instead the Kent post went to a soldier with considerable police experience, including senior positions with the Metropolitan Force and as Head of the Hendon Police College. So what was Tar to do?

Had money interested him he might have taken one or more City directorships; his connections, his judgment, his interest in, and his instinct, for people would have been an asset to any boardroom. But instead he chose to farm. It was a bold move. Hardly one which would make him rich. But it was one which gave him much pleasure for some ten years. From a Whitehall perspective, Masterman commented in his memoirs, '. . . I think his decision at the end of the war to leave the service in order to farm, was one of the greatest losses MI5 ever suffered.'[5]

Notes

1. Sillitoe, Sir Percy Joseph, 1888–1962.
2. Simkins, Charles Anthony Goodall, CB, CBE, 1912–2003.
3. Liddell stayed on as Deputy Director until he retired in 1953 to become Security Adviser to the Atomic Energy Authority. He is said to have been discomfited by the defection of Guy Burgess, known to be one of his friends; Blunt had been one of his protégés and he also knew Philby well.
4. Trevor-Roper's intellectual curiosity took him down many idiosyncratic byways. He may well have shared with Tar his irreverent views that the supposedly ancient traditions – kilts, clans, tartans and bagpipes – which made up Scotland's 'moral apparatus' were in fact invented only after the Act of Union with Britain in 1707. If so, Tar would have been mollified by his judgment that trews were 'a mark of social distinction' worn by chieftains and 'great men'. See Essay in Hobsbawm et al.
5. Masterman, *On the Chariot Wheel*, p. 219.

39

On Bredon Hill . . .

Farming is hard work, and does not really qualify as retirement, but at least in terms of the world of intelligence and counter-espionage, Tar had apparently 'retired'. The word is not often applied to a healthy, gregarious man of 39. Nor did it reflect the cheerful energy with which he approached his new life. The Robertson's first house had been in the suburban anonymity of Putney Hill. As the war rumbled on and the risks from the night sky grew ever greater, the Robertsons moved briefly to Farnham Common in Buckinghamshire, then to Round Bush House in the Hertfordshire village of Letchmere. After a brief stopover almost literally *à la recherche du temps perdu*, to Tar's first British home in Tunbridge Wells, Aunt Peg's house, they found rather grander quarters, Leighton Manor in the high Weald of Kent near Edenbridge, shielded by some 400 acres of land, and a bodyguard of oaks along the long drive. So grand in fact that it was most probably not purchased outright but leased from a family who had perhaps sought safer climes. In 2010 it was for sale at a 'Guide Price' of a mere £5 million.

Charming though the Weald was, with its oast houses, lanes and orchards, Joan Robertson loved the Worcestershire countryside and taught Tar to love it too, though the fate of its ancient county town, unscathed by the war only to be butchered by planners and developers is a sad reflection on post-war Britain.

Tar and Joan bought a 120 acre farm on the slopes of Bredon Hill, towering 900 feet over the Vale of Evesham, certainly moved less by Alfred Houseman's poem than by Tar's itch, first generated by a herd of Jersey cows which had surrounded the house at Tunbridge Wells, to try his hand at a rural life. He had sheep, pigs whose periodic dispatch to the local market always gave him a pang, cows and an orchard whose juicy apples and pears went into cider and perry vats. ZIGZAG, TRICYCLE, not to say Ritter and all the others would have been amused and admiring as he turned the handle of a washing mangle to crush root vegetables into animal feed.

But had he seen a 'Top Secret' memorandum written by Dick White in July 1950, Tar would have felt he had made the right decision. White described B Division, in an echo of David Petrie, as 'gripped by a crisis in management and a crisis in manpower'. The mission of the service remained the same – combating espionage, sabotage and subversion, though this now meant 'in practice . . . defending the realm in peace and war against Russian and satellite espionage, in time of peace defending the constitution, (which in its widest sense includes our industrial stability), against attempts to overthrow it by subversive means and in time of war preventing Fifth Column actions of all kinds'.

A ten-strong team had just finished a three year analysis of the Soviet and satellite intelligence services, and there is a note of grudging professional respect in White's comments about the NKVD's tradecraft, its 'most rigid security' and 'virtually exclusive use of methods of communication not susceptible to penetration by normal counter-measures', or more simply put, codes and ciphers GCHQ were not yet able to read even though the wartime Soviet intelligence traffic known as VENONA was already being laboriously unravelled. Since Philby was well aware of the breakthrough, Moscow's heightened communications security may have been a direct result of his warnings. Surveillance, trawling for defectors and the use of penetration agents remained MI5's main weapons. White was not to know that Blunt had given Moscow a unique insider's view of all these techniques.

That aside, it is still surprising that Tar never mentioned any approach to lure him back to the MI5 fold. Given White's comments, he would surely have had an important rôle to play. Nor is there any sign of his trying to retrace his steps even if only out of boredom or the 'decompression blues' which afflicted so many who had been at full and exciting stretch during the war.

Some in his family recalled (a memory recycled in several obituaries) that he moved early in his retirement to boost his income with a job as Director of Security at the former GC&CS, in the early days of its massive enlargement and rebranding as 'Government Communications Headquarters', (GCHQ) in Cheltenham. But GCHQ has no trace of him in its records, as an employee or even a consultant.[1]

The explanation lies in a conflation of family memories, understandable after so many years, mixing GCHQ with Tar's brief flirtation with his old friends at SIS. In the early 1950s, Tar felt himself in a financial squeeze; he had sunk much of his capital into the farm and the livestock. His farming income was under pressure and land prices were sliding in tandem, so if he sold he would face a sizeable loss. A more regular income might be no bad thing. It would be foolhardy to try to capture this in figures; rudimentary research into farmers' incomes in 1952 produces rough averages at best and since 1971 alone the value of sterling has depreciated so much that trying to arrive at a meaningful comparison is impossible. The best that can be said is that based on a 1956 survey, average annual income from a farm of the scale of Tar's was measured in hundreds of pounds at best.

Though we can glimpse only one side of the story it is reasonable to assume that SIS would be intrigued at the idea of using his experience in a project such as 'Berlin Tunnel', a joint venture between SIS and the CIA to tap buried Soviet telephone and cable traffic, the complex planning for which began in 1952. GCHQ engineers and linguists played an important part, which may explain the misunderstanding about a job at Cheltenham. For whatever reason the tentative dialogue faded away – perhaps the farm outlook began to look brighter, perhaps he came into some money, perhaps whatever SIS had in mind was an advisory rôle, and not a position on the permanent staff, or perhaps simply because it was just not challenging enough to put himself in an organisational strait jacket and turn his back on the Virgilian charms of the countryside. The personal papers have no trace of a follow-up.

Since the Berlin scheme was betrayed to the Russians by the SIS turncoat George Blake,[2] Tar might thus have avoided the distinction of being 'blown' to the Russians twice, the first time by Blunt and Philby. A pity nonetheless since his experience would have been valuable in devising cover stories for the operation and its vast output of message transcripts. He would have been even more useful in the aftermath of Blake's treachery when Anglo-American counter-espionage focus was forced to shift to the embarrassing question of whether the Russians had used their knowledge of the Tunnel's existence to feed the West with what they called 'dezinformatsiya', or what Tar in earlier days had known as 'chaff'.

Nor is there any indication that he had the slightest interest in joining one of the major British companies, not least those in the oil business, the airlines, and banks who always felt more comfortable with a retired senior MI5 or SIS officer discreetly tucked away in the Executive Suite as their 'Head of Security'. It is remarkable that he was able to switch off so completely. This makes in a sense for a lopsided, even in narrative terms, anti-climactic, story. After all those plots and plans there is little to spark the reader's attention about the retirement years counting sheep, playing golf, breathing new life into a moribund local village cricket club, enjoying the social life of a country gentleman, if not a fully-fledged squire, and a genial paterfamilias. Embroidery and stamp collecting, both interests of his father's were a fulfilling substitute for ISOS decrypts. Happily there were no signs of the career after-effects prophesied by the late British Prime Minister Harold Macmillan, who once remarked that 'no-one could work for ten years or more in MI5 without losing his reason.'

By temperament and training he was not a man to hoard papers. The few he left show him dealing politely and discreetly over the years with enquiries about the 'real' Hess story and other MI5 adventures. He also found himself entangled with David Mure, whose notion of Abwehr complicity we mentioned above. In 1979 Mure was on a different trail, the so-called Pearl Harbour Questionnaire. (Tar would have met Mure when he flew to Cairo to brief the cross-dressing Dudley Clarke on how the deception game was played in London.) The questionnaire listed detailed information about the US naval and military base in Hawaii which the Abwehr had instructed TRICYCLE to ferret out when he moved to New York in 1941, ostensibly as an official of the Yugoslav Government in exile but in fact, as the Abwehr thought, to build an intelligence network for them. They were once again mistaken and misled. TRICYLE was being run by SIS' New York Station on behalf of MI5.

As has been told and retold elsewhere TRICYCLE and his playboy lifestyle, were anathema for a man with J Edgar Hoover's visceral mistrust of all double agents and supposedly puritan instincts, (though the FBI Chief himself led an unconventional private life with his long-term colleague and companion Clyde Tolson), and the expensive US project came to an early and awkward end. But the questionnaire became another fixation for those who sided with the skullduggery school, Mure evidently among them, after its text was first published by J. C. Masterman. If it had been passed to the US General Staff, Mure argued, experienced eyes would have appreciated that an attack was being planned, and the US would have been better prepared to face or even avert the Japanese onslaught at dawn on 7 December 1941, immortalised by President Franklin D. Roosevelt as a 'day that will live in infamy'.

Instead it went no further than Hoover's desk. Why, Mure asked? Was it a Red plot in which Philby and Guy Liddell were accomplices, aimed at trying to keep the information away from the planners. If American suspicions were visibly aroused, the Japanese might call the plan off and instead turn on the Soviet Union, forcing Stalin to divert resources to fight on a potentially disastrous second front. Alternatively, Mure wrote, evidently warming to his theme, was it just a case of amateurish mishandling by the W Board and the Double Cross Committee, with Masterman and Ewen Montagu responsible for 'the worst staff mistake of the war, making the slight misunderstanding as to what the Light Brigade should attack at Balaclava appear as no more than a minor solecism.'

Tar responded to this, and to other criticisms by Mure of MI5's shortcomings, in a characteristically equable tone which must have concealed considerable irritation. Guy Liddell had passed the questionnaire to Hoover as they were close friends, and Hoover was effectively his counterpart in the US system. 'Much as I would like to implicate Philby in some plot to sabotage our war effort, I simply cannot find any motive for such an action.' As to Mure's speculation that Liddell was 'perhaps the Third or Fourth Man', this was quite feasible 'if you base your suggestion on the fact he knew the Philby, [Tomas] Harris, Burgess clique. You could say the same of me. I knew them all well and a number of far more sinister types . . . We put up with these characters, as Winston [Churchill] said, so long as they could help us to win the war . . .' Mure himself conceded in a draft he sent Tar, that for Liddell to go drinking with Burgess was not in itself evidence of anything. 'It is no crime to be friends with a drunken and disreputable pansy.'

Indeed Mure himself admitted in what might have served Graham Greene as the setting for a story, that in the 'world turned upside down' of post-war London he too had often drunk in a Chelsea pub run by a prominent member of one of Britain's notorious razor-wielding 'racecourse gangs', whose clientèle included 'Security officers', Philby, the latter's then lodger Charlie Dundas, (often identified in the literature as an SIS officer, though formally working for the British Council), Burgess, Liddell, an unnamed (fortunately for him) Admiral of the Fleet and the playboy murderer Neville Heath, an "Essex boy" given to grand aliases such as Lord Dudley, Lieutenant Colonel Armstrong and Group Captain Rupert Brook.[3]

On Mure's more substantive charge that Cairo's A Force had done a better job in deception than the team in London, Tar reminded Mure with a slight touch of asperity that the two organisations had fought entirely different wars. A Force was 'active operationally' while MI5's aim was 'long term strategic'. In fact St. James's Street had a twofold task – to build up a team of agents in whom the Germans had total confidence and at the same time, as part of its broader remit of defending the Realm to make sure there were no uncontrolled German agents working on British soil. 'Your successes in A Force were undoubtedly considerable in their way. I disagree – you can hardly expect me to think otherwise – that our life apart from OVERLORD was made up of failures.' Tricking the Germans into keeping their U Boats out of a wide swathe of the seas off the south coast of Ireland, and into altering the range of their V1 and V2 flying bombs, were notable achievements. In addition 'our intelligence bonus was staggering, and this as I have said was our prime target'.

Tar also became involved in a less tendentious initiative to tell the Double Cross story. Dick White had been put out by Prime Minister Margaret Thatcher's decision to defer publication of the fifth volume of the official series *British Intelligence in the Second World War*, covering security and counter-intelligence, (written by Sir Michael Howard, it was not published until 1990). Like many others he had also been offended by Masterman's unauthorised revelations and limelight-hogging. As Tom Bower relates in his careful and perceptive biography, White introduced the already knowledgeable author Nigel West to Tar and his fellow case officers to make sure their history was written. It was, and well. And just as well. When the fifth volume eventually saw the light of day, Tar's name was not to be found in the index. Nor were those of most of the other case officers though Liddell, Masterman and White did rate brief citations.

In October 1981 there was a reunion which brought together surviving officers and several of the key agents mentioned in our story. The stiffly formal photograph (see illustration) which was among Tar's few papers shows men and women of an age and gravitas hard to associate with their talents to deceive, and the extraordinary things they accomplished some forty years earlier. Given the secrecy and 'need to know' compartmentalisation with which they had all lived and because of which they had survived, Tar must have found it hard to imagine that ZIGZAG, BRUTUS, MUTT and JEFF would ever have turned up in the same room, meeting not just case officers they knew but agents and other officers of whose existence, like that of the entire intricate Double Cross system, they had been quite unaware. The image also reflects not just the camaraderie of the team but also the last vestiges of MI5 as a 'family firm'. We know of Tar's relationship with Sir Vernon via John Kell. The lady seated at the left of the front row is Sir Vernon's secretary, Mrs. Kenyon Jones. Standing next to her, his hand on her chair, is her husband William, a senior MI5 officer in the Middle East who had run the successful double agent CHEESE. A further 'inwardness' is that BRUTUS is holding a book to show off its cover. Much squinting through a lens reveals it to be Nigel West's groundbreaking study of MI5 which was published that same month and which may have been the catalyst for the get-together.

Many happy years came to an end when Joan Robertson died in 1980. A new phase of contentment began in 1983 when Tar married Rachel Chance, née Cameron, widow of another prominent Worcestershire man, Sir Hugh Chance.[4]

Some of the group got together again in June 1984, the 40th anniversary of D-Day when Juan Pujol, GARBO, was brought to London for an audience with the Duke of Edinburgh to meet up again with Tar and his case officers. According to the *Daily Mail* report SIS had expressed a view 'after the war' that the most prudent cover story was to put it about that GARBO was dead. Cyril Mills, co-proprietor with his brother of the eponymous family circus, and who had taken over as one of GARBO's case officers in the run-up to D-Day had been told this tale by Tar, and accepted it.[5] For Mills, the Spaniard's reappearance, another coup by Nigel West, thus had some of the aspects of a real resurrection, though his wartime experiences should have taught him that the truth in the secret world was a fluid and relative concept. The *Mail* report was one of the few clippings Tar kept in his file. Tar was also in contact with TATE, now living quietly in Watford, when the latter was inadvertently 'outed' over, of all things, an issue related to the Poll Tax register. Any memories of what might have happened to TATE on the way to Wales were airbrushed away.

His papers show several approaches by writers and TV producers looking for his story. Again the 'straight bat' was generally brought into play though when the 50th anniversary of D-Day approached, he, Christopher Harmer and Hugh Astor found themselves rubbing up gratingly against MI5's continuing reluctance to have them tell their stories in a proposed TV progamme, a reluctance they found hard to understand – as would many observers – given that so much had been in the public domain for years. The outcome was a highly qualified consent from the service's legal adviser telling them they could take part provided that any material they disclosed was in the public domain already and if it was not, that its disclosure would not directly or indirectly damage national security. This slippery *Catch 22* – how would it be possible for anyone so long out of active service to know what this wording might cover – did not in the event prove an obstacle and Tar's papers show no feedback or repercussions.

Tar died on 10 May 1994. Just two weeks earlier he and Rachel had been holidaying in Portugal, 'enjoying themselves to the full'. As Rachel's brother Peter Stormonth Darling[6] put it: 'He knew he was in overtime and he made the most of it.' There were private and public farewells.

First, he was laid to rest in the churchyard of St John's in Birlingham a church rebuilt in 1784 on 15th century foundations. Birlingham, its roots recorded in the Domesday Book, is a setting any Tourist Board would covet, lying in a verdant loop of the Avon a few miles outside Pershore, with one pub and its own cricket pitch on the village green. The essence, in a way, of the Realm Tar and his colleagues had undertaken to defend. Few outside the family would have realised the underlying contrast, the parabola which linked the farewell in an utterly English setting and Tommy's birth in the humid, spice-scented air on the banks of the Boebera. So many miles away, so many years and so many adventures ago.

Then there was the sadness and pride of the lunch. For many years the dwindling band of talented amateurs who had been the wartime members of Tar's Section had met annually over lunch or dinner. The lunch they had planned for 19 June 1994 was freighted with special meaning. Like that final IP Dinner remembered by Constance Kell, it was to be the last such get-together, though on a much smaller scale. Only two members of the team were now left – Christopher Harmer and Hugh Astor. With their special guest, Dame Stella Rimington, the first woman to serve as Director of their old Service and a worthy successor to Vernon Kell, they had planned to pay a special tribute to Tar and also to mark the fiftieth anniversary of his and their crowning accomplishment, the FORTITUDE D-Day deception, the biggest confidence trick of all time.

Rachel Robertson decided that the lunch should go ahead, even though Tar's chair was to be empty; she and his daughter Belinda joined the others in 'paying a silent tribute to our absent Chief and friend', in Harmer's words.

The next day, 20 June Tar's many friends and his extended family – a 'veritable clan', one recalled – gathered to celebrate his life at the church of the Holy Cross, better known as Pershore Abbey. Relatives close and distant, and friends of whom the same could be said, shuffled, rustled, smiled and nodded, in a setting which had been a place of Christian worship for over 1300 years. The Avon, flowing through the meadows behind the town's immaculately preserved Georgian façades carried the silt of centuries of history.

In trying to sum up Tar's life – in which so much achievement was compressed into a period of a few years – his character and his contribution to his country, we do not need to go much beyond the two main tributes paid at the Thanksgiving Service. Understandably these are always upbeat, positive affairs, with never an unkind word spoken, though those gathered to pay tribute may be aware that there might have been skeletons in the closet, odd episodes or predilections best left unmentioned. Where Tar stands out is that a career spent dealing and double-dealing with heroes and villains, patriots and traitors, self-serving scoundrels, Whitehall bigwigs, military 'brass hats', turf-protecting and manipulative SIS officers, bitchy academics, and less successful colleagues, left nothing negative to be said or hinted at. A rare thing in a life so complex, landmined with opportunities for backstabbing, jealousies, even bitter feelings of betrayal.

Christopher Harmer was unable to be there. His remarks, read by Tar's step-grandson Mathew Carr, evoked Tar the leader, who had created '. . . the happiest and most united environment in which I ever worked . . .' He attributed this to 'the unfailing even-handed fairness, enthusiasm and encouragement he gave to all of us.' Tar 'had the total and unquestioning loyalty of the whole team and we all remained firm friends for the rest of our lives'.

(Tar could not respond. The files can. When Harmer temporarily transferred out of MI5 in 1944 to head the SCI in Paris, Tar wrote to him in response to a request for advice on a longer term career choice – MI5 versus the Army – graciously telling him: '. . . how grateful I am for all the work you did for me in B1a. It was quite invaluable and it is accepted by all who have a brain to think that you are far and away the best operator we ever had in the Section. I am extremely grateful to you for everything you did and the way you worked so loyally for me.')

Peter Stormonth Darling spoke of Tar the man. 'It was people that counted with Tommy and they all started equal in his eyes . . . he saw the best in everyone and rarely disliked anyone though he could disapprove strongly of other people's actions or words . . .' Without knowing anything of the history of men like SNOW and CELERY, Stormonth Darling put his finger on the spot when he told those gathered in the Abbey that Tar '. . . was non-judgmental and had a soft spot for the unusual types including the odd rogue with a bit of charm . . .' In capturing Tar the cricketer he also highlighted the essence of counter-intelligence: 'True to character he was both an attractive right-handed batsman and a crafty left handed slow bowler.'

Tributes to Tar's innate leadership skills, his knack of getting results by persuasion rather than command, his charm and diplomacy are to be found across the spectrum of intelligence literature. They are also testimonials to Guy Liddell's management style in letting Tar have his head without regard to the niceties of rank.

We can fairly ask, though there is no real answer, whether without the unique opportunity presented by SNOW's wireless and the inspired guidance of the unflappable Guy Liddell indeed without the challenge of war itself, Tar would otherwise have had the chance to make the most of his talents. In a cliché much favoured by UK sports journalists: 'Cometh the hour, cometh the man.'

Equally unknowable, is quite what Vernon Kell saw in him that led him not just to take Tar on but even to think of him as a his prospective Personal Assistant. There was nothing in his background to suggest he would make a good counter-intelligence man or would even be interested in trying. Kell would certainly have watched his evolution from popular schoolboy to officer cadet, a dashing Seaforth officer, a man about town and a short-lived, bored man about the City. He trusted his son's judgement, and though perhaps some of their companionable racketing around town might have made him and Constance raise their eyebrows, what he now saw – a well-tailored, charismatic Child of Empire, popular at school, a good record at Sandhurst and a spell in a good regiment – struck the right note. Loyalty and honesty were not an issue. No battery of tests could really dig out what he was looking for. Writing many years after the war a senior MI5 officer tried to capture[7] the qualities that made for success in the Service: 'While no doubt integrity is the first qualification, it is closely followed by stability, a sense of responsibility and purpose, stamina, humour, tolerance and generosity . . . A Security Service officer must work as a team. To be humourless, opinionated or personally over ambitious is a serious defect.'

All of these were Tar hallmarks, much admired by all who knew him. And he was manifestly free of all the negative traits as well as a brilliant organiser and a gifted Whitehall diplomat. What he wasn't despite several such descriptions in the literature was a 'professional soldier' or a 'regular officer', tags which so often imply a mixture of courage and a 'Blimpishly' narrow 'by the book' mindset.

His time in the Seaforth was brief, and he did not particularly enjoy it. But that aside, his work in counter-intelligence called for another, less perceptible ingredient, more difficult to define and less easy to spot, though Kell's radar, fine tuned by years of experience may have picked it up. It is the ability to be two-faced, to wear the mask of Janus.

A successful agent-runner has to be able to make men and women from any background feel he is genuinely interested in them, that he sympathises with them whatever twisted path they may have taken to end up in his hands, that he trusts them and they can trust him even if he sends them into danger, that he will do his best for them whatever happens. We can cite Tar's support for CELERY, his efforts to help TRICYCLE track down the Abwehr playboy Johnny Jebsen after the war, his eventually unsuccessful support for ZIGZAG when his case officer was urging he be fired for indiscretion in the bars of Soho. Even his solicitude for TREASURE, before they fell out, bringing her flowers when she was ill in hospital, and his post-Dartmoor concern for SNOW.

But behind the façade, the bonhomie and sharing of confidence, the engaging chuckle, the protestations of trust, there has to be a pity-proof partition, allowing the other half of the agent-runner's mind to apply detached observation and cool judgment to assess in real time whether what he is hearing is true. If he senses falsehood, equivocation, dangerous doubts, he must act dispassionately, deceptively and if necessary ruthlessly, sending the agent into the limbo of the lost, all ties cut, or as in war, deploying more drastic counter-measures – expulsion to a hostile home country, jail or the threat of death. We have seen this chillier side of Tar, such as the comments on various files threatening agents that if they double-crossed him or misbehaved. 'I could not answer for the consequences.' 'You will not return to this country'; 'if you give us any trouble, you'll be sent to jail and handed over for trial to the French authorities', or 'I will not hesitate to have him removed.' We remember him sending SNOW to jail, and his son into internment, and entertaining TATE at home while coolly arranging for him to be shot if there was a risk of his falling into German hands. Even his obsessive hounding of TREASURE over her book. In their different ways, SNOW and ZIGZAG could look after themselves when dallying with the Abwehr and play the double game adroitly. But sending CELERY into Germany, or even initially encouraging the Duke of Hamilton to go to Lisbon to meet a leading Nazi required at the least a sense of professional detachment.

It is the constant balancing and rebalancing of velvet glove and iron fist, in circumstances of extraordinary strain, without losing his sense of proportion and humour or his eye for detail, his "networking" and organisational talents, and his imagination, that made Tar a master spymaster. Echoes again of Alfred Hitchcock, who once remarked, 'There is nothing to winning, really, if you happen to be blessed with a keen eye, an agile mind and no scruples whatever.' The latter phrase is not applicable to Tar but his operating style could and did reflect what Truffaut's perception of Hitchcock's unique blend of 'sincerity and . . . savagery'. So did his psychological understanding of how to deceive the Abwehr. 'A good screenplay', Hitchcock once counselled, 'must be told through the minds of the audience – pull them along and they begin wanting more.' In his many rôles on the intelligence stage from ingénue to leading actor, Tar was truly a man who could say 'I have done the state some service . . .' Tar's obituary in *The Times* described him as 'perhaps the most unsung of his country's wartime servants'. We can only hope this account has helped to make the song heard.

Notes

1. I am indebted to the GCHQ Historian Tony Comer for his help on this point.
2. Born George Behar, November 1922. Joined SIS in 1948. In 1961 he was sentenced to 42 years in jail for his work for the Russians. In 1966 he escaped to Moscow from MI5's old home at Wormwood Scrubs.
3. Heath, Neville George Cleveley, 1917–46, executed for the murder of two young women.
4. Chance, Sir William Hugh Stobart, 1896–1981.
5. Mills, Cyril Bertram, 1902–91, educated at Harrow and Cambridge, where he read engineering. Mills is remembered by one of the children of a Section B1a parent as a 'blusterer', but a man who delighted them by showing them his antique circus wagon, complete with leaded-light windows, and giving them ringside seats when the family circus pitched its Big Top at Olympia. One account claims he continued his association with the intelligence world during the Cold War.
6. Stormonth Darling, Peter, 1932–, soldier, banker, author.
7. Andrew, *Defence of the Realm*, pp. 330–1.

Acknowledgements

My principal debt is to Tar's extended family – his late brother Ian, his daughter and son in law Belinda and David McEvoy, his step-son and daughter Daniel Carr and Dr Caroline Keenan, and Rachel Robertson's brother Peter Stormonth Darling. They encouraged me to go ahead with what has proved to be a most enjoyable task, and shared their memories, answered sometimes intrusive questions and commented on my drafts. Peter Stormonth Darling did me the invaluable kindness of reading and commenting very helpfully on the final version. But any errors and omissions are my responsibility.

The documents, photographs and background they provided not least a family note by Tar's late brother Ian and the recollections of Mrs. John Kell and Mrs. Christopher Harmer are collectively referred to as 'personal papers'. I owe equal appreciation to my friend and mentor Professor M. R. D. Foot who read a draft of the entire book with his usual eagle eye and exemplary patience, and in the process saved me from many howlers. Professor Foot also pointed me in the direction of E. D. R. Harrison's paper on RSS. Not for the first time my task has been made much easier by dialogue with Mark Seaman, whose knowledge of all these fields and files is encyclopedic and who rivals Tar in his ability to get to the heart of things. Dr Calder Walton also read the text and offered much-appreciated suggestions and directed me to Emily Jane Wilson's dissertation. In turn, I thank Professor Christopher Andrew for introducing me to Dr Walton.

Valuable help has also come from Richard Aldrich, who directed me to the *Timewatch* TV programme, Andrea Baumann of Lincoln College, Oxford whose research into the Abwehr literature and Tar's correspondence with David Mure was of great assistance, Sarah

Brain at the Standard Chartered Banking Group, Svetlana Chervonnaya in Moscow, Tony Crassweller, GCHQ's Historian Tony Comer, Dave Cross, Keeper of the West Midlands Police Museum, Jim Davies and Keith Hayward at British Airways Archives and Museum, Jennifer Duffy of the National Archives of Scotland, Michael Hermann of Nuffield College, Alison Laitner of the Birmingham City Archives, Dr A R Morton of the Royal Military Academy, Hayden Peake, Dr Alex Pravda and Roy Giles of St. Antony's College Oxford, Chris Sheppard and Richard High of the Brotherton Library, University of Leeds for kindly researching the Anthony Blunt manuscript in the British Library, Charlie Turpin at the Guildhall City Library, Anne Wheeler, Archivist of Charterhouse School, the Central Chancery of The Orders of Knighthood, Di Webb at The National Sheep Association, Ben White of The Bank of England Archives, and Lynda Unchern of the Cambridge University Library. In Paris, Madame Francoise Gicquel and Madame Emmanuelle Broux-Foucard of the Paris Police Archives gave me valuable points on the Skoblin affair.

As always, Angela Burgess, a friend for many years, has provided essential logistical and moral support.

It is a touch coy to thank those individuals whose assistance in tying up loose ends was invaluable, but who prefer to remain anonymous; they know who they are, and how obliged I am for their help.

The principal published sources are listed below. It will be apparent that *The Times* archives, the *Oxford Dictionary of National Biography* and *Who Was Who*, all accessed via the London Library, have also been invaluable, as was the official website of the Security Service, an 'open society' concept with which Vernon Kell, David Petrie and even Dick White might have found it hard to come to terms. Professor Christopher Andrew's authorised history, *Defence of the Realm*, has saved me from meandering up several blind alleys, and has provided key new insights; I and all those who study the intelligence field owe him a great debt. I am also obliged to the Imperial War Museum and the British Library, who hold Blunt's *apologia pro vita sua*. But the main seams that have been mined are those of the UK National Archive. Though purists may disagree, to footnote each single reference in the text would have created for the regular reader a distracting picket fence of superscripts, all the more since as cases such as SNOW and CELERY overlap on multiple several files with considerable potential for confusion. I have thus simply listed the files which I have tapped, with the knowledgeable help of researcher Bob O'Hara.

CAB 154/105, HO 45/25689, HW 1/1, HW 74/16

KV 2: 16, 41, 100, 162, 171, 271, 278, 280, 325, 326, 327, 444, 445, 447, 448, 449, 450, 451, 453, 462, 463, 464, 466, 468, 528, 674, 845, 861, 1280, 1685

KV 4: 1, 2, 3, 16, 32, 88, 100, 122, 124, 127, 129, 131, 132, 151, 161, 170, 171, 172, 213, 214, 215, 217, 243, 259, 260, 270, 272, 411, 413, 444

Bibliography

Aldrich, R., *GCHQ – The Uncensored Story of Britain's Most Secret Intelligence Agency*, Harper Press, 2010.

Anderson, D. G., 'British Rearmament and the "Merchants of Death": the 1935–36 Royal Commission on the Manufacture and Trade in Armaments', in *Journal of Contemporary History*, Vol. 29, No.1 (January 1994) pp. 5–37.

Andrew, Christopher, *The Defence of The Realm, The Authorized History of MI5*, Allen Lane, 2009.

Anon, *MI5 The First Ten Years, 1909-1918*, Public Record Office, 1997.

——, *Mail Interception & Telephone Tapping in Britain*, Housmans Bookshop, c. 1970.

Bhageria, P. and Mahotra, P., *Elite Clubs of India*, Bhageria Foundation, @ www.eliteclubsofindia.com

Baillie-Stewart, N., (with Murdoch, J.), *The Officer in the Tower*, Frewin, 1967.

Baylis, Dr. G. M. [Introduces] The Black Book. *Sonderfahndungsliste* GB, Imperial War Museum, 1989.

Benton, K., 'The ISOS Years', in *Journal of Contemporary History*, Vol. 30, No. 3, (July 1995), p. 3.

Black, A., and Brunt, R., 'Information Management In MI5 Before Computers', in *Intelligence and National Security*, Vol. 16, No 2, (Summer 2001).

Blunt, A., *A Personal Memoir*, unpublished, held by The British Library.

Boston, A., *Leslie Blanche: Inner Landscapes, Wilder Shores*, John Murray, 2009.

Bower, Tom, *The Perfect English Spy: Sir Dick White and The Secret War, 1935–90*, William Heinemann, 1995.

Brammer, U. *Spionageabwehr und "Geheimer Meldedienst", Die Abwehrstelle X im Wehrkreis Hamburg 1939-1945*, Verlag Rombach, Freiburg, 1989.

Bucheit, G., *Der Deutsche Geheimdienst, Geschichte de militärischen Abwehr,* List, Munich, 1960.

Buiskoll, D. A., 'Medan', a paper delivered to the First International Urban Conference, Surubaya, 2004, accessed via http://www.indie-indonesie.nl

Campbell, D., 'Phonetappers & The Security State', in *New Statesman,* NS Report, No. 2, 1981.

Campbell, John P., 'A Retrospective on John Masterman's "The Double Cross System"', in *Journal of Intelligence and Counterintelligence,* Vol. 18/2, (2005) pp. 320-353.

Chapman, J., *The British at War – Cinema, State and Propaganda,* IB Tauris, 1998.

Connor, J. T. H., 'The Victorian Revolution In Surgery', in *Science,* Vol. 304, No. 5667, (April 2004).

Cocquart, E., *Marthe Richard – De la petite á la grande vertu,* Payot, Paris, 2006.

Crowdy, T., *Deceiving Hitler: Double-cross and Deception in WWII,* Osprey Publishing, 2008.

Curry, John, *The Security Service 1908–1945, The Official History,* PRO Publications, 1999.

Delmer, Sefton, *The Counterfeit Spy,* Hutchinson, 1973.

Denniston, R., *Thirty Secret Years, AG Denniston's work with signals intelligence, 1919-1944,* Heritage Press, Polperro, 2007.

Devine, T. M., *Scotland's Empire 1600–1815,* Allen Lane, 2003.

Doerries, R., *Walter Schellenberg, Hitler's Last Chief of Intelligence,* Frank Cass, 2003.

Douglas Hamilton, Lord James, *Motive for a Mission: The Story Behind Hess's Flight to Britain,* Mainstream Publishing, Edinburgh, 1979.

Elliott, G. and Shukman, H., *Secret Classrooms,* Little Brown/St. Ermin's Press, 2002.

Erickson, J., [Introduces], *Invasion 1940 – the Nazi Plan for the Invasion of Britain,* St. Ermin's Press, 2000.

Fischer, B., [CIA History Staff] a.k.a. 'Dr Rantzau': 'The Enigma of Major Nikolaus Ritter', in *Centre for the Study of Intelligence Bulletin,* Washington, DC, 2000. Accessed at http://permanent.access.gpo.gov/lps19742/www.cia.gov/csi/bulletin/csi11.html#toc7

Foot, M. R. D., *Memories of an SOE Historian,* Pen & Sword, 2008.

——, Dear, C.B., *The Oxford Companion to World War II,* OUP, 2001.

Gannon, Paul, *Colossus – Bletchley Park's Greatest Secret,* Atlantic, 2006.

Gardiner, J., *The Thirties, An Intimate History*, Harper Press, 2010.

Gray, M., Le Général Meurt à Minuit, Plon, Paris, 1981.

Handel, M. I., Muller, K-J., Campbell, J. C., Cubbage, T. L., Glantz, D.M., [contributions to] *Intelligence and National Security*, Vol. 2, No 3, London, 1987.

Harrison, E. D. R. 'British Radio Security and Intelligence 1939-1943', in *The English Historical Review*, February, 2009.

Hastings, Selina, *Somerset Maugham*, John Murray, 2009.

Hennessey, Thomas, and Thomas, Claire, *Spooks: The Unofficial History of MI5*, Amberley Publishing, Stroud, 2009.

Hesketh, R., *FORTITUDE, the D-Day Deception Campaign*, Little Brown/St. Ermin's Press, 1999.

Hoare, O., [Ed.], *Camp O20*, Public Records Office, 2000.

Hinsley, F. H., et al and Howard, Sir M., *British Intelligence in the Second World War*, Vols. 1–5, HMSO, 1981–1990.

Hogenhuis, A., *Des Savants dans la Résistance – Boris Vild et le R seau de Musée de l'Homme*, CNRS Editions, Paris, 2009.

Holzman, M., *James Jesus Angleton, the CIA, and the Craft of Counterintelligence*, University of Massachusetts Press, Amherst, 2008.

Jeffery, Keith, *MI6 – The History of The Secret Intelligence Service 1909-1949*, Bloomsbury, 2010.

Kahn, David, *Hitler's Spies: German Military Intelligence in World War II*, Hodder & Stoughton, 1978.

Kell, Sir V., *Diary*, and Kell, Lady C., *A Memoir of Sir Vernon Kell, together on* Imperial War Museum Microfilm, PP/MCR/120.

Knabe, H. et al, *West-Arbeit der MfS": das Zusammenspiel von "Aufklärung" und "Abwehr"*, LinksVerlag, Berlin, 1999.

Lander, Sir Stephen, [then Director of MI5] Speech to the Public Records Office Conference, "The Missing Dimension" London, 2001.

Lee, Y. K., 'Private Practitioners and Private Hospitals in Singapore, (1819-1872)', in *Singapore Medical Journal*, Vol. 46(9), (2005) pp. 489 et seq.

Leigh Fermor, Patrick, *A Time of Gifts*, John Murray, 1977.

Leverkühn, P., *der geheime Nachrichtendienst*, Bernard und Graefe, Frankfurt, 1957.

Mackenzie, C. A., *Realm of Silver*, Routledge, 1958.

Macintyre, B., *Agent Zigzag*, Bloomsbury, 2007.

——, *Operation MINCEMEAT*, Bloomsbury, 2009.

Masterman, J. C., *The Double-Cross System of the War of 1939-45*, Yale

University Press, London and New Haven, 1972.

——, *On the Chariot Wheel: An Autobiography*, OUP, 1975.

Montagu, E., *Beyond Top Secret U*, Davies, 1977.

Miles, J., *The Nine Lives of Otto Katz*, Bantam, 2010.

Morozan, V. V., Tereshchuk, A. V., Firsov S. L., Introduction, *Nadezhda Plevitskaya, Dezhkin Karagod*, Logos, St Petersburg, 1994.

Mueller, M., [trans. Brooks, G.], *Canaris*, Chatham Publishing/Lionel Leventhal, 2007.

Muggeridge, Malcolm, *The Thirties In Great Britain*, Hamish Hamilton, 1940.

Mure, D., Private papers, Imperial War Museum Archive 67/321/1-3, Box 3.

Murphy, C. J., *Security and Special Operations, SOE and MI5 During the Second World War*, Palgrave Macmillan, 2006.

Nabokov, V., *Collected Short Stories*, Penguin, 2010.

Paillole, P., *Services Spéciaux 1939–1945*, Laffont, Paris, 1975.

Paine, Lauran, *The Abwehr, Germany's Military Intelligence Service in the Second World War*, Hale, 1984.

Philby, Kim, *My Silent War*, MacGibbon & Kee, 1968.

Philby R, with Hayden Peake and Mikhail Lyubimov, *The Private Life of Kim Philby*, trans. by Geoffrey Elliott, St Ermin's Press, 1999.

Popov, D., Spy, *Counter Spy*, Weidenfeld & Nicolson, 1974.

Popov, V. V., *Sovyetnik Korolevy – Superagent Kremlya*, ['The Queen's Advisor and the Kremlin's Super-Agent'], Novina, Moscow, 1995.

Rankin, Nicholas, *Churchill's Wizards: The British Genius For Deception*, 1914–45, Faber and Faber, 2008.

Ratcliff, R. A., 'Searching for security – The German investigations into Enigma's security', in *Intelligence and National Security*, Vol. 14:1, pp 146–167, 1999.

Reile, O., *Treff Lutetia Paris*, Munich, Welsermuhl, 1973.

Ritter, N., *Deckname Dr Rantzau*, Hamburg, Hoffman u. Campe, 1972.

Ryan, O., *The Anglo-Spanish Shadow War, 1939–1945*, draft Ph.D Dissertation, Faculty of History, Cambridge University, 2009.

[Seaman, M. Introduces] *Garbo – the Spy Who Saved D-Day*, Public Record Office, 2000.

[Stafford-Smith J. ed.] *In the Mind's Eye: The Memoirs of Dame Elizabeth Hill*, The Book Guild, 1999.

Sergueiew, L., [Nataliya], *Seule face à l'Abwehr*, Fayard, Paris, 1966.

——, *Secret Service Rendered*, Kimber, 1968.

——, *Mon Voyage à Pied*, Paris-Warsovie, Susse, Paris, 1946.

——, *Routes, Risques, Rencontres*, Susse, Paris, 1943.

Sisman, Adam, *Hugh Trevor-Roper, The Biography*, Weidenfeld & Nicolson, 2010.

Smith, Michael, *Foley: The Spy Who Saved 10,000 Jews*, Hodder & Stoughton, 1999.

Smyth, D., *Deadly Deception: The Real Story of Operation Mincemeat*, OUP, 2010.

Stamp, G., *Britain's Lost Cities*, Aurum Press, 2007.

Ten Cate, A. W. N., *Deli in Woord en Beeld*, De Boussy, Amsterdam, 1905.

Thurlow, Richard, *The Secret State: British Internal Security in the Twentieth Century*, Blackwell, Oxford, 1994.

Trevor- Roper, Hugh, *The Philby Affair*, Kimber, 1968.

——, 'Sideways into SIS', Peake, H. & Halpern, S., [Eds.], *In the Name of Intelligence – Essays in Honor of Walter Pforzheimer*, NIBC Press, Washington DC, 1994.

——, [Essay In] Hobsbawm, E. and Ranger, T., [Eds.], *The Invention of Tradition*, CUP, 1983

Truffaut, F., *Hitchcock*, Touchstone, New York, 1985.

West, Nigel, *MI5 – British Security Service Operations 1909–1945*, Bodley Head, 1981.

——, *Seven Spies Who Changed the World*, Secker & Warburg, 1981.

—— [Ed.], *The Diaries of Guy Liddell, Vols 1 & 2*, Routledge, 2005.

——, 'More Observations on Abwehr in the UK', in *Journal of Intelligence and Counterintelligence*, Vol. 18/2, pp. 757–8, 2005.

West, Nigel and Tsarev, Oleg, [Eds.], *TRIPLEX, Secrets from the Cambridge Spies*, Yale University Press, London and New Haven, 2009.

Wheeler, Douglas L., 'The Price of Neutrality – Portugal, The Wolfram Question and World War II', in *Luso-Brazilian Review*, Vol. 23, No. 1, 1986.

Williams, W. H., *Who's Who in Arms*, Labour Party Research Department, 1935.

Wilson, Emily Jane, *The War In the Dark – The Security Service and the Abwehr 1940–1944*, University of Cambridge Ph. D. Dissertation, 2003.

Wright, Peter, *Spycatcher*, Viking, New York, 1987.

Index